Democracy and Other Neoliberal Fantasies

DEMOCRACY AND OTHER NEOLIBERAL FANTASIES

Communicative Capitalism & Left Politics

JODI DEAN

DUKE UNIVERSITY PRESS : DURHAM & LONDON 2009

© 2009 Duke University Press
All rights reserved
Printed in the United States of America on acid-free paper ∞
Designed by Jennifer Hill
Typeset in Arno Pro by Keystone Typesetting, Inc.

Library of Congress Cataloging-in-Publication Data
appear on the last printed page of this book.

For Paul, with love and disagreement

CONTENTS

ACKNOWLEDGMENTS

The chapters of *Democracy and Other Neoliberal Fantasies* began as responses. Some were responses to specific invitations. All were responses to the worsening political situation in the United States under the regime of George W. Bush and his global war of terror. I have substantially reworked the arguments here since I first delivered or published them, and I am grateful to those who took the time to respond to the early versions, to question or provoke me, and to offer suggestions and opportunities. Early versions of the first two chapters were published in *Cultural Politics*; the first appeared as "Communicative Capitalism: Circulation and the Foreclosure of Politics," in volume 1, number 1 (2005); the second appeared as "Enjoying Neoliberalism," in volume 4, number 1 (2008). Chapters 3 and 4 grew out of articles published in *Theory and Event*: "The Democratic Deadlock," from volume 10, number 4 (2008); and "Evil's Political Habitats," from volume 8, number 2 (2005). The fifth chapter reworks material from my contribution to Terrell Carver's and Samuel A. Chamber's *Judith Butler's Precarious Politics* (Routledge, 2008).

In writing this book, I have benefited from the work of numerous people. I try to thank by name those who extended invitations that enabled me to present and develop my ideas. Yet I want also to acknowledge my appreciation of the work of those who arranged flights and hotels, offices and meals, receptions and translators, but remain unnamed, behind the scenes. Thanks to Gonzalo Portocarrero for the opportunity to deliver a series of lectures inaugurating the Master's Program in Cultural Studies at Catholic University, Lima, Peru (and Alexandra Hibbet, who worked tirelessly as a translator and guide); Zoran Rosko and Petar Milat for the opportunity to present an early version of the first chapter at MAMA Multimedia Institute in Zagreb; Heiko Feldner and Fabio Vighi for arranging a research fellowship and lectures at Cardiff School of European Studies; Lars Iyer for the invitation to Newcastle upon Tyne; David Garcia for the invitation to speak in connection with the exhibit "Faith in Exposure" at Montevideo in Amsterdam; Steven Shaviro for inviting me to give a lecture in the DeRoy Lecture Series in the English Department at Wayne State University; James Maggio for the invitation to the University of Florida; Davide Panagia for the invitation to the Center for Theory, Culture, and Politics at Trent University; Keith Topper for the invitation to participate in the conference on weak ontologies at Northwestern University; Ross Cisneros for the invitation to the summit "Regarding Evil" at MIT; and, Michael Norquist for the invitation to speak with the graduate students in political theory at the University of Minnesota, Minneapolis.

Thanks to Steven Johnston and Jane Bennett for introducing me to my editor at Duke, Courtney Berger, and thanks to Courtney for supporting this project. Thanks also to John Armitrage, Ryan Bishop, Hubertus Buchstein, Sam Chambers, Mladen Dolar, Andrew Norris, Lee Quinby, Mike Shapiro, and Adam Thurschwell for comments on specific chapters. Thanks to Jackie Stevens and Ken Wark for their careful reading of the manuscript. And thanks to Cynthia Blacklaw for her work in preparing the manuscript.

Paul Passavant read and commented on the papers and essays that became this book. Surprisingly, he still doesn't agree with quite a bit of it. I am as grateful for his disagreement as I am for his love.

Geneva, New York
July 2008

Post-Politics and Left Victory

The end of the Bush administration and the crisis in capitalism confronting the world economy are opportunities not
simply for reflecting on the bankruptcy of conservatism and
neoliberalism but also for addressing the yet more significant
failures of the left. They present opportunities, in other words,
for confronting the ways that the true believers in the Republican message were actually leftists and Democrats. For many of
us on the American left, the election of 2000 indicated less
a divided populace than it did the consolidation of conservative hegemony. We read George W. Bush's assumption of the
presidency as exposing the underlying truth of the country, despite the fact Al Gore won the popular vote and the election's
outcome rested with the Supreme Court. A Bush presidency
seemed inevitable, almost foreordained. Trapped in what appeared as one enormous red state and overlooking the pervasive
blue and purple, we wallowed in our misery.[1] That over half the
voters did not want Bush somehow seemed unimportant. That
the Republicans remained significantly behind the Democrats
with respect to voters' party identification barely registered.[2] We
were convinced that the country was Republican, conservative,
capitalist, Christian fundamentalist, and evangelical (as if these
were all the same). It's almost as if we believed in their strength
and unity, their power and influence, more than they did themselves. So we submitted to what we loudly lamented as our own
worst nightmare. We turned a split election into the fact, the
victory, of conservatism. And ever since, many of us on the

academic and typing side of the U.S. left have interpreted this conservatism as the essential core of America's present politics.

Why did we do this? Why, instead of taking to the streets after the
decision to stop the count of Florida votes, did the majority of those who
position themselves on the U.S. left accept defeat? Why did we see an
overall and resounding right-wing victory and why did we submit? Why
was this election, in the minds of so many on the left, the beginning of a
new status quo rather than a minor setback we could use to strengthen our
resolve and invigorate our fight?

One should interrupt this line of questioning—what do you mean
"we"? There wasn't a unified left in 2000 and there isn't a unified left now.
Denying this unity is the article of faith unifying those who deny it *as*
leftists. (Conservatives already know the left exists—that's how they know
whom to oppose.) To presume some kind of left support for Gore in 2000
is thus ill-informed and naive. Let's recall: a number of us voted for Ralph
Nader (some blame us for the Bush presidency). Still others, whether they
voted or not, emphasize the futility of electoral politics under conditions
of communicative capitalism, which I define as the materialization of
ideals of inclusion and participation in information, entertainment, and
communication technologies in ways that capture resistance and intensify
global capitalism.[3] Gore was hardly a left-wing candidate. He was backed
by the business-friendly Democratic Leadership Council and major financial interests. The activist street theater group protesting at the party
conventions during the summer of 2000 was known at the time as Billionaires for Bush and Gore, not just Billionaires for Bush. So isn't the
assertion of a "we" inaccurate as well as misleading?

No. However valid these objections to the idea of a unified left may be,
they can't account for the emptiness in the streets in the wake of the
decision in *Bush v. Gore.* They point in the opposite, more radical direction, one of a vehement opposition to Bush that should have found its
expression in massive protests and dissent. Leftists opposed to Gore were
even more opposed to Bush. Thus, it *is* possible to invoke a "we" in this
regard—those of us opposed to Bush, those of us opposed to the Supreme
Court's decision, those of us opposed to stopping the Florida recount,
those of us beginning to suspect that the tenacity of the right's opposition
to President Bill Clinton and the relentlessness with which the Republicans were fighting their battles were slowly and not so subtly changing

American politics, those of us coming to think of our political position—and future—as trapped within conservative hegemony.

Lack of faith in Gore did not lead the left to concede defeat. We lacked something in ourselves. Call it faith, conviction, resolve—even the very notion of an "ourselves" that could be or be called a "we." Acquiescing to the fantasy of a conservative United States enabled us to deny this lack.

Consider the theme of "Clinton fatigue" so frequently invoked during the 2000 campaign. Conventional wisdom held that the United States was tired of Bill Clinton, tired of the endless qualifying, the slickness and scandal. Specifically left Clinton fatigue can be understood as the desire to get away from the Clinton years, from certain deeper feelings of guilt we didn't want to confront. This guilt likely resulted in part from our enjoyment of the Lewinsky affair (the president's sexual involvement with a White House intern that led the House to undertake impeachment proceedings). Talking about sex was great fun—and presidential sex was sordid *and* politically important, an ideal site for the typing left's political correctness and cultural superiority. Feeling guilty for enjoying Clinton's excesses could have made us feel like we deserved to be punished and that our punishment was losing the election, losing the power we never really had. Clinton proved to us—in a way we could not openly acknowledge—that we couldn't lead, that the left (even the middle!) is what the right says we are, *liberal*, both in terms of licentiousness and economic liberalism or neoliberalism.

Although such an explanation for Clinton fatigue on the left may be appealing, my wager is that the left's retroactive determination of the 2000 election as the truth of conservatism was also an effort to avoid confronting a more fundamental failure: our failure to take responsibility for the overwhelming neoliberalization of the U.S. economy that culminated during the Clinton administration in the defeat of universal health care, rollback of welfare state provisions (which were already sporadic, poorly delivered, and minimal), "reinvention of government" as a private contractor and market actor, and expansion of the freedoms of financial and banking concerns in the haze of a dot-com euphoria that trampled on the poor. The left had assumed and enjoyed the values of neoliberalism, firing its own salvos at the state and celebrating the imaginary freedoms of creativity and transformation offered by communicative capitalism. The unique singularity of each would replace the constraints of thinking in terms of, much less trying to build, something collective, something like an all. No wonder, then, that we could neither take to the streets nor see ourselves as us.

Left Enjoyment or Victory in Defeat

The political, economic, and social changes associated with the decline of disciplinary society, obsolescence of Fordist production, and defeat of the Keynesian welfare state have been accompanied by increased emphases on the singular, individual, and personal.[4] Commodities are no longer marketed to broad types—housewives, teenagers—but are individualized such that consumers can specify the features they desire in a product: *I'll take a grande half-caf skinny latte with extra foam: I'll design and order my own sports shoes; I'll save television shows, edit out the commercials, and watch them when it's convenient for* me. Media, ever smaller and more integrated, are not just many-to-many, as early internet enthusiasts emphasized, but me-to some-to me. The rise of the consumer as producer hyped as Web 2.0 and signaled by Facebook, MySpace, and YouTube designates a shift in media such that increasing numbers of people present their own artistic work (videos, photography, music, writing), express their own views, and star in their own shows. They want to make themselves known and visible —not just read or hear or see others (one example: 93 percent of U.S. teenagers use the Internet; 39 percent of them post their own art, stories, and video online).[5] At the same time, the experience of consuming media has become progressively more isolated—from large movie theaters, to the family home, to the singular person strolling down the street wearing tiny headphones as she listens to the soundtrack of her life or talks in a seeming dementia into a barely visible mouthpiece. This isolation in turn repeats the growing isolation of many American workers as companies streamline or "flexibilize" their workforce, cutting or outsourcing jobs to freelance and temporary employees. Insofar as too many on the academic and typing left have celebrated isolation as freedom and consumption as creativity, we have failed to counter the neoliberalization of the economy. Even worse—we have failed to provide good reasons to support collective approaches to political, social, and economic problems.[6] It's easier to let the market decide.

Rather than accepting responsibility for this failure and for our own enjoyment of the benefits and pleasures of networked, consumer-driven entertainment and communications media, though, we continue to blame the other guys—conservatives and neoconservatives, Republicans, mainstream Democrats, neoliberals, religious fundamentalists. After all, casting blame is infinitely easier than envisioning alternatives to global capitalism, combating climate change, or securing peace in the Middle East. As long as leftists see ourselves as defeated victims, we can refrain from having to admit that we are short on ideas—or that the ones we have seem unpopular, outmoded. Thus, we *need* a strong, united enemy. If the right is weaker than we are prepared to admit, then our retreat, our cowardice, is all the more shameful: *We gave in, gave up, before we needed to. We actually didn't lose. It's worse than that. We quit.*

Turning the contingent outcome of the 2000 election into the truth of conservative hegemony had other benefits besides that of relieving us of a responsibility we want to deny. It enabled us to embrace our failure (and then compromise with Democrats via rhetorics of electability, conciliation, unity, cooperation, and change). As victims of a stolen election, we could deny and accept our weakness and incapacity at the same time (the same dynamic accompanies the 2004 election, also alleged to have been stolen). *Losing is not our fault. It's not our fault that we are losers. The other guys cheated! They stole from us!*

The position of victim (rather than victor) grows out of a prominent strain of contemporary American politics, namely, the rights discourse associated with movements for civil rights, women's rights, and the rights of sexual minorities.[7] Although often linked to left political correctness, speaking as a victim is at odds with the long history of the labor movement as well as with the politics of the new left. One need but recall a whole series of claims to power: "Black power," "Sisterhood is powerful," "We're here; we're queer; get used to it," "Power to the people." Reducing political speech to testimony to the suffering of victims inverts these claims to power and subverts the movements' activist spirit.[8]

Shrinking the scope of political claims to those of victims needing recognition and redress also traps claimants in a double bind: to speak at all they have to demonstrate how they are harmed and vulnerable, how they are weak, inadequate, or suffering. They must speak as those who have lost, those who are losers.[9] One who feels the political impulse to struggle, who is ready for a fight against injustice, is not injured enough to speak. For many leftists, the attraction of the position of the victim is thus double: one is always morally correct—for who can deny the suffering of the victim?—and never politically responsible—for victims are too weak and injured to govern.

The language of victimization thrives in a variety of discursive habitats, not just those on the left. To take one example, some Christian evangelicals and fundamentalists speak as victims. They take nails for Christ as they endure the temptations of secular society. Identifying as victims enables these Christians to present themselves as a persecuted religious minority (as if the majority of American citizens were not Christian; as if the U.S. Constitution did not protect religious freedom).

Accompanying the presumed weakness of the victim is a taste for cruelty. In the United States, claims for the rights of victims have stimulated increases in the brutality of the criminal justice system. Families of victims demand ever harsher penalties in the name of achieving "closure."[10] The criminal as the singular locus and cause of the monstrous injustice suffered by the victim is a necessary component of this demand (which, in chapter 2, I consider in light of the fantasy of free trade). Neoliberalism's inevitable losses are displaced from systematic problems in need of collective solutions and concentrated onto the fantastic image of the individual criminal to be imprisoned, punished, tortured, and killed.

Communicative capitalism's consumerism, personalization, and therapeutization create ideal discursive habitats for the thriving of the victim identity. One might think here of gated communities (for huge houses with loads of closet space), surveillance cameras (I need to be sure that I'm safe), global positioning systems (where am I, anyway?), and RFID tags (no child left behind) as well as mini-furors over tainted pet food and ill-constructed toys. Moreover, particularly since leftists adopted the neoliberal language of hostility to regulation, constraining and penalizing corporations has seemed limited to the possibility of locating innocent, aggrieved victims—as if obscene inequities in corporate salaries and benefits weren't themselves criminal. Innumerable foundations organized around health and disease likewise struggle on behalf of victims, trying to secure ever-intangible "awareness." As Samantha King demonstrates with respect to breast cancer, such foundations form alliances with corporations engaged in cause-related marketing to reconfigure political action as consumption, volunteerism, and fundraising.[11] Finally, since September 11, 2001, the entirety of the population of the United States has seemingly

acquired the right to speak as victims, as violated, as aggrieved, and therefore as fundamentally nonresponsible for violence enacted in our name.

The American left has done little to challenge the hegemony of the
victim. Instead, we have embraced and encouraged the current condition
wherein those who don't speak as victims lack standing. The trap is
deadly: those who don't speak as victims aren't supposed to complain
(*they are privileged; what do they have to gripe about? what do they know of
suffering?*) and the political trajectory that follows from the complaints of
victims enhances surveillance and control, policing and security. Precisely
because the victim-security matrix is so tightly structured, the left is either
left out of the current matrix or doomed to reinforce it.

The 2000 presidential election is not the only instance when the American left failed to acknowledge victory. The left also won the culture wars
fought throughout the universities, arts, and media during the eighties and
nineties. Slavoj Žižek helps explain how such a victory functions. He
writes: "The true victory (the true 'negation of the negation') occurs
when the enemy talks your language. In this sense, a true victory is a
victory in defeat. It occurs when one's specific message is accepted as a
universal ground, even by the enemy."[12] Žižek uses the example of British
prime minister Tony Blair to make his point. Blair secured the victory of
the battle fought by his seeming opponent Margaret Thatcher in her
attack on the British welfare state. Bill Clinton is the U.S. equivalent of
Blair. Clinton achieved a dismantling of social services surpassing the
right's wildest dreams. Speaking a neoliberal language that made the state
just another market actor, Clinton realized the victory of Reaganism.

The victory of the academic left in the culture wars should be understood along similar lines: the prominence of politically active Christian
fundamentalists, Fox News, and the orchestrations of Bush advisor Karl
Rove all demonstrate the triumph of postmodernism. These guys take
social construction—packaging, marketing, and representation—absolutely seriously. They put it to work. The right's will to construct (and
deconstruct) reality to fit their interests reached new extremes during the
Bush administration: it paid the conservative commentator Armstrong
Williams to endorse the president's No Child Left Behind program, that is,
to impersonate a journalist while promoting a specific political agenda.
Similar fake news was distributed by the Transportation Security Administration (a report praising airport security), the Department of Health

and Human Services (television spots advertising the Medicare prescrip-
tion drug benefit), and the State Department (segments of good news
from U.S. military efforts in Afghanistan and Iraq).[13] As the *New York
Times* columnist Frank Rich writes, "The same conservatives who once
deplored postmodernism and moral relativism were now eagerly promoting a brave new world in which it was a given that there could be no
empirical reality in news, only a reality you wanted to hear (or they wanted
you to hear)."[14] Is it so surprising, then, that when empirical reality is up for
grabs many may start to doubt any claim made by the administration, even
one as seemingly basic as its account of the events of 9/11?

Corporate capitalism similarly embodies the triumph of postmodernism. Wink and guerrilla marketing, targeting specific groups, and identifying potential "tipping points," not to mention more basic advertising
strategies around branding, apply to consumers insights into the generation of affect and desire celebrated by scholars in critical theory, philosophy, and cultural studies. Amplifying this point, Žižek calls Gilles Deleuze
the "ideologist of late capitalism."[15] Is not the intense circulation of affects
in ways that bypass persons in a multiplication of intensities that Deleuze
celebrates a key feature of communicative capitalism? What about toys
like Transformers that can be reshaped as dinosaurs or machines and the
prominence of morphed images throughout the media sphere? These
morphings exemplify the continual transmutation of divides between machine and organism, human and animal, animal and computer. They are
virtual enactments of Deleuzian becoming.[16]

In a similar vein, Thomas Frank describes the underlying consensus
between cultural studies and corporations that consolidated during the
1990s. He notes the challenges confronting marketers when consumers are
fickle and styles change rapidly. Because consumers are already skeptical,
he explains,

> The intellectual task at hand is not just legitimation, it is infiltration,
> and suddenly questions like the oppositional or subversive potential of
> *The Simpsons* aren't quite as academic as they once seemed. Given the
> industry's new requirements, the active-audience faith of the cult stud
> becomes less an article of radical belief and more a practical foundation
> for the reprioritized audience research being done by the new breed of
> marketing experts, who can be found commenting lucidly on the post-

modern condition in highbrow business publications like the *Journal of Consumer Research*, laying out plans to "reenchant" the brand with a "liberatory postmodernism," and warning advertisers to create with the active, emancipation-hungry consumer in mind.[17]

Enthusiasm for diversity, multiplicity, and the agency of consumers actively transforming their lifestyles unites left academics and corporate capital. For many on the academic and typing left assertions of difference, singularity, and the fluidity of modes of becoming are radical. Yet insofar as they ignore their common cause with neoliberalism (a willful ignorance on the part of many left supporters of Barack Obama in the 2008 presidential campaign), they miss the truth of this radicality—the radical redistribution of wealth to the very, very rich and the radical reconstruction of the state into the authoritarian tool for their protection. Capitalism is more revolutionary than the left has ever been.

Ideological victory can look just like ideological defeat. When one's enemy accepts one's terms, one's point of critique and resistance is lost, subsumed. The dimension of antagonism (fundamental opposition) vanishes. Other, smaller conflicts emerge. Conflicts that are less significant, less crucial, become sites of intensity, sucking up political energies. Confusions arise as the multiplicity of small antagonisms, each seemingly central, make finding the key division difficult.

Confronting the implications of ideological victory is what many of us who identify as leftists fail to do. Some academics repeat terms from old battles, as if the problem of the contemporary right is its investment in essentialism and origins, as if the right doesn't already accept (and benefit from) the impact of representations and mediations. Some feminists continue to think that exposing pornography as sexist male domination is radical and insightful. They fail to recognize that this is part of pornography's appeal—*Why are you telling me this is domination when I know it's domination? That's why I like it! That's what gets me off!* Some new media activists celebrate, even fetishize, the latest communication gadgets, unaware that their message is indistinguishable from Apple's. Too often what passes for left politics is little more than the denunciation of all possibility of knowledge and truth, as if communicative capitalism was not already implicated in fundamental changes to the conditions of possibility for credibility, changes that activism for 9/11 truth demands that we confront.

Perhaps the most difficult instance of the contemporary problem of left victory, though, is left enthusiasm for democracy, as I explore in chapter 3. The aggressive war waged in Iraq has been fought in the name of democracy, seemingly taking left desire for democratic governance at its word: *You want democracy? This is what democracy looks like!*

Not Post-Political

When one's opponent takes over one's position, one is confronted with its realization, with its repercussions. This is what many of us don't like; this is what we want to avoid. So we say, "No! That's not it," but because our enemy has taken over our language, our ideals, we've lost a capacity to say what we want, even to know what we want. We can't even dream something else. Žižek writes: "In a radical revolution, people not only have to 'realize their old (emancipatory, etc.) dreams'; rather, they have to reinvent their very modes of dreaming."[18]

Such a reinvention is an enormous, perhaps impossible task. It's not furthered, though, by the diagnosis of "depoliticization," a diagnosis offered by political theorists the increased currency of which calls out for critique. If depoliticization means anything, it is the retreat into cowardice, the retroactive determination of victory as defeat because of the left's fundamental inability to accept responsibility for power and to undertake the difficult task of reinventing our modes of dreaming. Depoliticization is a fantasy, an excuse whereby the left says "We know collective action is possible theoretically, but we don't believe we exist." The term marks the gap between the commitment to common approaches to systemic problems constitutive of left thought for over two centuries and the isolating individualism of consumption and entertainment-driven communicative capitalism. The very diagnosis of depoliticization functions fetishistically to prevent the left from confronting the truth of its victory.

This view of depoliticization as an excuse or fetish covering over a failure of responsibility, however, is not widely shared. On the contrary, depoliticization and the correlative notions of post-politics, de-democratization, and postdemocracy are offered as terms for designating what is specifically new in the current political-economic condition. Over the past decades, a number of political theorists have attempted to analyze the contemporary conjuncture as post-political or postdemocratic.[19] Re-

versing the terms of the "end of ideology" thesis offered by neoconserva-
tive (Francis Fukuyama) and "third way" (Anthony Giddens) thinkers,
these theorists critically redescribe the orientation toward consensus, administration, and technocracy lauded as benefits of the post–Cold War
age. Several aspects of this redescription stand out, namely, the primacy of
the economy, the individual, and the police.

The current conjuncture is post-political, the argument goes, because
the spread and intensification of neoliberal economic policies have sub-
jected states to the demands of corporations and the seemingly inevitable
logic of the market. To the extent that state authority is increasingly less
able to constrain corporate power, politics matters less. This inability of
democratic politics to produce viable solutions to social and economic
problems, moreover, resonates with the celebration of the individual in
communicative capitalism. The individualization of politics into com-
modifiable "lifestyles" and opinions subsumes politics into consumption.
That consumer choices may have a politics—fair trade, green, vegan,
woman-owned—morphs into the sense that politics is nothing but consumer choices, that is, individuated responses to individuated needs. Zygmunt Bauman makes the point well:

> being an individual *de jure* means having no one to blame for one's own
> misery, seeking causes of one's own defeats nowhere except in one's
> own indolence and sloth, and looking for no other remedies other than
> trying harder and harder still. . . . With eyes focused on one's own
> performance and thus diverted from the social space where the contra-
> dictions of individual existence are collectively produced, men and
> women are naturally tempted to reduce the complexity of their predica-
> ment. Not that they find "biographic solutions" onerous and cumber-
> some: there are, simply, no "biographic solutions to systemic contradic-
> tions," and so the dearth of solutions at their disposal needs to be
> compensated for by imaginary ones. . . . There is therefore a demand
> for individual pegs on which frightened individuals can collectively
> hang their individual fears, if only for a brief moment.[20]

With politics seemingly reduced to consumer choice, government similarly contracts, now concerning itself with traumatized victims. Its role is
less to ensure public goods and solve collective problems than to address
the personal issues of subjects. Accordingly, pollsters assess individual

preference and satisfaction, as if the polled were the same as the politicized people. Finally, insofar as the economy alone cannot fulfill all the functions of government, one element of the state rises to the fore—security. Thus, accompanying diminished political influence on economic and social policy is the intensification and extension of the state as an agency of surveillance and control.

The neoliberal capitalist economy, the fragile, consuming individual, and the surveilling, controlling state are aspects of the diagnosis of depoliticization well worth emphasizing. Yet post-politics, depoliticization, and de-democratization are inadequate to the task of theorizing this conjuncture. The claim that states are decreasing in significance and impact because of the compulsions of the market ignores the millions of dollars regularly spent in political campaigns. Business and market interests as well as corporate and financial elites expend vast amounts of time and money on elections, candidates, lobbyists, and lawmakers in order to produce and direct a political climate that suits their interests. Capitalizing on left critiques of regulation and retreats from the state, neoliberals move right in, deploying state power to further their interests. Similarly, social conservatives in the United States persistently fight across a broad spectrum of political fronts—including local school boards, statewide ballot initiatives, judicial appointments, and mobilizations to amend the Constitution. The left-wing lament regarding post-politics not only overlooks the reality of politics on the ground but it cedes in advance key terrains of activism and struggle. Not recognizing these politicized sites as politicized sites, it fails to counter conservative initiatives with a coherent alternative.

Claims for post-politics are childishly petulant. Leftists assume that our lack of good political ideas means the end of politics as such. If the game isn't played on our terms, we aren't going to play at all. We aren't even going to recognize that a game is being played. To this extent, the claim for post-politics erases its own standpoint of enunciation. Why refer to a formation as post-political if one does not have political grounds for doing so? If one already has such grounds, then how exactly is the situation post-political? If one lacks them, then what is the purpose of the claim if not to draw attention to or figure this lack? Figuring a lack may be the strongest contribution of the rhetoric of depoliticization, one to which we on the left should attend, and one which makes debates among political theorists important for leftists looking to reinvent our modes of dreaming. It makes sense, then, to consider these debates in some detail.

Accounts of post-politics tend to slip between two different positions: post-politics as an ideal of consensus, inclusion, and administration that must be rejected and post-politics as a description of the contemporary exclusion or foreclosure of the political. Chantal Mouffe and Jacques Ranciere hold versions of the former view, Žižek takes the latter, and Wendy Brown specifies this latter point in terms of de-democratization.

Mouffe is the most compelling and precise as she takes aim at third way politics, the liberalism of John Rawls, and the deliberative democracy of Jürgen Habermas. Arguing that these approaches "negate the inherently conflictual nature of modern pluralism," she concludes, "They are unable to recognize that bringing a deliberation to a close always results from a *decision* which excludes other possibilities and for which one should never refuse to bear responsibility by invoking the commands of general rules or principles."[21] Consensus-based ideals fail to acknowledge that politics is necessarily divisive. A decision for one course rather than another excludes some possibilities and positions. Part of the challenge of politics is taking responsibility for such exclusion.

Key to the strength of Mouffe's argument is her careful use of Carl Schmitt's critique of liberal parliamentarianism. Schmitt argues that liberalism seeks to evade the core political opposition between friend and enemy, attempting instead "to tie the political to the ethical and subjugate it to economics."[22] Yet the political cannot be avoided, and attempts to submerge or efface it as intellectual deliberation or market competition result only in the displacement of the intensity characteristic of the political to another, potentially even more violent, realm. In Schmitt's words, "The political can derive its energy from the most varied human endeavors, from the religious, economic, moral and other antitheses. It does not describe its own substance, but only *the intensity of an association or dissociation* of human beings whose motives can be religious, national (in the ethnic or cultural sense), economic, or of another kind and can effect at different times different coalitions and separations."[23] The political marks the intensity of a relation, an intensity that characterizes the antagonism constitutive of society (around which society forms).

Mouffe's emphasis on the unavoidability of antagonism and division indicates a weak point in Ranciere's discussion of post-politics (and post-democracy, since for him democracy and politics are interchangeable). While attuned to the ways contemporary practices of counting opinions and managing preferences presume community and disavow political conflict and division, Ranciere tends to write as if the disappearance of politics were possible, as if the evacuation of politics from the social were a characteristic of the current conjuncture.[24] For example, he argues that today "the identification between democracy and the legitimate state is used to produce a regime of the community's identity as itself, to make politics evaporate under a concept of law that identifies it with the spirit of the community."[25] Ranciere is right to emphasize the convergence between presumptions of democracy and of legitimacy. But he is wrong to imply the existence of a string of identifying moves that turn politics into law and law into unified community. In the United States, at least, law is the site of open and avowed political conflict that undermines even the fiction of community, a conflict that brings to the fore the relations of power and privilege already (and necessarily) inscribed in law. Ranciere's claim that "the state today legitimizes itself by declaring that politics is impossible" simply does not apply to the United States post–September 11.[26] From the firing of the attorneys in the civil rights division of the Justice Department, to the manipulations of law undertaken in the justification of torture, to the abolition of habeas corpus in the Military Commissions Act, to the employment of presidential signing statements designed to undermine the laws they ostensibly endorse, law remains a highly contentious political site, indeed, the site of a counterrevolution endeavoring to install the vision of a unitary chief executive above the law.

Žižek's account of post-politics grows out of his reading of Ranciere.[27] Thus, he too oscillates between post-politics as the risky ideal behind the neoliberal third way, liberal multiculturalism, and the therapeutic administrative state and post-political as a description of today's "liberal-democratic global capitalist regime."[28] Although Žižek's position is weakest when he uses the term "post-political" descriptively, his explanation is nonetheless insightful: what makes the contemporary setting post-political is the exclusion of the possibility of politicization. Žižek's point here is that politicization entails raising the particular to the level of the universal. A specific crime, issue, or event comes to stand for something more than itself. Rather than a singular problem to be resolved, it indicates a series of problems confronting the system as a whole.[29] It is the symptomal point of antagonism in a given constellation. For example, the civil rights movement in the United States was not about the difficulties facing this or that particular person. It was a movement to change basic social practices, institutions, and regimes of visibility so as to guarantee African Americans basic rights as equal citizens. A more recent example can be found in Democrats' attempts to politicize the Bush administration's leaking of the identity of CIA agent Valerie Plame so that it would appear not simply as the matter of a singular leak but as harassment of Plame's husband, Joseph Wilson, for his criticism of the Bush administration for using information that it knew to be false to increase fear that Iraq had a viable nuclear weapons program. The Democratic strategy was to make this event stand in for a widespread and deliberate plan to deceive the U.S. public into supporting aggressive war against Iraq. "What post-politics tends to prevent," Žižek explains, "is precisely this metaphoric universalization of particular demands: post-politics mobilizes the vast apparatus of experts, social workers, and so on, to reduce the overall demand (complaint) of a particular group to just this demand, with its particular content."[30] As the Plame example indicates, politicization does occur today. The right did it particularly well when they presented liberals, feminists, gays, and Al Gore as standing in for the larger crime of contemporary selfishness, prurience, weakness, decadence, and general un-Americanism.

Žižek attributes contemporary post-politics to "the depoliticization of economics, to the common acceptance of Capital and market mechanisms as neutral tools/procedures to be exploited."[31] Taken as a broad description of U.S. politics, this argument is unconvincing: jobs, deficits, surpluses, taxes, inflation, interest rates, out-sourcing, the strength of the dollar, trade imbalances, consumer spending, subprime mortgages, bubbles, and budgets are key terms in the contemporary political lexicon. The economy appears as the site of politics, its most fundamental concern. Žižek's point, then, is better read as a critique of the left—the real political problem today is that *the left* accepts capitalism. The left is caught in a post-political situation because it has conceded to the right on the terrain of the economy: it has surrendered the state to neoliberal interests. Present leftists rarely view capitalism and its effects as evil (and part of Reagan's genius as president, as I explore in chapter 4, is his redirection of the language of evil away from capitalism). Instead, most view the problem as the state. "Depoliticized" thus well describes the contemporary left's inability to raise particular claims to the level of the universal, to present issues or problems as standing for something beyond themselves. The academic and typing left prides itself on just this unwillingness, an unwillingness to say "we" out of a reluctance to speak for another as well as an unwillingness to signify or name a problem, to take it out of its immediate context and re-present it as universal.

While Žižek's version of post-politics is helpful in identifying the failure of the contemporary left, it is wrong as a general point. In the United States, the right actively politicizes school curricula, climate science, stem cell research, Christmas, the judiciary, marriage, adoption, punishment, and the family. Every issue is made to stand for something beyond itself, an indication of weakness or resolve, a sign of support for us or them. Conservatives are not seeking individualized, therapeutic, or administrative answers. They want the intervention of law. They raise their claims to the status of a universal. They appeal to values of chastity, decency, piety, unity, order, and civility as universally valid principles and ideals. Neoliberals similarly argue in terms of universals. Their claim is that the market is the best way to arrange production, distribution, and consumption, not that it is the best way only for the privileged and wealthy. Here again, the notion of depoliticization fails to click on the imbrications of capitalism and democracy, the injunctions and failures to enjoy, and the intertwinings of certainty and skepticism characteristic of the current conjuncture. A premise of this book is that a political theory informed by recent work in psychoanalysis (primarily Žižek's Lacanian Marxism) is one way to access these sites and contribute to the project of politicizing the left.[32]

To be sure, the American left is not completely without vision. It uniformly asserts the primacy of democracy (which I critique in chapter 3) and less uniformly but equally unfortunately advocates generosity and responsiveness (which I critique in chapter 5).[33] Left enthusiasm for democracy leads me to Wendy Brown's analysis of contemporary U.S. politics in terms of de-democratization. In a rich discussion of the convergence of neoliberalism and neoconservatism, she highlights de-democratization as its central force and threat. The details of Brown's analysis are evocative, but her overall account is unpersuasive because it both presumes a prior democracy, a previous acceptance and practice of democracy that is now unraveling, and neglects the hegemony of democratic rhetoric today. Democracy has long been a contested category in U.S. politics, subordinated to individual and states' rights, valued less than elites' property and privilege, and easily pushed aside in times of war, cold and otherwise. Anxieties over the tyranny of the majority, the great unwashed, immigrants, Catholics, workers, women, blacks, and the young have infused the American system since its inception. The combination of civil rights, students, and new social movements in the 1960s with rapid expansion in communications media enabling people to register their opinions, contact representatives, and organize gatherings and protests has, *contra* Brown, realized democratic aspirations to a previously unimaginable degree. Even as banal a statistic as voter turnout supports my claim that the current conjuncture is not well conceptualized with the notion of de-democratization: the turnout of the voting age population in the United States in the 2004 election was the highest it has been since 1968.[34] To this extent, the presidential election of 2008 was less an exception than a trend, one marked as much by participation as it was by spending: the candidate who spends the most wins.

Expansions in networked communications media reinforce the hegemony of democratic rhetoric. Far from de-democratized, the contemporary ideological formation of communicative capitalism fetishizes speech, opinion, and participation. It embeds us in a mindset wherein the number of friends one has on Facebook or MySpace, the number of page-hits one gets on one's blog, and the number of videos featured on one's YouTube channel are the key markers of success, and details such as duration, depth of commitment, corporate and financial influence, access to structures of decision-making, and the narrowing of political struggle to the standards of do-it-yourself entertainment culture become the boring preoccupations of baby-boomers stuck in the past. Chapter 1 details how communicative capitalism materializes and repurposes democratic ideals and aspirations in ways that strengthen and support globalized neoliberalism. The proliferation, distribution, acceleration, and intensification of communicative access and opportunity produce a deadlocked democracy incapable of serving as a form for progressive political and economic change. So the problem isn't democratization. It's the left's failure to think beyond democracy and defend a vision of equality and solidarity, its unwillingness to reinvent its modes of dreaming.

When democracy appears as both the condition of politics and the solution to the political condition, neoliberalism can't appear as the violence it is. Yet under communicative capitalism, this is precisely what has occurred. Right and left share the same rhetoric of democracy, a rhetoric merging ethics and economics, discussion and competition so that each is a version of the other. In the absence of distinctions, conviction is indistinguishable from knowledge and certainty triumphs over evidence. (*Can we ever really know the truth? What is verification, anyway?*) So preemptive war is fought in the name of spreading democracy even as critics of the same war use the same terms to voice, to imagine, their opposition. The contemporary left is in a position of true victory, of victory in defeat. Our enemy speaks our language. And because our enemy has adopted our language, our ideals, we lack the ability to say what we want. Our present values thus become horrific realizations of their opposites, entrapping us in psychotic politics.

Technology

THE PROMISES OF COMMUNICATIVE CAPITALISM

Although mainstream media in the United States supported the Bush administration in the run-up to the March 2003 invasion of Iraq, critical assessments of the government's justifications for war circulated throughout global capitalism's communications networks. Alternative media, independent media, and non–U.S. media provided thoughtful reports, insightful commentary, and critical evaluations of the "evidence" of weapons of mass destruction in Iraq. They highlighted the falsity and venality of the administration's articulation of the attacks of September 11 with Iraq, its elision of Osama bin Laden into Saddam Hussein as public enemy number one. Amy Goodman's syndicated radio program *Democracy Now* regularly broadcast shows intensely opposed to the militarism and unilateralism of the Bush administration's national security policy. The *Nation* magazine offered detailed and nuanced critiques of the justifications offered for attacking Iraq—particularly those cloaked in humanitarian good will. Antiwar activists working to supply citizens with opportunities to make their opposition known circulated lists of congressional phone and fax numbers via email. On websites, they posted petitions and announcements for marches, protests, and direct-action training sessions. As the administration's preparations for a seemingly inevitable war proceeded, thousands of antiwar bloggers commented on each step, citing other media to support their positions. True, the mainstream news media failed to cover demonstrations such as the protest in September 2002 by 400,000 people in London or march on

Washington in October 2002, when 250,000 people surrounded the White House. Nonetheless, myriad progressive, alternative, and critical left news outlets supplied frequent and reliable information about the action on the ground. All in all, a strong antiwar message was out there.

But the message was not received. It circulated, reduced to the medium. Bush acknowledged the massive worldwide demonstrations of February 15, 2003. He even reiterated the fact that a message was out there: the protestors had the right to express their opinions. He didn't actually respond to their message, however. He didn't treat the words and actions of the protestors as sending a message to him that he was in some sense obliged to answer. Rather, he acknowledged the existence of views different from his own. There were his views and there were other views. All had the right to exist, to be expressed. But that in no way meant, or so Bush made it seem, that these views were involved with each other, that they inhabited a common space, that they were elements to be considered and integrated in the course of reaching a consensus on American foreign policy.

The terabytes of commentary and information, then, did not indicate a debate over the war. On the contrary, in the days and weeks prior to the U.S. invasion of Iraq, the antiwar messages morphed into so much circulating content, just like all the other cultural effluvia flowing through communicative capitalism's disintegrated spectacles.

We might express this disconnect between engaged criticism and national strategy as the difference between the circulation of content and official policy. Both are politics, just politics of different sorts, at different levels. Terms like *democracy*, it would follow, confuse matters by blurring these levels. So on the one hand, we have media chatter—from television talking heads, radio shock jocks, and the gamut of print media to websites with RSS (Real Simple Syndication) feeds, blogs, podcasts, email lists, and the proliferating versions of instant text messaging. In this mediated dimension, politicians, governments, and activists struggle for visibility, currency, and, in the now quaint term from the dot-com years, mindshare. On the other hand are institutional politics, the day-to-day activities of bureaucracies, lawmakers, judges, and the apparatuses of the police and national security state. These institutional or state components of the system seem to run independently of the politics that circulates as content. They go about their work, the business of politics, and the other level reports on it, talks about it, treats it as content about which it opines.

Anyone even slightly familiar with democratic ideals should reject out of hand this distinction between politics as the circulation of content and politics as the activity of officials. The fundamental premise of liberal democracy is the sovereignty of the people. Governance by the people is exercised through communicative freedoms of speech, assembly, and the press; it relies on norms of publicity that emphasize transparency and accountability; it consists of the deliberative practices of the public sphere. Democratic communication steers, influences, or, more minimally, informs politics as the governing and legislating activity of elected officials. Ideally, the communicative interactions of the public sphere, the circulation of content and media chatter, not only impact but also constitute official politics.

In the United States today, however, they don't. Less bluntly put, there is a significant disconnect between politics circulating as content and official politics. Pundits gesture to this disconnect when they refer to the bubble of concerns "inside the Beltway" and the "real concerns" of "ordinary voters." So multiple opinions and divergent points of view express themselves in myriad intense exchanges, but this circulation of content in dense, intensive global communications networks actually relieves top-level actors (corporate, institutional, and governmental) from the obligation to answer embedded in the notion of a message. Reactions and rejoinders to any claim are always already present, presupposed. In this setting, content critical of a specific policy is just another story or feature in a 24/7 news cycle, just another topic to be chewed to bits by rabid bloggers. Criticism doesn't require an answer because it doesn't stick as criticism. It functions as just another opinion offered into the media-stream. So rather than responding to messages sent by left activists and critics, top-level actors counter with their own contributions to the circulating flow of communications—new slogans, images, deflections, and attacks; staged meetings or rallies featuring their supporters; impressive photo-ops that become themselves topics of chatter. Sufficient volume (whether in terms of the number of contributions or the spectacular nature of a contribution) gives these contributions their dominance or stickiness.

Contestations today rarely employ common terms, points of reference, or demarcated frontiers. In our highly mediated communications environments we confront instead a multiplication of resistances and assertions so extensive as to hinder the formation of strong counterhegemonies. The proliferation, distribution, acceleration, and intensification of communicative access and opportunity result in a deadlocked democracy incapable of serving as a form for political change. I refer to this democracy that talks without responding as communicative capitalism.[1]

The concept of communicative capitalism reformats as a criticism the neoliberal idea of the market as the site of democratic aspirations, indeed, as the mechanism by which the will of the demos manifests itself. In Thomas Frank's words, "To believe in the people is to believe in their brands."[2] Consider the circularity of claims regarding popularity. McDonald's, Wal-Mart, and reality television are depicted as popular because they seem to offer what people want. How do we know they offer what people want? People choose them—*they must be popular*.

This equation treats commercial choices as the paradigmatic form of choosing. In so doing, it displaces attention from the fact that the market is not a system for delivering political outcomes, even as many of us can't tell the difference between political campaigns and advertising. Unlike marketing's catch-phrases and jingles, political decisions—to go to war, say, or to establish the perimeters of legitimate relationships—involve more than the mindless reiteration of faith, conviction, and unsupported claims. They rest on contestable and divisive assertions of justice and right generally, potentially universally. Unlike the economy under neoliberal capitalism, moreover, the political is not a domain for the extraction of work and value from the many to enrich the few. It is, rather, the terrain upon which claims to universality are raised and defended. Political claims are partisan claims made in the name of and on behalf of a larger group, indeed, of an all that can never be fixed or limited (and so remains non-all), a group perhaps best understood as composed of anyone. Such claims are general rather than individual, and they require those who make them to think beyond themselves as specific individuals with preferences and interests and consider what is best for anyone.

The concept of communicative capitalism designates the strange merging of democracy and capitalism in which contemporary subjects are produced and trapped. It does so by highlighting the way networked communications bring the two together. The values heralded as central to democracy take material form in networked communications technologies. Ideals of access, inclusion, discussion, and participation come to be realized in and through expansions, intensifications, and interconnections of global telecommunications. Changes in information and communication networks associated with digitalization, speed (of computer processors as well as connectivity), and memory/storage capacity impact capitalism and democracy, accelerating and intensifying some elements of each as they consolidate the two into a new ideological formation.[3]

Expanded and intensified communicativity neither enhances opportunities for linking together political struggles nor enlivens radical democratic practices—although it has exacerbated left fragmentation, amplified the voices of right-wing extremists, and delivered ever more eyeballs to corporate advertisers. Instead of leading to more equitable distributions of wealth and influence, instead of enabling the emergence of a richer variety in modes of living and practices of freedom, the deluge of screens and spectacles coincides with extreme corporatization, financialization, and privatization across the globe. Rhetorics of access, participation, and democracy work ideologically to secure the technological infrastructure of neoliberalism, an invidious and predatory politico-economic project that concentrates assets and power in the hands of the very, very rich, devastating the planet and destroying the lives of billions of people.

Saskia Sassen's research on the impact of economic globalization makes clear how the speed, simultaneity, and interconnectivity of electronic communications produce massive distortions and concentrations of wealth.[4] Not only does the possibility of superprofits in the finance and services complex lead to hypermobility of capital and the devalorization of manufacturing but financial markets themselves acquire the capacity to discipline national governments. As David Harvey explains, neoliberalism's endeavor "to bring all human action into the domain of the market" requires "technologies of information creation and capacities to accumulate, store, transfer, analyze, and use massive databases to guide decisions in the global marketplace."[5] Sassen's and Harvey's work supplies powerful empirical evidence for the convergence between networked telecommunications and globalized neoliberalism into communicative capitalism.

In the United States, the proliferation of media has been accompanied by a shift in political participation.[6] Rather than actively organized in

parties and unions, politics is a domain of financially mediated and professionalized practices centered on advertising, public relations, and rapid
adaptation to changes in the technologies and practices of communication. The commodification of communication reformats ever more domains of life in terms of the market: *What can be bought and sold? How can
a practice, experience, or feeling be monetized?*[7] Bluntly put, the standards
of a finance- and consumption-driven entertainment culture produce the
setting of democratic governance today. Changing the system—organizing against and challenging communicative capitalism—seems to entail strengthening the system. How else can one get a message across?
Doesn't it require raising money, buying television time, registering domain names, building websites, making links, and increasing awareness?

I am not claiming networked communications never facilitate political
resistance. One of the most visible examples to the contrary is the experience of B92 in Serbia. Radio B92 used the Internet to circumvent governmental censorship and disseminate news of massive demonstrations
against the Milosevic regime.[8] My point is that the political efficacy of
networked media depends on the setting. Under conditions of intensive
and extensive proliferation of media, conditions wherein everyone is presumed to be a producer as well as a consumer of content, messages get
lost. They become mere contributions to the circulation of images, opinion, and information, to the billions of nuggets of information and affect
trying to catch and hold attention, to push or sway opinion, taste, and
trends in one direction rather than another. What in one context enhances
the potential of political change, in another submerges politics in a deluge
of circulating, disintegrated spectacles and opinions. Differently put, the
intense circulation of content in communicative capitalism occludes the
antagonism necessary for politics, multiplying antagonism into myriad
minor issues and events.[9] In relatively closed societies, that antagonism is
not only already clear but also apparent at and as the very frontier between
open and closed.

Communicative capitalism is a political-economic formation in which
there is talk without response, in which the very practices associated with
governance by the people consolidate and support the most brutal inequities of corporate-controlled capitalism. One way to understand the
hold of communicative capitalism is to consider its animating fantasies,
fantasies that, for many on the left, are inextricable from their faith in

democracy. This chapter takes up three such fantasies, those of abundance, participation, and wholeness. The hold of these fantasies on the political imaginary, the promises and aspirations they inscribe in the ideological structure of our most basic communicative activities, helps account for the persistence of belief in democracy in the face of knowledge of the way that the democratic form continues to strengthen the place and power of the wealthy and diminish the lives and opportunities of the poor.

In the months before the 2002 congressional elections, just as Congress abdicated its constitutional responsibility to declare war to the president, mainstream media frequently employed the trope of "debate." Democratic leaders, with an eye to this "debate," asserted that questions needed to be asked. They did not take a position or provide a clear alternative to the Bush administration's emphasis on preventive war. Giving voice to the ever-present meme regarding the White House's public relations strategy, people on the street spoke of whether Bush had "made his case." Nevertheless, on the second day of Senate debate on the use of force in Iraq, *no one* was on the floor—even though many were in the gallery. Why, at a time when the means of communication have been revolutionized, when people can contribute their own opinions and access those of others rapidly and immediately, why has democracy failed as a political form? Why has the expansion and intensification of communication networks, the proliferation of the very tools of democracy, coincided with the stunting of left political ideals and the diminishment of progressive political struggle? These are the questions the idea of communicative capitalism answers.

The Fantasy of Abundance:
From Message to Contribution

The delirium of the dot-com years was driven by a tremendous faith in speed, volume, and connectivity.[10] The speed and volume of communicative transactions would generate new "synergies" and hence wealth. Although that bubble burst (to be followed by a smaller one encompassing social networking sites, the user as producer, and the Web 2.0 meme), a similar belief underlies the conviction that enhanced communications access facilitates democracy. The belief begins with the observation that more people than ever before can make their opinions known. The Internet enables millions not simply to access information but to register their points of view on websites and blogs, to agree or disagree, to vote, and to send messages. Communications, media, and information enthusiasts point to this abundance of messages as an indication of the democratic potential of networked technologies.

Optimists and pessimists share this fantasy of abundance.[11] Those optimistic about the impact of networked communications on democratic practices emphasize the wealth of information available on the Internet and the inclusion of millions upon millions of voices or points of view into "the conversation" or "public sphere." Pessimists worry about the lack of filters, the data smog, and the fact that "all kinds of people" can be part of the conversation.[12] Despite their differing assessments of the value of abundance, both optimists and pessimists characterize networked communications in terms of exponential expansions in opportunities to transmit and receive messages.

The fantasy of abundance covers over the way facts and opinions, images and reactions circulate in a massive stream of content, losing their specificity and merging with and into the larger flow of data. Any given message is a contribution to this ever-circulating content, a drop in the ocean of cultural and political stuff engulfing us. This morphing of message into contribution is a constitutive feature of communicative capitalism.

One of the most basic formulations of the idea of communication is as a message and the response to the message.[13] Under communicative capitalism, this changes. Messages are contributions to circulating content— not actions to elicit responses. The exchange value of messages overtakes their use value. So a message is no longer primarily a message from a sender to a receiver. Uncoupled from contexts of action and application—as on the Web or in print and broadcast media—the message is simply part of a circulating data stream. Its particular content is irrelevant. Who sent it is irrelevant. Who receives it is irrelevant. That it need be responded to is irrelevant. The only thing that is relevant is circulation, the addition to the pool. Any particular contribution remains secondary to the fact of circulation. The value of any particular contribution is likewise inversely proportionate to the openness, inclusiveness, or extent of a circulating data stream: the more opinions or comments that are out there, the less of an impact any given one might make (and the more shocking, spectacular, and new a contribution must be in order to register or have an impact). In sum, communication functions symptomatically to produce its own negation.

Communication in communicative capitalism, then, is not, as Jürgen Habermas would suggest, action oriented toward reaching understanding.[14] In Habermas's model of communicative action, the use value of a message depends on its orientation. A sender sends a message with the intention that the message be received and understood. Any acceptance or rejection of the message depends on this understanding. Understanding is thus a *necessary* part of the communicative exchange. In communicative capitalism, however, the use value of a message is less important than its exchange value, its contribution to a larger pool, flow, or circulation of content. A contribution need not be understood; it need only be repeated, reproduced, forwarded. Circulation is the setting for the acceptance or rejection of a contribution.

How a contribution circulates determines whether it has been accepted or rejected. Does it circulate widely, among a variety of differentiated groups such that teenagers in the United States, accountants in Estonia, and indigenous groups in the Amazon speak in its terms, wear its logo, or hum its jingle? Does it circulate narrowly and influentially? Does it catch on but in an ironic, counterintuitive way, a way potentially counter to its original intention or reception? The questions alert us to how the sender (or author) becomes immaterial to the contribution, just as the producer, labor, drops out of the picture in commodity exchange. The circulation of logos, branded media identities, rumors, catch phrases, blog posts, urban myths, even positions and arguments exemplifies this point. The popularity, the penetration and duration of a contribution, marks its acceptance or success.

Thinking about messages in terms of use value and contributions in terms of exchange value sheds light on what would otherwise appear to be an asymmetry in communicative capitalism: the fact that some messages *are* received, that some discussions extend beyond the context of their circulation. It is also the case that many commodities are not useless, that people need them. But what makes them commodities is not the need people have for them or, obviously, their use. Rather it is their economic function, their role in capitalist exchange. Similarly, the fact that messages can retain a relation to understanding in no way negates the centrality of their circulation. Indeed, this link is crucial to the ideological reproduction of communicative capitalism. Some messages, issues, debates, are effective —public relations, advertising and political consulting are some of the industries depending on the production of such efficacy. Some contributions make a difference. But more significant is the system, the communications network. Even when we know that our specific contributions (our messages, blog posts, podcasts, video uploads, books, articles, films, letters to the editor) simply circulate in a rapidly moving and changing flow of content, in contributing, in participating, we act as if we do not know this. This action manifests ideology as the belief underlying action, the belief that reproduces communicative capitalism.[15]

The fantasy of abundance both expresses and conceals the shift from message to contribution. It expresses the shift through its emphases on expansions in communication—faster, better, cheaper; more inclusive, more accessible; high-speed, broadband, and so on. Yet even as it emphasizes these multiple expansions and intensifications, this abundance, the fantasy occludes the resulting devaluation of any particular contribution. It presumes that all contributions, all sites, are equal, equally likely to be heard or to make a difference. Enthusiastically reiterating the idea that anyone and everyone can participate, contribute, express themselves, and create, the fantasy of abundance also prevents us from recognizing the underlying inequalities inextricable from complex networks.

Recent developments in network science demonstrate structure in seemingly random networks. On the Web, for example, sites are not equally likely to have the same number of links. Nor are links randomly distributed among sites in a predictable, bell-curve fashion. Instead, there are clusters and hubs wherein some sites are nodes to which many sites link. These hubs serve as connectors for other nodes. In his path-breaking work on structure in complex networks, Albert-László Barabási finds hubs on the Web, in Hollywood, in citation networks, phone networks, food webs in ecosystems, and even cellular networks where some molecules, like water, do much more work than others.[16]

Barabási explains that degree distribution in networks with hubs, most real networks, follows a power-law. He writes, "Power laws mathematically formulate the fact that in most real networks the majority of nodes have only a *few* links and that these numerous tiny nodes coexist with a few big hubs, nodes with an anomalously high number of links. The few links connecting the smaller nodes to each other are not sufficient to ensure that the network is fully connected. This function is secured by the relatively rare hubs that keep real networks from falling apart"(70). In most real networks, nodes don't have an average number of links. Rather, a few have exponentially more links than others. Barabási describes the difference between random networks and networks that follow a power-law degree distribution with the term *scale*. In random networks, there is a limit to the number of links a node can have as well as an average number of links. Random networks thus have a characteristic "scale." In most real networks, however, "there is no such thing as a characteristic node. We see a continuous hierarchy of nodes, spanning from the rare hubs to the numerous tiny nodes"(70). These networks don't scale. They are "scale free."

Barabási notes that others have observed power-law degree distributions. The Italian economist Vilfredo Pareto noticed that 20 percent of his peapods produced 80 percent of the peas—nature doesn't always follow a bell curve. He also found that 80 percent of the land in Italy was owned by 20 percent of the population. In business and management circles, Pareto's law is known as the 80/20 rule (although he did not use the term) and is said to apply in a variety of instances: "80 percent of the profits are produced by only 20 percent of the employees, 80 percent of customer service problems are created by only 20 percent of consumers, 80 percent of decisions are made during 20 percent of meeting time, and so on"(66). Further examples might be Hollywood's "A list" or the "A list" that emerged among bloggers. Like scale-free networks, Pareto's law alerts us to distributions that follow power-laws.

How can power-laws be explained? Is some kind of sovereign authority redirecting nature out of a more primordial equality? Barabási finds that power-laws appear in phase transitions from disorder to order (he draws here from the Nobel prize-winning work of the physicist Kenneth Wilson). Power-laws "are the patent signatures of self-organization in complex systems" (77). Analyzing power-laws on the Web, Barabási identifies several properties that account for the Web's characteristics as a scale-free network. The first is *growth*. New sites or nodes are added at a dizzying pace. If new sites decide randomly to link to different old sites, old sites will always have an advantage. Just by arriving first, they will accumulate more links. But growth alone can't account for the power-law degree distribution. A second property is necessary, *preferential attachment*. New sites have to prefer older, more senior sites. Differently put, new sites will want to link to those sites that already have a lot of links. They don't link randomly but to the most popular sites which thereby become hubs.

Barabási argues that insofar as network evolution is governed by preferential attachment, one has to abandon the assumption that the Web (or Hollywood or any citation network) is democratic: "In real networks linking is never random. Instead, popularity is attractive" (86). Nodes that have been around for awhile, that have to an extent proven themselves, have distinct advantages over newcomers. In networks characterized by growth and preferential attachment, then, hubs emerge.

The fantasy of abundance—anyone can build a website, create a blog, express their opinions on the Internet—misdirects some critical media theorists away from the structure of real networks. Alexander R. Galloway, for example, emphasizes "distributed networks" that have "no central hubs and no radial nodes."[17] He claims that the Internet is a distributed network like the U.S. interstate highway system, a random network that scales, to use Barabási's terms. Embracing Gilles Deleuze's and Félix Guattari's image of the rhizome, Galloway notes that in a rhizome any point can be connected to any other; there are no intermediary hubs and no hierarchies. For him, the Web is best understood rhizomatically, as having a rhizomatic structure. Barabási's work demonstrates, however, that on the Web, as in any scale-free network, there are hubs and hierarchies. Some sites are more equal than others. Imagining a rhizome might be nice, but rhizomes don't describe the underlying structure of real networks. Hierarchies and hubs emerge out of growth and preferential attachment.

Networked communications are celebrated for enabling everyone to contribute, participate, and be heard. The form this communication takes isn't concealed. People are fully aware of the media, the networks, even the surfeit of information. But they act as if they don't have this knowledge, believing in the importance of their contributions, presuming, say, that there are readers for their blogs, articles, and books. People tend to believe, then, in both abundance and registration. They believe that there is too much out there *and* that their own specific contribution matters. Why? As I explain in the next section, networked communications induce a kind of registration effect that supports a fantasy of participation.

The Fantasy of Participation: Technology Fetishism

In their online communications, people are apt to express intense emotions, intimate feelings, some of the more secret or significant aspects of their sense of who they are. Years ago, while surfing through Yahoo's homepages, I found the page of a guy who featured pictures of his dog, his parents, and himself fully erect in an s/m–style harness. At the bottom of his site was the typical, "Thanks for stopping by! Don't forget to write and tell me what you think!" This quaint image suggests how easy many find it to reveal themselves on the Internet. More contemporary examples are blogs, image-sharing sites like Flickr, video-sharing sites like YouTube, and social-networking sites like MySpace or Facebook. Not only are people accustomed to putting their thoughts online but also, in so doing, they believe their thoughts and ideas are registering—*write and tell me what you think*! They imagine themselves brave participants in a combative arena or prostrate confessors acknowledging their shortcomings. One *believes* that one's contribution matters, that it means something to and within a context broader than oneself. Contributing to the information stream thus has a subjective registration effect detached from any actual impact or efficacy.

Because of this registration effect, people treat their contribution to circulating content as communicative action. They believe that they are active, making a difference by clicking on a button, adding their name to a petition, or commenting on a blog. Slavoj Žižek describes this kind of activity with the term *interpassivity*. When we are interpassive, something else, a fetish object, is active in our stead. Žižek explains: "You think you are active, while your true position, as embodied in the fetish, is passive."[18] The frantic activity of the fetish works to prevent actual action, to prevent something from really happening. Activity on the Internet, contributing to the circulation of affect and opinion, thus involves a profound passivity, one that is interconnected, linked, but passive nonetheless. Put back in terms of the circulation of contributions that fail to coalesce into actual debates, that fail as messages in need of response, we might think of this odd interpassivity as content that is linked to other content but never fully connected. Linking or citing stands in for reading, which stands in for engaging. At each juncture, there is a gap.

Networked communication and information technologies are exquisite media for capturing and reformatting political energies. They turn efforts at political engagement into contributions to the circulation of content, reinforcing the hold of neoliberalism's technological infrastructure. Political intensities become shorn of their capacity to raise claims to the universal, persisting simply as intensities, as indications of subjective feeling (a phenomenon taken up in greater detail in chapter 4). The more strident the voices, the more intense the feelings, the stronger is the pull of communications media in their myriad, constant, and ever-ready forms. Media circulate and extend information about an issue or event, amplifying its affect and seemingly its significance. This amplification draws in more media, more commentary and opinion, more parody and comic relief, more attachment to communicative capitalism's information and entertainment networks such that the knot of feedback and enjoyment itself operates as (and in place of) the political issue or event. Attention focuses on reflecting and commenting on the tangle of intensities—for the moment. More energies are invested in it. And the problem or issue is neglected, left to continue along its course, undeflected and unchanging despite the massive amount of interest and energy it has generated.

This capture of political energies and investments and their reformatting as contributions is enabled by the reduction of politics to communicative acts, to speaking and saying and exposing and explaining, a reduction key to a democracy conceived of in terms of discussion and deliberation. Struggles on the Internet are able to reiterate and thereby displace political struggles in local and institutional settings precisely because these latter struggles are envisioned as communicative engagements. In turn, this displacement protects the activities of corporate and governmental officials who are able to market and monitor, expropriate and privatize, unencumbered even as their activities are observed and discussed.[19] That people know what corporations and governments are doing doesn't mean they can change them. That they are aware of a problem, have an opinion, and make their opinion known doesn't mean they have developed the infrastructure necessary to write new legislation, garner support for it, and get it passed, much less carry out a revolution (a term the left has abandoned and the right embraced).[20] When communication serves as the key category for left politics, whether communication be configured as discussion, spectacle, or publicity, this politics ensures its political failure in advance: doing is reduced to talking, to contributing to the media environment, instead of being conceived in terms of, say, occupying military bases, taking over the government, or abandoning the Democratic Party and doing the steady, persistent organizational work of revitalizing the Greens or Socialists.

Under communicative capitalism, communication functions fetishistically as the disavowal of a more fundamental political disempowerment or castration. If Freud is correct in saying a fetish not only covers over a trauma but in so doing helps one through a trauma, what might serve as an analogous sociopolitical trauma today? A likely answer can be found in the left's role in the collapse of the welfare state: its betrayal of fundamental commitments to social solidarity. A thorough account of this collapse is beyond the scope of my analysis here. Three aspects of left failure nonetheless mark the political trauma underlying technology fetishism: its abandonment of workers and the poor; its retreat from the state and repudiation of collective action; and its acceptance of the neoliberal economy as the "only game in town."

In brief, the late 1960s and early 1970s witnessed a set of profound changes in the world economy, changes associated with declines in economic growth and increases in inflation and unemployment. As the following chapter explores, powerful figures in the corporate and finance sectors took this opportunity to dismantle the welfare state (by privatizing public holdings, cutting back on public services, and rewriting laws for the benefit of corporations). For the most part, the American left seemed relatively unaware of the ways business was acting as a class to consolidate political power—a fundamental component of which was the passage of a set of campaign finance laws establishing the rights of corporations to contribute unlimited amounts of money to political parties and political action committees.[21] Instead, coming out of the movements associated with 1968, increasingly prominent voices on the left emphasized and fought for personal freedoms, freedoms from parental and state constraints as well as freedoms for the expression of differences of race, sex, and sexuality. While these ideals were situated within movements for social justice, their coexistence was precarious, as tensions at the time between workers and students made clear. Harvey writes, "Pursuit of social justice presupposes social solidarities and a willingness to submerge individual wants, needs, and desires in the cause of some more general struggle . . . It has long proved difficult within the U.S. left, for example, to forge the collective discipline required for political action to achieve social

justice without offending the desire of political actors for individual freedom and for full recognition and expression of political identities."[22] Just
as corporate, business, and financial interests were coming together politically, those on the left were fragmenting into particularities.[23]

Identity politics proved a boon for the right, enabling the alliance
between social conservatives and neoliberals. The former opposed the
welfare state for the way it allegedly undermined morality and family
values, encouraged criminality, abortion, and sex outside of marriage, and
benefited the drug-addicted and lazy more than the sober and diligent.
Engaged in struggles against social conservatives on all these fronts, many
leftists embraced the emphasis on freedom and attack on the state prominent among neoliberals. The state seemed but another repressive authority, its provisions tied to the sexism of the traditional family and the racism
of the white mainstream.[24] Unions appeared corrupt, already part of a
status quo limiting opportunities to the white and the male. Likewise, in
the wake of more than a quarter century of anticommunism, ever fewer
leftists found in Marxism a viable language for expressing political aspirations. Observing how oppression occurs along multiple axes, they argued
that a focus on class obscures the diversity of political struggles.[25] The
economic problems plaguing the welfare state, moreover, suggested to
some the limits of political attempts at regulation and redistribution. The
economist Michael Perelman notes that "by the time of the Carter administration, many liberals joined conservatives in opposing regulation."[26]
Deregulation came to seem like a respectable policy. Given the impera-
tives of complex systems, even leftists started to agree that some form of
capitalism would and should persist; what was needed were guarantees for
the rights and differences of all within capitalist societies, a more radical or
participatory approach to democracy.

Yet as they echoed the criticisms of the state prominent on the right,
leftists failed to provide a compelling vision of a new form of social
solidarity. Instead, they continued to emphasize the plurality of struggles
on a variety of social and cultural terrains and to affirm different modes
of living. Such an emphasis and affirmation enabled an easy coexistence
with consumer capitalism insofar as choices of fashion and entertainment
could be quickly read as politically significant. Antiracist? Wear a Malcolm
X t-shirt. Gay-friendly? Fly a rainbow flag. The ease of political expression,
the quick availability of the affective thrill of radicality, could let more

people feel that they were politically engaged even as the shift in political parties from person-intensive to finance-intensive organization strategies reduced the political opportunities open to most Americans to voting or giving money.

In short, the American left responded to the attack on the welfare state, collapse of Keynesianism, and emergence of a neoliberal consensus by forfeiting its historical solidarity with workers and the poor, retreating from the state, and losing the sense that collective solutions to large-scale systemic inequalities are possible and necessary. The failure of solidarity was manifest perhaps most acutely in President Bill Clinton's destruction of welfare guarantees (aid to families with dependent children) in favor of Temporary Assistance to Needy Families (capped at five years) in the Personal Responsibility and Work Opportunity Reconciliation Act of 1996. Republicans didn't eliminate welfare; Democrats, the party associated with the interests of the poor and the working class since the Depression, did.

This failure of solidarity is closely linked to the left's withdrawal from the state—even as various elements on the right developed strategies for funding and winning electoral campaigns, interpreting the Constitution, and rewriting laws, even as corporate and business interests steadily increased their political investments, the left failed adequately to defend what had long ago been won, namely, the notion that the most fundamental role of the state is ensuring a minimal social and economic standard below which no one is allowed to fall. Indeed, many dismissed the state as useless and outmoded, preferring to theorize instead a politics beyond the state (a move which left an open field for conservative strategists).[27]

Finally, as it overlapped with a reluctance to offend any particular desires for freedom, backing away from the state resonated with a sense that there is no alternative to the market. And rather than simply an approach to the distribution of goods and services, this sense is more profoundly a sense of political inefficacy: *we* can't do anything about anything. In part, the loss of agency results from the prior acceptance of the inevitability of capitalism. But it results as well from an underlying skepticism toward uttering the word *we*, toward speaking for others and thereby risking overlooking their specific differences.

The splintering and collapse of the left constitutes a political trauma. Technology fetishism responds to this trauma, acknowledging and denying it at the same time. For many, new media let them feel as if they are making a contribution, let them deny the larger lack of left solidarity even as their very individualized and solitary linking and clicking attests to the new political conditions.

In the last decades of the twentieth century, information and communication technology spread beyond government and university settings on the promise of political empowerment. Ted Nelson, Stewart Brand, and the People's Computer Company reconfigured images of commuting away from IBM and its technocratic experts and toward the emancipation and empowerment of ordinary people.[28] In the context of the San Francisco Bay Area's antiwar activism during the early seventies, they held up computers as the means to renew participatory democracy.[29] This was the setting for Apple's presentation of its Macintosh computer as changing the world, as saving democracy by bringing technology to the people. In 1984, the company ran an advertisement with an image of a Mac next to a picture of Karl Marx; the slogan: "It was about time a capitalist started a revolution." During the nineties Al Gore and Newt Gingrich promised ordinary citizens' access to government. They appealed to the possibility of town meetings for millions opened up by the Internet. Their rhetoric of democratization and education drove the Information and Infrastructure Technology Act, the National Information Infrastructure Act (both passing in 1993), and the 1996 Telecommunications Act.[30] Networked communications technologies would ensure real political efficacy and governmental responsiveness. Democracy would be enhanced as all citizens acquired the ability to access information and express their opinions.

This promise of participation was not simply propaganda. It was and remains a deeper, underlying fantasy wherein technology covers over our impotence and supports a vision of ourselves as active political participants. Think of the rhetoric encasing any new device, system, code, or platform. A particular technological innovation becomes a screen upon which all sorts of fantasies of political action are projected.[31]

Peer-to-peer file sharing, especially in light of the early rather hypnotic, mantra-like appeals to Napster, provides a clear example. Napster—despite that fact that it was a commercial venture—was heralded as a sea change; it would transform private property, bring down capitalism. More than piracy, Napster was a popular attack on private property itself. Nick Dyer-Witheford argues that Napster, and other peer-to-peer networks, present "real possibilities of market disruption as a result of large-scale copyright violation." He contends: "While some of these peer-to-peer networks—like Napster—were created as commercial applications, others —such as Free Net—were designed as political projects with the explicit intention of destroying both state censorship and commercial copyright. . . . The adoption of these celebratory systems as a central component of North American youth culture presents a grassroots expansion of the digital commons and, at the very least, seriously problematizes current plans for their enclosure."[32] Lost in the celebratory rhetoric is the fact that capitalism has never depended on one industry. Industries rise and fall. Corporations like Sony and Bertelsmann can face declines in one sector and still make astronomical profits in other ones. Worries about the loss of the beloved paperback book to unwieldy e-books weren't presented as dooming the publishing industry or assaulting the very regime of private property. Why should sharing music files be any different? "Sharing" at one level (files) enables ownership at others (hardware, network access).

Even the much-lauded "consumer as producer" fails to attack private property. On the one hand, large commercial sites like Amazon claim ownership rights to all content—book reviews, lists—placed on their site. On the other, production is always and necessarily a kind of consumption, whether of raw materials or labor power.[33] Joshua Gamson's point about the legacy of Internet-philia is appropriate here: wildly displaced enthusiasm over the political impact of a specific technological practice results in a tendency "to bracket institutions and ownership, to research and theorize uses and users of new media outside of those brackets, and to allow 'newness' to overshadow historical continuity."[34]

Napster is a technological fetish onto which all sorts of fantasies of political action were projected. In this instance, the fantasy is one deeply held by music fans: music can change the world. Armed with networked personal computers, the weapons of choice for American college students in a not-so-radical oh-so-consumerist entertainment culture, the wired revolutionaries can think they are changing the world, comforted all the while that nothing really changes (except the price of compact discs).

The technological fetish covers over and sustains a lack on the part of the subject. It protects the fantasy of an active, engaged subject by acting in the subject's stead. The technological fetish "is political" for us, enabling us to go about the rest of our lives relieved of the guilt that we might not be doing our part and secure in the belief that we are, after all, informed, engaged citizens. The paradox of the technological fetish is that the technology acting in our stead actually enables us to remain politically passive. We don't have to assume political responsibility because, again, the technology is doing it for us.

The technological fetish also covers over a fundamental lack or absence in the social order. It protects a fantasy of unity or wholeness, compensating in advance for this impossibility. Technologies are invested with hopes and dreams, with aspirations to something better. A technological fetish is at work when one disavows the lack or antagonism rupturing (yet producing) the social by advocating a particular technological fix. The "fix" lets us think that all we need is to extend a particular technology and then we will have a democratic or reconciled social order.

Gamson's account of gay websites illustrates this fetish function. Gamson argues that in the United States, the Internet has been a major force in transforming "gay and lesbian media from organizations answering at least partly to geographical and political communities into businesses answering primarily to advertisers and investors."[35] He focuses on gay portals and their promises to offer safe and friendly spaces for the gay community. What he notes, however, is the way that these safe gay spaces now function primarily "to deliver a market share to corporations." As he explains, "Community needs are conflated with consumption desires, and community equated with market."[36] Qua fetish, the portal is a screen upon which fantasies of connection can be projected. These fantasies displace attention from their commercial context.

In communicative capitalism, the technological fetish has three primary modes of operation: condensation, displacement, and denial.

Condensation occurs when technology fetishism reduces the complexities of politics—of organization, struggle, duration, decisiveness, division, representation, and so on—to one thing, one problem to be solved and one technological solution. For example, democracy might be treated as a singular problem of information: people don't have the information they need to participate effectively.[37] Bingo! Information technologies intervene to provide people with information. This sort of strategy, however, occludes the problems of organizing and political will. For example, as Mary Graham explains in her study of the politics of disclosure in chemical emissions, food labeling, and medical error policy, transparency started to function as a regulatory mechanism precisely at a time when legislative action seemed impossible. Agreeing that people had a right to know, politicians could argue for warning labels and more data while avoiding hard or unpopular decisions. Corporations could comply—and find ways to use their reports to improve their market position. "Companies often lobbied for national disclosure requirements," Graham writes. "They did so," she continues, "because they believed that disclosure could reduce the chances of tougher regulation, eliminate the threat of multiple state requirements, or improve competitive advantage. . . . Likewise, large food processing companies and most trade associations supported national nutritional labeling as an alternative to multiple state requirements and new regulations, or to a crackdown on health claims. Some also expected competitive gain from labeling as consumers, armed with accurate information, increased demand for authentically healthful productions."[38] Additional examples of condensation appear when theorists and activists emphasize singular websites, blogs, and events. Such spikes in the media sphere may well seem impressive, but they conform to the dictates of broadcast media spectacle, momentary eruptions that anchor people to their screens, calling upon them to register their opinions, to contribute. They don't provide alternative practices of collective engagement, challenge corporate ownership of the telecommunications infrastructure, or redirect financial flows toward the most disadvantaged.

The second mode of operation of the technological fetish is displacement. A tendency among some political and new media theorists is to displace politics onto the activities of everyday or ordinary people as if academics, activists, and politicians were somehow extraordinary. What everyday people do in their everyday lives is supposed to overflow with political activity: conflicts, negotiations, interpretations, resistances, collusions, cabals, transgressions, and resignifications. The Internet—as well as cell phones, beepers, and other communications devices (though, weirdly, not the regular old telephone, likely because of its confinement in domestic and office space)—is teeming with politics. To put up a website, to deface a website, to redirect hits to other sites, to deny access to a website, to link to a website are construed as real political actions. Bloggers and blogging allegedly reactivate politics, operating as forces reshaping politics and journalism, despite the continued role of the mainstream media *even for bloggers* and the continued domination of large-scale financial interests

in electoral politics. The emphasis on networked communication strategies displaces political energy from the hard work of organizing and struggle. It also remains oddly one-sided, conveniently forgetting both the
larger media environment of these activities, as if there were not and have
not been left print publications for years, and the political setting of
networked communications. After all, the Republican Party as well as all
sorts of other conservative organizations and lobbyists use the Internet
just as much as, if not more than, progressive groups.

Writing on Many-2-Many, a group weblog on social software, Clay
Shirky uses a similar argument to explain Howard Dean's poor showing in the Iowa caucuses following what appeared to be his remarkable
successes on the Internet during the 2000 presidential campaign. Shirky
writes:

> We know well from past attempts to use social software to organize
> groups for political change that it is hard, very hard, because participa-
> tion in online communities often provides a sense of satisfaction that
> actually dampens a willingness to interact with the real world. When
> you're communing with like-minded souls, you *feel* [emphasis in origi-
> nal] like you're accomplishing something by arguing out the smallest
> details of your perfect future world, while the imperfect and actual
> world takes no notice, as is its custom.
>
> There are many reasons for this, but the main one seems to be that
> the pleasures of life online are precisely the way they provide a respite
> from the vagaries of the real world. Both the way the online environ-
> ment flattens interaction and the way everything gets arranged for the
> convenience of the user makes the threshold between talking about
> changing the world and changing the world even steeper than usual.[39]

Interacting with others online feels good. It feels like action, like one is
doing something, like one is making a difference. One might argue on a
blog for hours on end, failing to convince another person of a single point,
and *still* feel efficacious and involved. But this feeling is unconnected from
any larger collective practice that might actually affect change.

My point is not that Web-based activities are trivial or that social
software is useless. The Internet is an important medium for connecting
and communicating, and the Dean campaign was innovative in its use of
social software to build a vital, supportive movement around Dean's can-

didacy. But media pleasures should not displace our attention from the ways political change demands much, much more than networked communication and the ways intense mediality provides barriers to action on the ground (it's hard to find time to go door-to-door when one blogs twenty hours a day). As the Dean campaign also demonstrates, without organized and sustained action, without building relationships with caucus attendees in Iowa, say, Internet politics remains precisely that—a politics of and through new media, and that's all.

The last operation of the technological fetish follows from and is enabled by the previous two: denial. The political purchase of the technological fetish is presumed in advance; it is immediate, understood. File-sharing *is* political. A website *is* political. Blogging *is* political. This assertion of immediacy, however, is an energetic form of denial. The presumption that a left politics necessarily attaches to a technological fix denies what the media activist or technology enthusiast already knows to be the case—that democracy in practice is the rule of the wealthy, the protection of a governmental elite who serves their interests, and the constant chatter and opining of everyone else in the circuits of communicative capitalism.

In his account of fetishism, Freud describes how the young boy's belief in the fetish enables him to retain and give up this belief at the same time.[40] He can know his belief that his mother has a penis is false but continue to believe it nevertheless—this is what the fetish allows him to do. Crucial to Freud's account is the reason for the boy's underlying attachment to his false belief—fear of castration. If he accepts what he knows, the boy must acknowledge castration, and this is what he cannot bear. He would rather retain the fiction of a mother with a penis than acknowledge a world of lack or accept the possibility of his own dependence or diminishment.

The power of the technological fetish operates in a similar fashion. A condition of possibility for asserting the immediately progressive political character of something—web-radio or open-source software, say—is a prior exclusion of knowledge of their antagonistic conditions of emergence, their embeddedness within the brutalities of global capitalism, their dependence for existence on systemic violence and nationalized and racialized divisions. Advocating the extension of information and communication technologies accepts and denies these conditions at the same time. Even as the proliferation of communication technologies serves

neoliberal financialization, accelerating the speed of monetary transactions and consolidating networks of privilege, the left advocate of participation, deliberation, and fundamental rights to communication can—
and must—energetically deny this context. Why would leftists promise
that the technologies could fix democracy, if democracy was not broken, if
it was not failing as a political form? And if democracy's underlying
brokenness is the problem, the actual condition for the advocate's emphasis on communication and technology, why isn't this fundamental lack
or failure the central matter at hand? Communicative capitalism thrives on
the fetishistic denial of democracy's failure, its inability to secure justice,
equity, or solidarity even as it enables millions to access information and
make their opinions known.

The Fantasy of Wholeness: A Global Zero Institution

Communicative capitalism relies on the fantasy of abundance accompanying the reformatting of messages as contributions and the fantasy of
participation accompanying technology fetishism. These fantasies give
people the sense that our actions online are politically significant, that
they make a difference. A fantasy of wholeness further animates networked communications. This fantasy furthers our sense that our contributions to circulating content matter by locating them in the most significant of possible spaces—the global. But the world does not serve as a
space for communicative capitalism analogous to the one the nation provided for industrial capitalism. On the contrary, the space of communicative capitalism is the Internet. Networked communications materialize
specific fantasies of unity and wholeness as the global. These fantasies in
turn secure networked transactions as the Real of global capitalism.

The concept of the "zero institution" helps explain the way the Internet
functions as the key space for imagining the global.[41] A zero institution is
an empty signifier. It has no determinate meaning but instead signifies the
presence of meaning. It is an institution with no positive function. All it
does is signify institutionality as such (as opposed to chaos, say). As
originally developed by Claude Lévi-Strauss, the concept of the zero institution accounts for the way people with radically different descriptions
of their collectivity nevertheless understand themselves as members of the
same tribe. Žižek adds to the Lévi-Straussian idea insight into how both

the nation and sexual difference function as zero institutions. The nation designates the unity of society in the face of radical antagonism, the irreconcilable division and struggle between classes. Sexual difference, in contrast, suggests difference as such, a zero-level of absolute difference that will always be filled in and overdetermined by contextually given differences.

In light of the nation's failing capacity to stand symbolically for institutionality, the Internet has emerged as the zero institution of communicative capitalism. It enables myriad constituencies to understand themselves as part of the same global structure even as they radically disagree, fail to co-link, and inhabit fragmented and disconnected network spaces. The Internet is not a wide-open space with nodes and links to nodes distributed in random fashion such that any one site is equally as likely to get hits as any other site. This open, smooth, virtual world of endless and equal opportunity is a fantasy (and not simply because some countries censor and block). Barabási's research on directedness in scale-free networks demonstrates that the World Wide Web is broken into four major "continents" with their own navigational requirements (161–78). Following links on one continent may never bring a user to another continent; likewise, following links in one direction does not mean that a user can retrace these links back to her starting point. Despite the fact that its very architecture (like all directed networks) entails fragmentation into separate spaces, the Internet presents itself as the unity and fullness of the global. Here, through our communicative interactions, the global is imagined and realized. The Internet thus functions as a particularly powerful zero institution precisely because it is animated by the fantasy of global unity.

The Internet provides an imaginary site of action and belonging. Celebrated for its freedoms and lack of boundaries, this imagined totality serves as a kind of presencing of the global. On the one hand, the Internet imagines, stages, and enacts the "global" of global capitalism. But on the other, this global is nothing like the "world"—as if such an entity were possible, as if one could designate an objective reality undisturbed by the external perspective observing it or a fully consistent essential totality unruptured by antagonism.[42]

The oscillations in the 1990s debate over the character of the Internet can clarify this point. In the debate, Internet users appeared either as engaged citizens eager to participate in electronic town halls and regularly communicate with their elected representatives, or they appeared as Web-surfing waste-of-lives in dark, dirty rooms downloading porn, betting on obscure Internet stocks, or collecting evidence of the U.S. government's work with extraterrestrials at Area 51. In other versions of this same matrix, users were either innocent children or dreadful war-game-playing teenage boys. Good interactions were on Amazon. Bad interactions were under-ground and involved drugs, kiddie porn, LSD, and plutonium. These famil-iar oscillations remind us the Internet has always been particular and struggles over its regulation have been struggles over what kind of particu-larity would and should be installed. Rather than far-reaching, engaging, and accessible, the Internet has been constituted in and through conflict over specific practices and subjectivities. Not everything goes.

We might even say that those who want to clean up the Internet, who want to get rid of or zone the porn and the gambling, who want to centralize, rationalize, and organize commercial transactions in ways more beneficial to established corporations than to mom and pop shops, express as a difference on the Internet what is actually the starker difference between societies traversed and mediated through electronic communica-tions and financial networks and those reliant more on social, interper-sonal, and extralegal networks. As Ernesto Laclau argues, the division between the social and the nonsocial, or between society and what is other to it, external and threatening, can only be expressed as a difference internal to society.[43] If capital today traverses the globe, how can the difference between us and them be expressed? The oscillations in the Internet debates depict a difference between those who are sexualized, undisciplined, violent, irrational, lazy, excessive, and extreme and those who are civilized, mainstream, hard-working, balanced, and normal. Put in the terms of Lacanian psychoanalysis, the other on the Internet is the Real other—not the other I imagine as like me and not the symbolic other to be recognized and respected through abstract norms and rights. Efforts to clean up the Internet target more than gambling and porn; they involve the image of the global. Whatever disrupts the fantasy of unity on the Internet cannot be part of the global.

The particularity of the fantasies of the global animating the Internet is striking. Richard Rogers's research on linking practices on the World Wide

Web brings out the pervasive localism and provincialism. In his account of the Dutch food safety debate, Rogers observes "little in the way of 'web dialogue' or linkage outside of small Dutch 'food movement.' "[44] Critics of partisan bloggers as well as of the sheltered world of AOL click on a similar problem—the way the world on the Internet shrinks into a very specific image of the global.[45] How would English-speaking American high school students on Facebook or southern mommies uploading photos of their scrapbook pages come into contact with sites providing Qur'anic instruction to modern Muslims—even if there were no language problems? And why would they bother? Why should they? As a number of commentators have worried for a while now, opportunities to customize the news and announcements one reads—not to mention the already undigestible amount of information available on topics in which one is deeply interested— contribute to the segmentation and isolation of users within bubbles of views and opinions with which they already agree.[46] Segmentation and isolation are neither new nor unique to the Internet, but they run counter to the fantasy of the global on which communicative capitalism relies.

The particularity of these fantasies of the global is important because this is the global networked communications produce. Our networked interactions produce our specific worlds as the global of global capitalism. They create the expectations and effects of communicative capitalism, expectations and effects that necessarily vary with the setting. Because the global is whatever specific communities or exchanges imagine it to be, anything outside the experience or comprehension of these communities either does not exist or is an inhuman, otherworldly alien threat that must be annihilated. If everything is out there on the Internet, anything I fail to encounter—or can't imagine encountering—isn't simply excluded (everything is already there), it is foreclosed. Admitting or accessing what is foreclosed destroys the very order constituted through foreclosure. Thus, the imagined unity of the global, a fantasy filled in by the particularities of specific contexts, is one without fundamental conflict.[47] Circulating content can't effect change in this sort of world—it is already complete. The only alternative is the Real that ruptures my world, that is to say, the evil other with whom I cannot imagine sharing a world, the one I must eradicate. The very fantasy of a global that makes my networked interactions vital and important results in a world closed to politics and threatened by evil.

No Reponse

A Lacanian commonplace is that a letter always arrives at its destination. What does this mean with respect to networked communications? It means that a letter, a message, in communicative capitalism is not really sent. There is no response because there is no arrival. There is just the contribution to circulating content.

Many readers will likely disagree.[48] Some might bring up the successes of MoveOn. From its early push to have Congress censure Bill Clinton and "move on," to its efforts to organize its millions of members in opposition to the U.S. invasion of Iraq, MoveOn has become a presence in mainstream American politics. In addition to circulating petitions and arranging emails and faxes to members of Congress, one of MoveOn's best actions was a virtual sit-in: over 200,000 of us called into Washington, D.C., at scheduled times on the same day, shutting down phone lines into the Capitol for hours. In early 2004, MoveOn sponsored an advertisement contest: the winning ad would be shown during the Super Bowl football game. The selected ad, titled "Child's Play," illustrated the Bush administration's trillion-dollar deficit with images of children hauling trash, working in assembly lines, and carrying out other physically demanding tasks generally associated with low-pay, low-skill labor. It was great—but CBS refused to broadcast it.

Far from being evidence against my argument, MoveOn exemplifies technology fetishism and confirms my account of the reduction and capture of political energies into contributions to communicative capitalism's circuits of information and entertainment. MoveOn's campaigns director, Eli Pariser, says that the organization is "opt-in, it's decentralized, you do it from your home."[49] No one has to remain committed or be bothered with boring meetings. All one has to do is contribute—an opinion, a signature, or money. Andrew Boyd, in a positive appraisal of the group, writes that "MoveOn's strength lies . . . in providing a home for busy people who may not want to be a part of a chapter-based organization with regular meetings. . . . By combining a nimble entrepreneurial style with a strong ethic of listening to its members—via online postings and straw polls—MoveOn has built a responsive, populist and relatively democratic virtual community."[50] Busy people can think they are active—the technology will act for them, alleviating their guilt while assuring them that nothing will change too much. The virtual community won't place too many (actually any) demands on them. Its democracy is the democracy of communicative capitalism—opinions will circulate, views will be expressed, information will be accessed. By sending an email, signing a petition, responding to an article on a blog, people can feel political. And that feeling feeds communicative capitalism insofar as it leaves behind the time-consuming, incremental, and risky efforts of politics. MoveOn likes to emphasize that it abstains from ideology, from division. While this postideological gesture is disingenuous—MoveOn's politics are clearly progressive, antiwar, left-democratic—the emphasis on a nonposition is symptomatic of precisely that denial of the trauma of contemporary left politics that the technological fetish covers over: it is a refusal to offer a vision of collectivity, to stand for a solidarity premised not on individual particularities and desires (which is no solidarity at all) but on the painstaking and organized struggle for reclaiming the state as a force to be used against neoliberalism and its corporate beneficiaries.

One might find better reasons to disagree with me when one focuses on the role of the Internet in mass mobilizations, in connecting activists from all over the world, and in providing an independent media source. The mobilization on February 15, 2003, of ten million people worldwide to protest the Bush administration's push for war against Iraq is perhaps the most striking example, but one might also mention MoveOn's candlelight vigil on March 16, an action involving over a million people in 130 countries. Such uses of the Internet are vitally important for political activists—especially given the increasingly all-pervasive reach of corporate-controlled media. But these examples fail to address the question of whether such instances of intense social meaning drive larger organizational efforts and contribute to the formation of political solidarities with more duration. At the end of the first decade of the new millennium, there is little evidence that they do. On the contrary, left activists seem ever more drawn to spectacular events that raise awareness, momentarily, but do little in the way of building the institutions necessary to sustain a new political order. Networked communication technologies materialize democracy as a political form that formats political energies as communicative engagements. Valued as the key to political inclusion and democratic participation, new media technologies strengthen the hold of neoliberalism and the privilege of the top 1 percent of people on the planet. At the same time, globally networked communications remain the very tools and terrains of struggle, making political change more difficult —and more necessary—than ever before.

2

Free Trade

THE NEOLIBERAL FANTASY

Communicative capitalism strengthens the grip of neoliber-alism. Our everyday practices of searching and linking, our communicative acts of discussing and disagreeing, performing and posing, intensify our dependence on the information networks crucial to the financial and corporate dominance of neoliberalism. Communicative capitalism captures our political interventions, formatting them as contributions to its circuits of affect and entertainment—*we feel political, involved, like contributors who really matter.*

The fact of such formatting does not mean networked computing necessarily or inevitably leads to neoliberalism—or vice versa (after all, the Soviets had computers and the protocols underlying the Internet were developed as state initiatives). Neoliberalism is a political and economic project—there is nothing inevitable about it.[1] The sense that *there is no alternative* is a component of neoliberal ideology, one of the ways that the ideology installs in its subjects a belief in markets—*anything else fails, is inefficient, can't be funded, won't last, can't compete in a global arena . . .*

To succeed, though, neoliberalism depends on the organized political occupation and direction of governments, on the use of the bureaucratic, legal, and security apparatuses of the state in ways that benefit corporate and financial interests (the most obvious examples here include the Bush administration's support of and collusion with oil and energy interests as well as private military contractors and Clinton's revocation of the Glass-

Steagall Act in 1999 so as to enable the formation of financial superpowers composed of commercial banking, investment banking, and stock brokerage). Neoliberalism's supporters and adherents have to rely on political alliances and in so doing compromise some of the values and ideals they champion. At the same time, to retain its dominant position neoliberalism as an ideological formation has to offer something to the people whose lives it shapes. It has to structure their expectations and desires so that it *feels right, like the way things just are.* It can't say directly, "Hey, you guys go work really hard so that rich people can get even richer."

Lacanian psychoanalysis, particularly as reworked by Slavoj Žižek, helps explain the way ideological formations link together a set of often conflicting and contradictory promises for enjoyment and explanations for its lack (for people's failure to enjoy despite all the promises that they would). Enjoyment (*jouissance*) is the Lacanian term for an overwhelming, even agonizing, affective intensity.[2] It designates something we desire but can never fully get, and something we want to avoid but can never fully shake. It's that "something extra" for the sake of which we do what might otherwise seem irrational, counterproductive, or even wrong. And it's that "something extra" we can't help but suspect accompanies even those actions that we hope are rational, productive, and right. Ideological formations, then, work as economies of enjoyment to forbid, permit, direct, and command enjoyment.[3]

The category of enjoyment is an important addition to the theory of ideology insofar as it accentuates the way an ideological formation is more than a set of meanings, images, and the accumulated effects of dispersed practices. Rather, ideology "takes hold" of the subject at the point of the nugget of enjoyment outside the meaning or significance the ideological formation provides. This excess enjoyment marks the incompleteness of a formation, the limits of what it can explain, and the extra "kick" it promises. Fantasies organize these remainders, accounting for societies' failures, ruptures, and inconsistencies in ways that promise and produce enjoyment. In so doing, they bind subjects to certain sets of relations, structuring and confining their thinking and acting so as to attach them to seemingly inescapable patterns of domination, patterns they may well recognize as domination but keep following, nevertheless.

Chapter 1 takes up the fantastic investments in technology informing and attaching some leftists to democracy, the fantasies of abundance,

participation, and wholeness. This chapter considers neoliberalism's underlying fantasy of free trade and the kinds of enjoyment this fantasy
promises and provides. It highlights a specific problem neoliberalism creates for left politics, namely, the change in the subject positions available
for political deployment. Whereas the Keynesian welfare state interpel-
lated subjects into specific symbolic identities (such as the worker, the
housewife, the student, or the citizen), neoliberalism relies on imaginary
identities. Not only do the multiplicity and variability of such identities
prevent them from serving as loci of political action but their inseparabil-
ity from the injunctions of consumerism reinforces capitalism's grip.

What Is Neoliberalism?

In recent years, scholars have produced significant analyses of neoliberalism as a set of policy assumptions favoring corporations, as inseparable
from globalization and imperialism, as a "project for the restoration of
class power," as a specific form of governmentality, and as a new form
of the state.[4] The following sketch of neoliberalism synthesizes these
contributions.

Most generally, neoliberalism is a philosophy viewing market exchange
as a guide for all human action. Redefining social and ethical life in
accordance with economic criteria and expectations, neoliberalism holds
that human freedom is best achieved through the operation of markets.
Freedom (rather than justice or equality) is the fundamental political
value. The primary role of the state is to provide an institutional framework for markets, establishing rights of property and contract, for example, and creating markets in domains where they may not have existed
previously. Consequently, neoliberalism accords to the state an active
role in securing markets, in producing the subjects of and conditions for
markets, although it does not think the state should—at least ideally—
intervene in the activities of markets.

In his unpublished lectures on governmentality, Michel Foucault emphasizes two fundamental differences between early political liberalism
and contemporary neoliberalism.[5] First, neoliberalism inverts the early
model of the state as a limiting, external principle supervising the market
to make the market form itself the regulative principle underlying the
state. Second, neoliberalism relies on a different notion of the individual

or subject. For classic liberals, such as Thomas Hobbes and John Locke, the free, rational individual is the very foundation of the state, that which grounds and limits legitimate government. Neoliberals neither anchor their account of the rational chooser in a domain of natural freedom nor make the rational chooser the ground and limit of government. Rather, they see the subject as acting and reacting in accordance with various economic incentives and disincentives. For neoliberals, then, a goal of governance is to "construct responsible subjects whose moral quality is based on the fact that they rationally assess the costs and benefits of a certain act as opposed to other alternative acts."[6] In short, neoliberalism doesn't rely on preexisting conditions. It creates new ones, reformatting social and political life in terms of its ideal of competition within markets.

The key principles of neoliberalism were formulated by a group of economists, philosophers, and historians who gathered around the Austrian philosopher Friedrich von Hayek.[7] In 1947 they founded the Mount Pelerin Society (the name comes from the Swiss spa where they first met). Their commitment to the role of competitive markets in securing freedom vehemently opposed both Marxist theories of centralized state planning and Keynesian polices of state intervention in the economy.

Over subsequent decades, neoliberalism remained a marginal economic movement, far outside mainstream Keynesian's commitment to regulatory policies designed to stabilize capitalism and protect citizens from its worst excesses. Nonetheless, as they combated the hegemony of Keynesianism in academic and policy circles, neoliberals slowly gathered support from financial and political elites. A crucial element of this success was their establishment of alternative institutions. They created "a huge international network of foundations, institutes, research centers, publications, scholars, writers, and public relations hacks" who developed, packaged, and pushed neoliberal doctrine.[8] In 1974, von Hayek received the Nobel Prize in Economics. Two years later another key member of his circle won the prize as well, the neoliberal economist Milton Friedman, the primary figure in the Chicago School of economics.

Not until the elections of Margaret Thatcher in the United Kingdom in 1979 and Ronald Reagan in the United States in 1980 did neoliberal ideology come to dominate economic policy.[9] The preceding decades had been the heyday of Keynesian policies wherein the role of the state was to guide the economy and distribute risk so as to shield the inevitable losers in a capitalist market. One such policy endeavors to ensure the stability of production by guaranteeing consumption, either by the state or private consumers. For Keynesians, a living wage is not just a moral issue. It's an economic one, a way to guarantee consumers' purchasing power and stabilize production. Michael Lebowitz explains: "Increased wages would increase aggregate demand, stimulate job creation and new investment . . . mass consumption, it was argued, is necessary for mass production. However, to realize these benefits the market itself would not suffice—state policies and micromanagement were seen as critical."[10] The Keynesian state protects production through oversight and intervenes in order to stimulate demand. The market by itself can't guarantee continued productivity.

By the 1970s, the consensus around Keynesianism was unraveling, in part in reaction to the "structural crisis" in the world economy. Duménil and Lévy note the main aspects of the crisis: "diminished growth rates, a wave of unemployment and cumulative inflation."[11] Elsewhere they identify the crisis as a decline in the rate of profit; unemployment, then, was not a cause of the crisis but an effect, a way for employers to control costs.[12] Other scholars draw attention to additional blows against the Keynesian economic orthodoxy: the collapse of the Bretton Woods Agreement in 1973, the dramatic increases in the price of oil ("oil shocks") brought about by OPEC in 1973 and 1979, and the failure of Keynesianism "to develop public understandings of the economy which could compete with the neoliberal rhetoric of 'free markets.'"[13] The previous chapter attributes this failure not to Keynesians but to leftists who joined the attack on the state and collective approaches to the economy. The left's failure to defend core Keynesian commitments to collectivizing risk, diminishing the impact of contingencies on all concerned (such as illness, natural disaster, economic crisis), and redistributing some portion of the economic surplus to ensure a minimal standard of living contributed to the hegemonic position of neoliberal ideology.[14] Indeed, this failure is the fundamental political trauma affecting the contemporary left. Absent an adequate defense of collective approaches to common problems and in the face of seeming acceptance of the fiction that *there is no alternative,* the left knows neither who or that it is, nor what it would advocate if it existed at all.

Thatcher and Reagan responded to rising unemployment and inflation in the UK and United States by tightening the money supply (already undertaken by Jimmy Carter in the United States), reducing the power and influence of the unions (Thatcher infamously breaking the coal miners union and Reagan firing the air-traffic controllers who refused to return to work), deregulating the economy (eliminating or loosening regulatory oversight in a slew of areas, including banking, communications, utilities, trading, airlines, and the railways so as to foster competition), and pursuing privatization strategies (involving both the subcontracting out of public services and their complete selling off to the private sector).[15] Reagan, and to an extent his predecessor, Jimmy Carter, specifically defended privatization in terms of neoliberal ideology, that is, as a means of forcing government to "embrace private marketplace models" and "respect capitalist measures of success."[16] Bill Clinton and Al Gore further extended neoliberal ideology. As became ever clearer during Clinton's first term, government was like any purchased good, a product offered to satisfy customers even as its production and provision demanded a mindful eye toward the constraints of the market.

Since the early eighties, increasing numbers of states worldwide have adopted neoliberal policies of privatization, deregulation, and financialization. Some of them have done so on their own (or, more accurately, as a response to pressures from ruling financial elites seeking to restore their class power). Others have been compelled by international institutions such as the World Bank and International Monetary Fund to remove price controls, accept inferior terms of trade, and dismantle their public sectors as a condition for aid and loans. Previously committed to a view of development emphasizing the managerial role of the state, these institutions came in the late seventies and early eighties to be dominated by the Washington Consensus, the conviction that neoliberalism provided the quickest and surest formulae for growth. Structural adjustment policies involving cuts to state budgets and programs for the poor were thus instituted throughout the Second and Third Worlds to encourage the development of markets (or to eliminate barriers to the flow of capital and capacity outside countries to more profitable investment sites). The former Soviet Union likewise underwent "shock treatments" as its state-owned and controlled economy was rapidly privatized.

By the end of the twentieth century, neoliberalism had replaced Keynesianism as the reigning approach to the economy, the state, and development.[17] As Robert Pollin observes: "The neoliberal economic agenda—of

eliminating government deficits and inflation, sharply cutting back government spending, deregulating labor and financial markets, and opening
national economies to free trade and multinational capital investments—
has become so dominant throughout the world over the past generation
that even thinking through serious alternatives presents itself as a daunting
task."[18] The charge led by Margaret Thatcher as she dismantled the British
welfare state and defeated the trade unions in the name of increasing
competition now prevails as the common sense of neoliberal ideology—
There Is No Alternative.

Free Trade

Neoliberal ideology relies on the fantasy of free trade. The fantasy promises that an unfettered market benefits everyone. Why? Because markets
are the most efficient ways of ensuring that everyone does what they are
best suited for and gets what they want. Michael Lebowitz describes this
faith: "The unfettered market, we are told, insures that everyone benefits
from a free exchange (or it would not occur) and that those trades chosen
by rational individuals (from all possible exchanges) will produce the best
possible outcomes. Accordingly, it follows that interference with the perfect market system by the state must produce disaster—a negative-sum
result in which the losses exceed the gains. So, the answer for all right-
thinking people must be, remove those interferences."[19] Everyone benefits,
not just some, all. The free market fantasy is that everyone will win. To
ensure that everyone will win, the market has to be liberated, freed from
constraints, unleashed to realize its and our full potential.[20] As free rational
agents armed with full information, people will make the right choices—
but, again, only so long as nothing biases or constrains these choices, so
long as nothing fetters the freeness of the market.

Four aspects of Slavoj Žižek's discussion of the role of fantasy in ideology are helpful for analyzing neoliberalism's fantasy of free trade. Žižek
argues, first, that the "external ideological ritual is the true locus of the
fantasy which sustains an ideological edifice."[21] Fantasy isn't hidden under-
neath official statements and policies. It's not like some kind of trick or
illusion duping the poor, gullible masses. Rather, fantasy is manifest in our
actual practices; these practices, what people actually do, are the location of ideological beliefs. Neoliberal ideology focuses on trade, that is,

on practices of exchange. The ordinary exchanges of everyday people—
cleaned up and understood as rational decisions made under ideal conditions—are trade. When neoliberals talk of free trade, most of us tend to
imagine these individual exchanges. We might think of small farmers and
local businesses or about how great it is to get to choose what we want
from abundant, alluring consumer items. We might imagine lemonade
stands or buying and selling on eBay. Only rarely and with great effort do
we focus on banks, credit cards, subprime mortgages, structured debt
vehicles, currency trading, or insurance companies' profit-oriented efforts
to deny payment to those who have dutifully paid their premiums for
years. Neoliberalism's fantastic appeal stems in part from the way individual exchanges stand in for global flows (upward) of capital.

Second, Žižek holds that fantasy answers the question "What am I to
the Other?"[22] In the United States, the typical answer to this question is
"free." To the Other, I am the one, we are the ones, who are free. After
September 11, 2001, "because we are free" answered the question "Why do
they hate us?" From the U.S. perspective, to cite an earlier example, the
Cold War was fought between freedom and totalitarianism. Neoliberalism
affirms and extends this self-understanding in terms of freedom (or, better,
freeness). Its emphasis on free trade answers the question of who we, as
Americans, are—we are those who trade freely, who value freeness. Ours is
the home of the free (despite or because there is no such thing as a free
lunch). Increasingly, neoliberalism affirms technology's fantasy of wholeness to tell us who "we" are in a global sense. We are those connected to
each other through exchange, the exchange of commodities as well as of
contributions. On the Internet, we are free to buy anything from anywhere
at any time.

Third, Žižek explains that fantasy occults an original deadlock.[23] In
neoliberal ideology, the fantasy of free trade covers over persistent market
failure, structural inequalities, the prominence of monopolies, the privilege of no-bid contracts, the violence of privatization, and the redistribution of wealth to the "have mores." Free trade thus sustains at the level of
fantasy what it seeks to avoid at the level of reality—namely, actually free
trade among equal players, that is, equal participants with equal opportunities to establish the rules of the game, access information, distribution,
and financial networks, and so forth. Paradoxically, free trade is invoked as

a mantra in order to close down possibilities for the actualization of free trade and equality.

We can see this closure at work in the slippage between ideas of competition and winning. On the one hand, neoliberal thought emphasizes the necessity of competition. As George points out, competition was Margaret Thatcher's central value and faith in competition was the governing precept of her destruction of the British public sector. George quotes Thatcher, "It is our job to glory in inequality and see that talents and abilities are given vent and expression for the benefit of us all."[24] On the other hand, even as neoliberalism emphasizes competition, it holds on to the notion that everyone is a winner, a notion clearly at odds with competition because in competition there are winners and losers. Thus, so-called Third World or "developing" countries are not told, "Sorry, losers, that's the breaks in a global economy." Rather, they are promised that everyone will win.[25] The Global Report on Human Settlements notes: "Conventional trade theories see increased trade and a liberalized trade regime as purely beneficial; but, as in all chance, there are, in fact, winners and losers. Those participating in the active, growing areas of the world economy or receiving (unreliable) trickle-down effects benefit. Those who do not participate at best receive no benefits, but, in fact, are usually losers, since capital tends to take flight from their countries or their industries to move to more productive zones, reducing work opportunities and business returns as currencies and wages fall or jobs disappear."[26] Just as the Washington Consensus promised the less-well-off countries that they would all benefit from free trade, so in the United States are workers advised not to worry about the decline in manufacturing and rise of outsourcing. New jobs will be created. With education, workers can be retrained. This same promise that no one will lose reappears at the level of the local school. Kids today are taught that everyone's a winner. Everyone gets some kind of prize or ribbon just for showing up. In some U.S. districts, schools no longer post grades or rankings out of fear of hurting the self-esteem of those students near the bottom. Perhaps surprisingly, the emphasis on testing inherent in George W. Bush's education policy, No Child Left Behind, is not accompanied by a corresponding ranking of students. Instead, schools and teachers are ranked and assessed—but not the students, because everyone is a winner.

Žižek writes, fourth, "Fantasy constructs a scene in which the *jouissance* we are deprived of is concentrated in the other who stole it from us."[27] I mentioned at the beginning of this chapter that in Lacanian psycho-analysis, enjoyment is something we desire but can never fully get. Žižek's insight here is that one of the ways fantasy keeps our desire intact as desire is by telling us why we haven't fulfilled it. It accounts for our failures to enjoy. We haven't fulfilled it, we haven't gotten it, we haven't *really enjoyed* because someone *stole* the enjoyment from us. But for them, we would enjoy. *I would have had a fabulous evening if you hadn't gotten drunk, flirted with the bartender, looked at me in that weird way.* This might be called the "excuses, excuses" role of fantasy.

Free trade stages the scene of stolen enjoyment as a deferred promise of fulfillment. When we carry out our exchanges in the market, our needs and desires will be met. This is the very definition of a perfect market. It will meet everyone's needs and desires. In a crude sense, financial, stock, bond, and commodities markets are bets on this future, investments in the promised fulfillment. We could also include here mortgages, loans, credit cards, all sorts of different financial instruments that rely on a presumption of future satisfaction.

To be sure, market exchanges do not actually provide *jouissance*. Or, more precisely, when the market serves as vehicle for *jouissance*, it is mesmerizing, repulsive, excessive (this is that aspect of enjoyment as that which we want to avoid but can't). The point is clearer when we distinguish between free trade's staging of the lack of enjoyment as a loss or theft and its figuring of the corresponding excess of *jouissance*. Recall, the fantasy of free trade tells us everybody wins. If someone loses, this simply indicates that trade was not free. Someone cheated. He didn't play by the rules. She had secret information, the benefits of insider knowledge or the advantages of an unfair monopoly. Within the frame of the fantasy, the solution to this failure to enjoy is oversight, preferably by those familiar with the industry or practice in question. The government can make sure that others are not out there stealing our enjoyment, the fruits of our labor, through their dishonest and unfair dealings.

There are risks, however, for which the fantasy allows. The government might get overinvolved. It might overstep its boundaries and impede "free trade." Although it might seem to be in tension with the fantasy of keeping trade free, the notion of oversight sustains enjoyment as stolen in a way that reinforces the hold of the fantasy. "Oversight" strengthens rather than undermines free trade as it shifts the location of thievery from the insider or cheat to the government itself—*the government might tax me too much; it might pay for the medical expenses of all sorts of illegal immigrants while I could lose my health insurance at any point; it might use my tax dollars to support tenured radicals (who look down their lazy, secular noses at me and my hardworking, God-fearing way of life) while I can't even afford my kids' tuition.* . . . The fantasy of free trade thus plays host to a series of tensions and anxieties associated with our failure to enjoy.[28] It displaces these anxieties away from the brutalities and uncertainties of the neoliberal market and onto the state as an institution for collective approaches to social, economic, and systemic problems.

Neoliberal ideology's fantasy of free trade also accounts for the lack of *jouissance* or enjoyment in terms of excess, that is, as the sacrifice or expenditure of "too much." The one who fails to enjoy fails because he has overdone something; there is something excessive in his relation to the market. A company expanded too fast; it tried to do too much too quickly. Perhaps it failed because it overpaid its workers, overproduced, or over-diversified (and hence lost touch with its fundamentals). Similarly, those who find their stock portfolios, retirement accounts, and pension funds decimated by falling markets are likewise alleged to have expended *too much.* They were overconfident; they didn't play it safe enough; they had too much faith in the market. They didn't temper their faith in the market with good old common sense or with an appreciation of the mysteries and vagaries of markets (which, perhaps oddly, are the same thing). Everybody knows that ordinary people can become overexuberant and that this can lead to speculative bubbles. The wise investor should believe in the market, *but not too much.* In the terms of the fantasy of free trade, these losers were irrational in their expectations. Perhaps they were even greedy. At the very least, they failed to achieve the proper balance necessary for the promised, inevitable market success.

How the fantasy accounts for losers is actually less interesting than the remarkable twists it employs to explain winners' failure to enjoy. Why don't they enjoy? One version of the neoliberal fantasy of free trade answers the question by differentiating between market and spiritual fulfillment and showing how the former depends on the latter.[29] Not only is success in the world empty when it is purchased at the cost of spiritual fulfillment but spirituality makes good business sense.

Accordingly, in the United States, materialistic varieties of evangelical Christianity play a vital role in supplementing neoliberalism. A full account of this supplementary work is more than I can provide here.[30] I want to flag, though, the reliance of some U.S. churches, particularly the megachurches throughout the exurbs and edge cities, on market and public relations approaches to growth. The pastors and leaders of these churches recognize that many of their potential congregants are recent transplants who have followed jobs and housing into areas of new development. These transplants are likely to have few friends and limited support networks. Out among exurbia's sprawl of big box stores and fast food restaurants, people have relatively few opportunities to meet others. There are few, if any, public parks and nearly everyone drives wherever they need to go. "In such locales," Michelle Goldberg writes, "megachurches fill the spiritual and social void, providing atomized residents instant community. Besides worship services, they offer dinners and parties, family counseling and summer camp, even sports leagues, gyms, and weight-loss programs. There's a McDonald's inside the Brentwood Baptist Church in Houston, and a Starbucks in the Covenant Celebration Church in Tacoma, Washington."[31] The churches respond to and reiterate the basic components of contemporary consumerism. They attempt both to fill gaps produced through neoliberal capitalism (the financial insecurities brought about by job loss and the social insecurities occasioned by the absence of community) and to respond by repurposing the lessons of advertising, marketing, and public relations. An element of the reassurance provided by many megachurches and popular evangelists is the promise of material abundance integrated into the spiritual message. Dr. Sam Storms created Enjoying God Ministries to help Christians experience the power of the Spirit. Revolution Church in Manitou Spring, Colorado, similarly aims to make it easier for people to enjoy God.[32] Each repeats the injunction to enjoy that is characteristic of communicative capitalism.[33]

Another way neoliberal ideology's free market fantasy accounts for winners' failures to enjoy combines the division between material and spiritual values with the problem of excess. Consider the figure of the entrepreneur or executive who seems to have it all, but actually doesn't.

What does "it all" actually mean? How much is necessary and for what? The fantasy of a free market defers answering insofar as buying and selling, investing, and even bequeathing never stops. The market continues, ever expanding and intensifying, without end. The entrepreneur can't have it all because there is no limit. His problem thus seems to be that he doesn't know this. He doesn't realize that capitalism necessarily generates a surplus and so he can't realize, make real in his own life, a limit to his desire.

Accordingly, the free-marketeer, the phantasmic businessman, corporation, or investment banker, has to be careful and not be *too* absorbed, *too* captivated, by the delights of the free market. The sacrifice is too much when it involves the marketeer's friends, family, and soul. Charles Dickens's character Ebenezer Scrooge is perhaps the most familiar reminder of what happens to those who fail to enjoy precisely because of their excessive investment in the market. Inverting Dickens's story of a miser who turns moderation into excess, the film *The Game* (1997, directed by David Fincher) offers a character for a neoliberal age, Nicholas Van Orten (played by Michael Douglas). More than a story of the cold investment banker, fabulously wealthy and successful yet nonetheless incapable of connecting with his wife, his brother, or a childhood trauma (he witnesses his father's suicide), the film treats Van Orten's financial and material success as profoundly boring and repetitive (in stark contrast to another Douglas character, the corporate raider Gordon Gekko in Oliver Stone's film *Wall Street* [1987]; in the earlier film, Gekko's success, even his coldness—as in the famous line "Greed is good"—appear as the ultimate objects of desire). In *The Game*, other white men at the top, the real players, are shown expressing their sense of boredom and entrapment. Persisting in a stultifying environment of pervasive enjoyment, they need desperately to install the gap necessary for desire. The solution is "the game," an unpredictable, high-risk game in which the players don't know the rules, the other players, the conditions, the limits, or even what determines a win or a loss. The game repeats in another space the brutality of the neoliberal market, returning to its players the possibility of desire that their successes had foreclosed.

The mistake involved in excessively sacrificing for the sake of success is one of overidentification, of identifying too much with neoliberal ideology. As Žižek argues, "An ideological identification exerts a true hold on us precisely when we maintain an awareness that we are not fully identical to it, that there is a rich human person beneath it."[34] The free-marketeer who sells himself, who sells out, who sells it all, overidentifies with neoliberal ideology, eliminating the place of the warm, interesting person that the system is supposed to serve, whose needs the system is supposed to meet. When he sacrifices everything to the system, the player, the investment banker or entrepreneur, acts as if such a sacrifice is necessary for success. He exposes the truth of the system—it *really does* demand all sorts of horrible, incalculable sacrifices; it *really does* brutally disregard real human needs and relationships. The overzealous executive thus fails to keep open the gap between the fantasy and the reality of the free market and thereby subverts the fantasy that we are all winners. *The Game*, incidentally, does not subvert this fantasy. In the end, Van Orten, having been, like Job, stripped of everything, confronts his trauma, becomes a full person, and reconciles with his family.

Another version of the overidentified, overinvested free-marketeer is the one who clearly delights in the game, in the risk, the hunt, the thrill of the market. A key motif in market-porn, that is, in memoirs of life in business, the fascinating-repulsive market predator exposes the obscene supplement of the free market fantasy, the violence or violation that underpins the system.[35] His enjoyment depends on the other's losing. He only wins when others lose. According to business memoir conventions, the predator ultimately has to lose in some domain—his business is taken over or collapses, he loses his family, or he loses his sense of self. This loss is thus accompanied by lessons, lessons now made available to everyone so we can avoid his mistakes and be ourselves winners in the free market.

I've been describing free trade as a fantasy that occludes and sustains the brutality of neoliberal capitalism. Free trade establishes possibilities through which we narrate our relation to enjoyment. Žižek argues that what makes desire possible in contemporary conditions is the "despotic figure which stands for the primary *jouisseur*," the one who appropriates all enjoyment.[36] My reading of the fantasy of free trade suggests otherwise. This fantasy provides a more complex organization of enjoyment, one that promises that everyone wins, uses losses to reconfirm the necessity of strengthening the system so everyone wins, and perpetually displaces the thieves of enjoyment throughout the system as warnings, exceptions, and contingencies.

From Symbolic to Imaginary Identity

The fantasy of free trade is but one of the fantasies animating neoliberalism as an ideological formation. The previous chapter considers fantasies linked to communication technologies, and there are still others remaining to be analyzed.[37] But important as the level of fantasy is for understanding how neoliberalism organizes enjoyment, the category of fantasy alone cannot explain the hold of neoliberalism. Thus, in this chapter, I've also mentioned neoliberalism's reliance on a religious supplement (specifically, some practices of evangelical Christianity) as well as its investment in its differences from and opposition to competing ideologies. Neoliberalism has to employ a variety of means to secure its dominance, as its understanding of the role of the state explicitly acknowledges.

Analyzing the changed functioning of the state under neoliberalism, Paul A. Passavant develops a compelling account of neoliberal governmentality.[38] A crucial element of this mode of governmentality is the consumer/criminal doublet. In what follows, I link Passavant's consumer/criminal doublet to Žižek's idea of the decline of symbolic efficiency in order to explain an additional aspect of neoliberalism as an ideological formation, namely, how it produces the subjects it needs. Under neoliberalism, the disciplined worker and consumer-citizen of the social welfare state fragment into myriad, shifting, imaginary identities that converge around the strange attractors of the insatiable shopper (shopaholic) and incorrigible criminal.

THE DECLINE OF SYMBOLIC EFFICIENCY

In his critique of risk society theory, Žižek introduces the idea of the decline of symbolic efficiency.[39] He draws from the later work of Lacan to describe a change in the functioning of the symbolic order. During the middle years of his teaching, Lacan understood the symbolic order as the order of language and meaning. The symbolic is what counts as our everyday experience, our understanding of the role of names and offices, our expectations regarding references. We might say that the symbolic here refers to what everybody knows. In his later work, Lacan introduces different modes in the operation of the symbolic. Hence, his four discourses—those of the master, hysteric, university, and analyst—are different forms of the social link established through language. By Seminar XX, rather than presuming a symbolic order held in place by a master signifier, Lacan theorizes a symbolic space held together by fragile and contingent knots of enjoyment (symptoms, quilting points).[40] In this later version, Lacan emphasizes the ways the imaginary, the symbolic, and the Real are entangled in one another, rupturing, filling in, and covering over their own excesses and lacks.

Žižek's notion of a decline in symbolic efficiency continues the theorization of this idea of a symbolic space permeated by enjoyment. He highlights our perpetual uncertainty, our sense that we never really know whether what we say registers with the other as what we mean as well as our sense that we are never quite sure what "everybody knows." There is no ultimate guarantor of meaning, no recognized authority that stops our questioning or assuages our doubts. For example, if we receive distressing medical news, we can—and are encouraged to—seek a second, third, and fourth opinion. Many of us will search for information on the Internet and explore alternative remedies. But we rarely find firm, reassuring answers, answers in which we are completely confident. There are myriad experts all offering their own specific advice—how can we choose among them? To take another example, how can we know the truth about global warming? Some scientists, politicians, and journalists have called it a hoax and a conspiracy to undermine capitalism.[41] Other scientists, politicians, and journalists tell us that the first group constitutes a minority; there is clear evidence for global warming and a scientific consensus that humans are causing it. Then we might worry *aren't minorities sometimes right*? Hasn't mainstream scientific opinion been *dead wrong* in the past? In the face of fundamental disagreement, how can one determine whom to believe—especially if we are already skeptical about the media, which some remind us is owned by corporations even as others emphasize its pervasive left bias? I return to these problems of credibility and certainty in chapter 6. For now, I simply want to tag this fundamental uncertainty, this fact that we cannot count on something like reality, as the decline of symbolic efficiency.

The change in the status of reality, of the symbolic order of language and meaning, has been noted by others besides Žižek—most directly, by the administration of George W. Bush. In an oft-cited article from the *New York Times Magazine*, Ron Suskind relates a discussion he had with a

White House aide. The aide dismissed journalists as being part of the "reality-based community." He continued, "That's not the way the world really works anymore. . . . We're an empire now, and when we act, we create our own reality. And while you are studying that reality—judiciously, as you will—we'll act again, creating other new realities, which you can study, too."[42]

The decline of symbolic efficiency links to Michael Hardt's and Antonio Negri's account of the shift from disciplinary society to the society of control.[43] As Hardt and Negri explain, disciplinary logics worked primarily within the institutions of civil society to produce subjects. These institutions—the nuclear family, union, school, neighborhood—are now in crisis. According to the 2000 census, for example, less than a quarter of Americans live in families comprised of a married couple and children.[44] Union membership has likewise declined such that in 2006 only 12 percent of workers were unionized and public sector employees were five times more likely than private to belong to a union.[45] Hardt's and Negri's point is that the old political subject, the citizen-subject of an autonomous political sphere, the disciplined subject of civil society, can no longer be said to exist.

The implications of this point are broad. For just as the disciplined subject of civil society can no longer be said to exist, so is there a fragmentation among the identities mobilized politically in and as civil society. Throughout the latter half of the twentieth century, the categories of social inclusion and exclusion were politicized and mobilized.[46] Social movements organized along lines of race, sex, ethnicity, and sexuality radically transformed everyday life as they sought to eliminate entrenched hierarchies. As a result of the critical work of these movements, as well as the accompanying decline of the welfare state and empowering of neoliberalism, racial, sexual, and ethnic identities are less fixed, less stable, less available as determinate subject positions. The category "we" seems permanently to have been called into question and in its place are fluid, hybrid, and mobile imaginary identities (Hardt and Negri use the term *singularities*).

Emerging in the context of the breakdown of determining social norms, the subjects inhabiting these identities are generally undisciplined, although subject to ever more controls. We might think here of changes in public schools away from practices of discipline and normalization and toward searching, surveilling, and policing. Contemporary subjects increasingly lack self-control, in part because they lack a strong sense of self that arises through discipline, and, as I detail below, look outside themselves for some authority to impose control. External control—through the direct or indirect use of force, through threats and fears, and through the mobilization and intensification of affects and desires—takes on more of the work previously done by internalized control.[47] In psychoanalytic terms, we can say that symbolic identity is increasingly fragile, uncertain, and meaningless in the society of control. Imaginary identities sustained by the promise and provision of enjoyment replace symbolic identities. And the multiplicity and adaptability of these identities does not mean that subjects are somehow freer or more liberated than they were under the discipline of the welfare state. Rather, they come under different sets of controls, different organizations of enjoyment.

Read together with Hardt and Negri, Žižek's notion of the decline of symbolic efficiency clarifies an effect of the shift from a Keynesian to a neoliberal ideological formation. The latter does not provide symbolic identities, sites from which we can see ourselves. Rather, it offers in their place new ways for me to imagine myself, an immense variety of lifestyles with which I can experiment. The variety of available identities and the mutability which characterizes contemporary subjects' relations to their identities, moreover, renders imaginary identity extremely vulnerable. The frames of reference that give it meaning and value shift and morph. Others who might challenge it can appear at any moment. Their successes, their achievements, their capacities to enjoy can all too easily call mine into question—*I could have had more; I could have been better; I could have really enjoyed.*

We thus encounter under neoliberalism a situation wherein "*symbolic* prohibitive norms are increasingly replaced by *imaginary* ideals (of social success, of bodily fitness . . .)."[48] These imaginary ideals combine with ferocious superego figures who command subjects to enjoy (thereby effectively ensuring that we cannot).[49] So neoliberal ideology does not produce its subjects by interpellating them into symbolically anchored identities (structured according to conventions of gender, race, work, and national citizenship).[50] Instead, it enjoins subjects to develop our creative potential and cultivate our individuality. Communicative capitalism's circuits of entertainment and consumption supply the ever new experiences and accessories we use to perform this self-fashioning—*I must be fit; I must be stylish; I must realize my dreams. I must because I can—everyone wins. If I don't, not only am I a loser but I am not a person at all; I am not part of everyone.* Neoliberal subjects are expected to, enjoined to, have a good time, have it all, be happy, fit, and fulfilled.

The end of the welfare state and decline of symbolic efficiency may appear to usher in a new era of freedom from rigid norms and expectations. But the fluidity and adaptability of imaginary identities is accompanied by a certain fragility and insecurity. Imaginary identities are incapable of establishing a firm place to stand, a position from which one can make sense of one's world. Moreover, their very mutability and normative indeterminacy configure imaginary identities as key loci for operations of control (rather than internalized discipline), particularly those operations affiliated with desire and fear as they promise and provide enjoyment. The flip side of the multiplicity of imaginary identities, then, is a reduction and congealing of identity into massive sites or strange attractors of affective investment.

STRANGE ATTRACTORS

The idea of the decline of symbolic efficiency enables us to read Passavant's "consumer/criminal doublet" as a specific figuring of enjoyment, as a site of phantasmic investment specific to neoliberalism as an ideological formation. Whereas the Keynesian welfare state produced the symbolic identities of consumers, workers, citizens, and prisoners (among others), neoliberal governmentality relies on the convergence of imaginary identities around the strange attractors of the consumer and the criminal. The consumer figures the possibility of enjoyment promised by neoliberalism. Consumption provides the terrain within which my identity, my lifestyle, can be constructed, purchased, and made over. Yet consumption is more than a terrain—the consumer is commanded to enjoy, compelled by the impossible demand to do more, be more, have more, change more . . . *not in step with the latest fashion but in advance of it, not looking at what's new but at what's coming up next.*[51] The consumer today is imagined as excessive, extreme, and unregulated. She is imagined, in other words, as a composite of the neoliberal market itself. Correspondingly, the criminal figures the ever present threat of loss, the losing that the fantasy of free trade disavows. Insofar as the criminal serves as the site of displaced anxiety over such loss and losing, he is the intolerable monster, the one who stands for the Real of violence and whose expulsion and eradication mobilize neoliberal governmentality.[52] The obverse of the frenzied, out of control consumer, the monstrous criminal must be controlled completely, for life, or better, to death.

In *A Consumer's Republic*, Lizbeth Cohen describes three waves of consumerism in the United States. Crucial to each wave is the symbolic role of the consumer, that is, of the consumer as a recognized identity in a democratic polity. In each time period, Cohen's consumers provide symbolic locations from which one might gaze at American society, positions from which citizens might see themselves and thus from which they might be effectively mobilized. Among her examples are the loyal female citizens of World War II whose consumer choices were central to the domestic front; the African Americans demanding equal treatment in restaurants, stores, theaters, parks, pools, and buses; the grassroots participants in mass campaigns for safe products, fair labels, and equitable credit. These consumers serve as ego ideals, points of symbolic identification, gazes in front of whom people might imagine themselves in their activities as consumers and thus view themselves and these activities as likeable, admirable.[53]

Cohen's active consumer-citizens differ significantly from neoliberalism's consumers. Whereas the activities and political engagements of consumers under Keynesianism centered on the consumption of necessities—food, transportation, housing—today's consumer is primarily a consumer of excess, armed with credit cards and perpetually revising her identity. Juliet B. Schor construes the "new consumerism" in terms of a compulsion to purchase luxury goods so as to keep up with televised images of affluence.[54] Other commentators similarly describe consumerism in terms of relentless marketing, obsessive purchasing, and luxury fever.[55] Crucial to their accounts is the image of the consumer as compelled to buy, as a manikin with a credit card driven to create a lifestyle for herself. Still others address the effects of neoliberalism's intensification of consumerism. Ronaldo Munck writes, "The whole consumer process—from conception to sale, through advertising, marketing and fashion building—has fragmented identities and made them more fluid as consumption is continuously revolutionized."[56]

Emerging from these descriptions is the consumer as a kind of strange attractor quite unlike the stable symbolic identities the welfare state endeavored to preserve and disciplinary society worked to provide. The excessive consumer is as dynamic, volatile, and free as the neoliberal market itself.

Not all accounts of consumption begin from excess or luxury—Daniel Miller in particular has done important work on consumption as provisioning.[57] Nonetheless, images of excessive consumers abound and in fact determined debate in the U.S. Congress over the (typically misnamed) Bankruptcy Abuse Prevention and Consumer Protection Act of 2005. In an argument characteristic of those offered in support of the legislation, Tim Kane, a research fellow at the conservative Heritage Foundation, rejected "the liberal line that some fifty percent of modern bankruptcies are driven by healthcare emergencies" and lauded the bill for "making it harder for people to abuse the system and feign poverty."[58] For him, as well as for the majority of senators and representatives who approved the bill, overhauling bankruptcy law was "essential" to helping "bankrupt Americans break the bad habits of over consumption." These voices, along with those of economists and sociologists considering consumerism strictly in terms of excess and luxury, have little to say about provisioning, or about the rising costs of healthcare, housing, education, and transportation, on the one hand, and the collapse of pension funds and increases in layoffs and unemployment, on the other. How they conceptualize consumption, in other words, has less to do with actual practices than it does with the image of the insatiable consumer, the strange attractor orienting or structuring their analyses. Moreover, even as they criticize the consumption of "experiences," that is, of travel, leisure, culture, and spirituality, they too often neglect the fact of the broader commodification and marketization of ever more aspects of daily life such that people have little opportunity to do anything other than consume.

The image of the excessive consumer saturates popular media. Magazines, newspapers, and television shows employ a vocabulary of abundance. Women are said to pick up "armloads" of sweaters or t-shirts—*one in every color!* Consumers scoop up or snatch up "must haves." In the United States, the market for mini storage facilities as well as for closet organizing systems is rapidly expanding as consumers run out of places to store their extra stuff. Mainstream media coverage of "Black Friday"—the Friday after Thanksgiving when shoppers eager to cash in on Christmas bargains send retailers into the black as they post their first profits of the year—features images of mobs and mayhem. A television news report from an ABC–affiliated station in the San Francisco area describes a common scene: "Stores created a shopping frenzy on the day after Thanksgiving that turned ugly and even violent. Here and across the country, shoppers fought over merchandise, and in one case, trampled others. The rush to get into a Michigan Wal-Mart store when the doors opened turned into a stampede. Shoppers fell and tripped over each other. A lady lost her wig and quickly put it back on as the melee continued. At the Best Buy store in San Carlos, early morning shoppers created a mob scene just to get bargain-priced laptops and other electronics."[59] The British novelist Sophie Kinsella has written a popular series featuring an excessive conumer—*Confessions of a Shopaholic, Shopaholic Takes Manhattan, Shopaholic Ties the Knot, Shopaholic and Sister,* and *Shopaholic Has a Baby.* The novels' protagonist is Rebecca Bloomwood, a compulsive shopper who spends in order to save and who, in the initial book of the series, works as a financial journalist, dispensing the advice she doesn't follow. Her purchases always make a kind of immediate sense, thereby reformatting the ostensibly responsible choices presupposed in descriptions of neoliberal markets as a kind of nonsense. Enjoined by the superego to shop, buy, and enjoy, she fails when she does and she fails when she doesn't. She fails when she does by overspending, overconsuming, running up debt, and risking bankruptcy. She fails when she doesn't because by not shopping she will lose her already fragile identity; she will have no way to signify who and that she is, where and how she belongs. The first book, *Confessions of a Shopaholic,* ends with Bloomwood—her credit cards maxed out—successfully avoiding bankruptcy in two quite predictable ways: she sells her belongings, thus confirming the importance of free trade, and marries a wealthy businessman.

The criminal is the other side of the consumer/criminal doublet. David Garland describes in detail the decline of the rehabilitative ideal in penal policy over the past thirty years. He explains: "Crime has been redramatized. The stock welfarist image of the delinquent as a disadvantaged, deserving, subject of need has now all but disappeared. Instead, the images conjured up to accompany new legislation tend to be stereotypical depictions of unruly youth, dangerous predators, and incorrigible career criminals. Accompanying these projected images, and in rhetorical response to them, the new discourse of crime policy consistently invokes an angry public, tired of living in fear, demanding strong measures of punishment and protection."[60] As Garland makes clear, criminals today figure as strange attractors in revenge fantasies. They stand in for the inexplicable, the unpredictable. As sites of loss, they embody and occlude neoliberal ideology's inability to account for, to allow for, loss and losers. Free-trade fantasy necessarily recuperates loss in a narrative of gain—*everybody wins*. Losses in the Real, Real losses, don't fit. They are overwhelming, excessive. The criminal is the imaginary figure covering over and sustaining this excess of loss. His monstrosity marks the horror of losing, our inability to account for inevitable contingencies. The neoliberal criminal, then, is outside the domain of calculable risk: we can never be insured against the loss he inflicts upon us. The logic, as Passavant points out, is one of zero tolerance.[61] No risk is acceptable; any risk is monstrous, unbearable.

During the era of the welfare state, criminology viewed crime in the context of functioning institutions, in terms, that is, of proper education, family socialization, and job opportunities.[62] According to the mainstream criminological discourse of the period, the criminal was a deviant, one who deviated from social expectations. In Garland's words, crime signified "an under-achieving socialization process" and could thus be remedied by state intervention in specific domains (15). The discourse of contemporary criminology, however, differs. It views crime as routine. Crimes are the responses of normal individuals to available choices and incentives. Criminals follow market incentives just like everybody else. Because crime can erupt anywhere, any time, the proper response is preemptive—*get them before they can get you*. Preemption takes a variety of forms, including zoning, surveillance, and an increase in the severity of penalties for repeat offenders. The goal is protecting the public, ensuring its safety, preventing the impossible. Appropriate measures keep *us* away from *them*. The daily business of the community has to be secured against the criminal disruption.

Corresponding to this shift from deviant to norm is a change in the focus of criminological concern. Welfare state criminology emphasized the criminal, bringing all the disciplines to bear in understanding him and his crime. In contrast, the society of control emphasizes the victim. "Victim impact statements," Garland writes, "are introduced to court in order to individualize the impact of the crime, to show how the offence affected this particular victim, in all her particularity, in all her human specificity" (179). As a result, the offender is rendered "more and more a projected image" (179). The criminal, in other words, is less a person than the image standing in for a horrifying, unbearable, contingent event. Injustice is what happens to the victim; the victim is the one unjustly deprived of opportunity, life, enjoyment. The criminal is imagined as the monstrous instrument of deprivation.

More can be and has been said about the criminal as an imaginary figure. Scholars attend to the proliferation of crime dramas on television, the spectacle of criminality that drives local news, and the rhetoric empowering appeals to strict sentencing and the death penalty. What my analysis of fantasy in neoliberal ideology adds is insight into the way the criminal is a strange attractor for displaced anxieties around the brutality of the neoliberal economy. Criminals seem particularly horrifying figures precisely because they are figures for the Real of loss. The more anxious and desperate economic conditions become, that is, the more false and fragile the fantasy of free trade is experienced as being, the more monstrous and deadly become those imagined as criminals in our midst and the more they will have to pay since no one else can. As Jonathan Simon notes, "The notion of retribution as an abstract requirement of justice is giving way to the ability of specific individuals to obtain satisfaction from cruelty."[63] The satisfaction one gets from the suffering of another, as we learn from Nietzsche, is then perhaps the greatest enjoyment one can expect (which may explain the lack of an outcry in the United States after the publication and circulation of the photos of tortured prisoners at Abu Ghraib—apparently, Americans were glad to see that Iraqi prisoners were being tortured; apparently, Americans enjoyed the photos).

Against Identity

Neoliberalism is an economic and political program benefiting the top 1 percent of the world's population as it sends billions into poverty. Forced upon many, it is chosen and embraced by some, particularly those privileged in the United States, United Kingdom, and European Union. Thus, neoliberalism also functions as an ideological formation offering a specific arrangement of enjoyment. The fantasy of free trade is a key aspect of this arrangement—neoliberalism promises that everyone will win. It also integrates its losses and failures into this arrangement as intensifications of the promised enjoyment—whether as stolen or excessive, enjoyment is still possible.

Yet neoliberal ideology relies on more than fantasy. It involves a restructuring of political possibility. Neoliberalism eliminates the symbolic identities made available under Keynesianism, providing instead a multiplicity of fluid and adaptable imaginary identities that converge around the strange attractors of the consumer and the criminal. Whereas the welfare state enabled the construction of political identities as sites for oppositional redeployment, neoliberal ideology forecloses such opposition in advance. Under the conditions of the decline of symbolic efficiency, identities are too fleeting and unstable to serve as sites of politicization.[64] In the rapidly shifting media environments of communicative capitalism or in the complexities of urban war zones, identifications morph and mutate so rapidly as to be politically inconsequential. Likewise insofar as brands themselves provide sites of identification that mobilize consumers, a focus on identity production as central to left political struggle affirms rather than contests corporate practice in a global neoliberal economy. How would climate change, for example, be rendered into the terms of political identity? Is it a matter of lifestyle? Of being the sort of person who drives a Prius and carries an attractive nylon bag to the grocery store? Such a reduction to an imagined "green identity" formats climate change as an issue of individual consumer choice, as a fashionable cause. Not only does such formatting reinforce, yet again, the supposition that the free market, left on its own, will find solutions to major problems but it is built on the exclusion of collective approaches to systemic problems.

The fantastic suppositions of neoliberal ideology have become part of the air we breathe, elements of our most fundamental assumptions about how the world works: everyone is an individual with a unique identity; the free market enables us to create and develop these unique identities; everybody wins; there is no alternative. Even leftists critical of big, bad corporations and the growing extremes of wealth and poverty find it extraordinarily difficult to think of alternatives to the present configuration of power. In part this is because we have been unable to give voice to values of collectivity, cooperation, solidarity, and equity strong enough to counter neoliberalism's free-trade fantasy. It is also because we can't imagine how we would realize, enact, bring about such a vision. Our very supposition of democracy, as the following chapter explores, entraps us in the inequalities of communicative capitalism.[65]

3

Democracy

A KNOT OF HOPE AND DESPAIR

A commonplace of media punditry in the twenty-first century concerns the deep divide in American politics. Whether in terms of political parties, red states and blue states, support or opposition to U.S. militarism in Afghanistan and Iraq, or the ongoing culture war between the religious right and the secular left, the United States is depicted as a nation split in its fundamental ethico-political self-understanding.

This depiction is misleading. Each side of the divide appeals to democracy. The administration of George W. Bush presented itself as actively engaged in bringing democracy to the Middle East and as encouraging countries throughout the world to strengthen their democratic institutions. To this extent, it repeated the rhetoric of the twentieth century's two world wars as well as its cold war, positioning itself and its allies as democracies and its enemies as, well, not democracies (as authoritarians, fascists, communists, terrorists, and, briefly, Islamo-fascists). The left, although seemingly opposed to the Bush administration, also appealed to democracy as that which it wishes to restore, redeem, or reach. Since the left enabled the ideal of socialism to wither away with the Soviet state, what democracy might mean, or the range of possibilities democracy is meant to encompass, remains unclear, to say the least. The economic and social guarantees fundamental to social democracy and the welfare state don't feature prominently in most left discussions of democracy. More pronounced are themes of participation and deliberation, immanence and inclusion, ideals that are necessary but impossible, perpetually deferred, forever to come.

Why does the left continue to appeal to democracy? Is democracy, as Slavoj Žižek asks, the ultimate horizon of political thought?[1] Is reiterating the ideological message of communicative capitalism the best the left can do in the face of neoliberal hegemony and the collapse of socialism? Is democracy the fallback position for left politics, all that remains of our wounded and diminished political aspirations? Or does the hope its evocation promises mark instead a pervasive left despair?

Real existing constitutional democracies privilege the wealthy. As they install, extend, and protect neoliberal capitalism, they exclude, exploit, and oppress the poor, all the while promising that everybody wins. The present value of democracy relies on positing crucial determinants of our lives and conditions outside the frame of contestation in a kind of "no-go zone." These suppositions regarding growth, investment, and profit are politically off-limits, so it's no wonder that the wealthy and privileged evoke democracy as a political ideal. It can't hurt them. The expansion and intensification of networked communications technologies that was supposed to enhance democratic participation integrates and consolidates communicative capitalism. Nevertheless, the left continues to present our political hopes as aspirations to democracy.

Despite democracy's inability to represent justice in the wake of political submission to a brutalized, financialized, punishing global market, left political and cultural theorists appeal to arrangements that can be filled in, substantialized, by fundamentalisms, nationalisms, populisms, and conservatisms diametrically opposed to social justice and economic equality. Calling for democracy, leftists fail to emphasize the divisions necessary for politics, divisions that should lead us to organize against the interests of corporations and their stockholders, against the values of fundamentalists and individualists, and on behalf of collectivist arrangements designed to redistribute benefits and opportunities more equitably. With this plea, leftists proceed as if democracy were the solution to contemporary political problems rather than symptomatic of them, rather than the name of the impasse in which we find ourselves.

Concerned with how continued adherence to democracy absorbs and incorporates hope so as to lodge politics in a field of already given possibilities, I consider here three current invocations of democracy: democracy as radical ideal, democracy as political practice, and democracy as theoretical justification for rule. These three invocations are primary ways democracy is figured today. In appealing to democracy, left political theory remains trapped in the terms and suppositions conditioning these invocations, terms and suppositions that I analyze by drawing upon Žižek's elaboration of Lacan's four discourses.

To the extent that the left—whether mainstream Democrats, deliberative democrats, radical democratic theorists and activists, or the typing left blogging and publishing in print media—accepts globalized neoliberal capitalism and acquiesces to a political arrangement inadequate to the task of responding to the gross inequality, immiseration, and violence this capitalism generates, it will fail to provide a viable alternative politics. Accordingly, this chapter explores the limitation of democracy as a contemporary political ideal, demonstrating how this organizational form and polemical concept serves highly particular interests and stands in the way of universalization.[2] It clicks on the links between contemporary theories of deliberative democracy (the most prominent democratic theories today) and the political arrangements of real existing democracy, arrangements that include activists and elected officials. While Hubertus Buchstein and Dirk Jörke present a persuasive account of the disconnect between highly professionalized (and commodified) academic democratic theory and everyday references to and identifications with democracy, I highlight the overlap among these invocations of democracy, the coincidence between actual and ideal participation that ultimately undermines dynamic, responsive, left politics.[3]

Theories of deliberative democracy tend to focus on the justification of democratic principles and practices. More than building models of democratic governance, they provide grounds that support claims for the superiority of democracy over other political arrangements. These grounds, moreover, have an interesting status. They are raised both in academic and popular debate, or, more precisely, *as both academic and popular debate*. Theories of deliberative democracy prioritize not simply claims regarding deliberation but actual practices of deliberation. For democratic theorists, then, there is a *necessary* link between theories and practices, a *necessary* connection to real life. Practices are legitimately democratic not when their outcomes can be imagined as the result of deliberation but when the practices are *actually* deliberative. Legitimacy follows from realization, from deliberative practice. And for democratic theorists the opposite holds as well: deliberative and democratic are the standards themselves determining legitimacy.

For example, crucial to Jürgen Habermas's account of universalization is the idea that normative claims to validity are actually debated, that the justification of norms requires and results from the actual discourses of actual people.[4] With Habermas's emphasis on constitutional forms, on the one side, and the corresponding alliance between liberal and deliberative democrats, on the other, we have a contemporary theory that finds justificatory elements in real-life political practices. Rather than providing rational reconstructions of everyday practices, the contemporary theory of deliberative democracy uses everyday practices as justifications for the validity of deliberative procedures.[5] Both normative and descriptive accounts of democratic procedures thus play key roles in theorists' accounts of deliberative democracy.

As it occupies this in-between space, this space between facticity and validity, democratic theory presents ideals and aspirations as always already present possibilities. In so doing, it brings utopia inside, eliminating it as an external space of hope. Yet by internalizing the hope that things might be otherwise, democratic theory destroys that hope: potential problems are solved in advance, through democratic channels. *We already know how to get there. We already have the procedures. Anything else is mere tweaking.* Despite all our problems with democracy, democracy is the solution to all our problems.[6] The idea that democracy marks an empty place where things can be otherwise, that democratic procedures incorporate already the keys to revising and reforming the practice of democracy, becomes the conviction that there is nothing but, no alternative to, democracy. To this extent, democratic theory presents democracy as realized, as adequate to its notion. If this is the case, the problem is in the notion.

University Discourse

We can go some way toward understanding the problem contained in the notion of deliberative democracy when we recognize how it has consolidated around ideas of argument and deliberation.[7] Democracy is envisioned as the exchange of reasons by participants in a discussion characterized by equality, inclusivity, reciprocity, and transparency. Such discussion among equals, however, is clearly but one particular model of discourse, one sort of idealized discourse among other possible configurations. Why just one?[8]

Lacanian psychoanalysis, especially as elaborated by Žižek, offers an account of four discourses, four different models of the social bond: discourses of the master, the hysteric, the university, and the analyst.[9] Lacan developed these four discourses in part to account for differences in the ways that discourses function, differences in the kinds of social links they provide and the kinds of suppositions and requirements that structure them. In brief, the four discourses are sets of formulae that distinguish between speaking and the place from which something is spoken. For example, my question "What are you doing?" can be understood in a variety of ways, depending on my addressee as well as on what underlies or supports my asking of the question. If I ask my young daughter, "What are you doing?" I am likely speaking from a parental position. If I ask a political leader, "What are you doing?" I may be challenging her authority, calling upon her to justify her policies and decisions. If I ask an associate in my laboratory, "What are you doing?" I may be speaking as a fellow scientist engaged in the production of knowledge. Lacan formulates the differences among these questions as different discourses, different ways that communication establishes a social link. These three situations are examples of the discourse of the master, the discourse of the hysteric, and the discourse of the university.

I can also participate in discourse without saying anything at all: I can just sit there, mute and impassive. In this way, I confront the other as a kind of object or catalyst. She will likely project different sorts of knowledge, desires, and motives onto me. I can accept this projection and claim this knowledge, positioning myself perversely as the one who knows the real truth behind her words. Or I can remain impassive, challenging her to accept that there really is no secret truth for me to know, challenging her, in other words, to accept responsibility for herself. This fourth situation, one in which an object is in the position of speaking agent, is the discourse of the pervert as well as the discourse of the analyst.

The discourse of the master is the first of Lacan's four discourses or four accounts of the social link provided in communication. Its structure is rooted in the absolute authority of the master's word. The master's word is law—even if it seems unfair or crazy. So the master can say, "Do this" or "Do that," "Pick that cotton," "Kneel!" or "Go fight that battle!" Any of these injunctions is acceptable within the discourse of the master simply because the master said it. The second discourse, the hysteric's, takes form when the subject challenges the master's word. Read politically, this discourse follows a logic of "protest and resistance," of demands that can never actually be met, that perpetually shift because they are never *really* about what is actually demanded.[10] In the third discourse, the discourse of the university, knowledge occupies the position of speaking agent. Consequently, Žižek reads the political bond established by this discourse as the rule of experts.[11] Finally, he argues that the political bond proper to the discourse of the analyst is "radical-revolutionary politics." Here, the excluded, symptomal point of the situation is the speaking position. The risks of such a political formation appear in the fact that this formula is also that of the perverse discourse. In the perverse discourse, the object that speaks positions itself as an instrument in behalf of the other, an instrument grounded in knowledge of what is best for the subject or other.

The theory of deliberative democracy follows the model of the discourse of the university wherein knowledge ostensibly speaks for itself even as the deliberations or interventions of those actually participating in contemporary democratic politics conform to the discourse of the hysteric and the pervert. Political antagonists may speak the same language, but they speak it in different ways, from differing positions of enunciation, to differing symbolic and imaginary others, and within differing discursive formations. Insofar as democratic theory ignores these differences and conforms to the discourse of the university, it fails to confront the current political impasse, disavowing its own underlying suppositions of power and authority and, as detailed in chapter 6, the changed conditions of credibility wherein such authority has already collapsed.

Invoking Democracy

Democracy as a radical ideal was invoked by a sign posted in a coffee shop in Trumansburg, New York, in early 2005. The sign urged people to "take back democracy." It advertised the showing of a film about Al Jazeera, *The Control Room*, and called upon people to come inform themselves, discuss the film, and, presumably, organize future actions. President George W.

Bush invoked democracy as a political practice in a speech he gave in 2003. He proclaimed the role of the United States in spreading democracy across the globe, his strategy for democracy in the Middle East, and his hopes for the future of a democratic Iraq.[12] Citing the lessons of World War II and the Cold War, lessons that teach us that sacrifices made for the sake of democracy are worthwhile, Bush noted that "now we must apply that lesson in our own time. We've reached another great turning point— and the resolve we show will shape the next stage of the world democratic movement." In their well-known and influential description of the current academic consensus around deliberative democracy, Amy Gutmann and Dennis Thompson invoke democracy as a theoretical justification for rule. They define deliberative democracy "as a form of government in which free and equal citizens (and their representatives) justify decisions in a process in which they give one another reasons that are mutually accept- able and generally accessible, with the aim of reaching conclusions that are binding in the present on all citizens but open to challenge in the future."[13] As an example, albeit an admittedly imperfect one, Gutmann and Thomp- son refer to George W. Bush's recognition of a need to justify his deci- sion to go to war, his persistence in making the case for preventive war against Iraq.

What might we make of these three invocations of democracy? A first pass might say that they are not talking about the same thing, that democ- racy, an empty signifier, is filled in with differing contents in each case. Here one might emphasize the differences between the protestors hailed by the sign in the coffee shop, the leader of a hegemonic power, and academics elucidating a second-order account of legitimacy in politics. Yet even with these differences is it not the case that, in each invocation, democracy is somehow missing, outside the frame? That democracy is standing in for aspirations to something lacking in the present, something more than what we have?

Democracy is missing from the protestors' sign when we imagine them saying that their voices have not been heard, that Bush's decision to go to war violated American constitutional principles. The Bush administration violated democratic norms in going to war against the wishes of the majority. The protestors are contesting this decision, saying that it was not in their name, that they do not authorize it, and that this lack of authoriza- tion is a lack of democracy. Democracy is outside Bush's frame when we recognize his self-image as a bringer of democracy, an instrument of the future. He looks outside of a present America, sees a global absence that threatens the United States, and acts to fill it. Democracy is missing from Gutmann's and Thompson's account insofar as the argument they make is normative, a theory of how things ought to be, not of how they are.

Gutmann and Thompson summarize the most widely accepted view of democratic legitimacy, synthesizing decades of work by John Rawls and Jürgen Habermas. Although disagreements among democratic theorists remain, which Gutmann and Thompson rehearse in detail, the general idea is that democracy is properly conceived not in terms of the collective will of the people but in terms of the quality of collective will formation. Democracy, then, does not rely on a simple identity between government and the governed, sovereign and subject, but consists in a mediated relation between the two. Democracy is a matter of the proper procedures. Political theorists don't install these procedures and get them to work. They establish what the proper procedures *should be* if democracy is to hold.

But is the matter of missing democracy really so simple? Does it make sense to render each of the three cases in terms of democracy to come? As a missing utopia? What if, instead, we think of each case in terms of the presence or realization of democracy, as what real existing democracy looks like? When we do, we see that the protestors invoke a democracy imagined as resistance. They appeal to practices of constitutionally protected questioning and critique. The organizers showing the Al Jazeera film are democratically engaged, active citizens. Like the protestors, Bush, too, is following and invoking a democratic script. He is carrying out his democratic mandate. He is executing a decision which, while necessarily in excess of the complex string of reasons and knowledge bearing upon it, takes place nonetheless within a space of power opened up and guaranteed by democratic procedures. And here, Gutmann and Thompson return as providers of insight into the knowledge of democracy. They don't decide to go to war or contest the decision to go to war. Rather they set out the procedures through which decisions should be made. And from their perspective, from the perspective of the neutral knowledge of the university, democracy is proceeding apace. This is what democracy looks like.

According to Gutmann and Thompson, the practices of the Bush administration exemplify the fundamental characteristic of deliberative democracy—the requirement to give reasons. They point out that the administration "recognized an obligation to justify their views to their fellow citizens" and that it gave reasons for preemptive war. These reasons, Gutmann and Thompson claim, "laid the foundation for a more sustained and more informative debate *after* the U.S. military victory" (2–3). As a commenter on my blog put it, it's as if they are saying, "One good thing you can say about the war is despite all the death and destruction, it reinvigorates the postwar political debriefing process."[14] Gutmann and Thompson concede that the administration did not exhaust nonmilitary options before shocking and awing the Iraqi people. Nevertheless, they marvel that "the remarkable fact is that even under the circumstances of war, and in the face of an alleged imminent threat, the government persisted in attempting to justify its decision" (2). They add that it is likely correct that "no amount of deliberation would have prevented the war" (2).

Both the missing and the present democracy readings are unsatisfying. Nevertheless, they are useful for elaborating a certain epistemological impasse in deliberative democracy, especially once we reread them in light of the different positions of enunciation at work in each explanation, that is, in light of the discourses of the hysteric, the pervert, and the university.[15]

The Lack of Democracy

If we frame the issue as one of missing democracy, the protestors seem to take on the position of hysterics. Why? One, because they address their claims to a master, challenging his authority as they say, *we need democracy, democracy is not what we have*; and, two, because the demands they make seem fantastic, incapable of being filled by the master they address.

The claim that democracy is missing is difficult to take seriously. An antiwar position was out there, made vivid by the millions all over the world out in the streets on February 15, 2003. A democratically elected Congress voted to authorize the president to carry out military operations should diplomacy fail. Where, then, is the failure of democracy? The emptiness of the concept of democracy is a problem insofar as it isn't clear what, exactly, the protestors might be demanding. What do they really want? Is it democracy or something else? And insofar as it isn't clear what the protestors are demanding, it seems impossible to give them what they want.

We should also ask whether the screening of the film is really intended to inspire democratic debate. Are pro-torture, anti-Islamists expected and encouraged to attend? Is this an opportunity for Christian conservatives to explain the benefits of Fox News or try to organize those at the screening to evict anti-American tenured radicals from the university? Since the answer to these questions is obviously no, the appeal to democracy seems disingenuous, a way of avoiding the true, partisan position of the protestors, of masking the fact that their appeal is actually ruptured by an excess of power or desire that they can't fully acknowledge. The organizers of the film viewing don't really want an inclusive conversation. They want organized political resistance, but they don't say this directly. Instead, they appeal to democracy, shielding themselves from taking responsibility for the divisiveness of politics.

Ultimately, insofar as the protestors address their demands to a master and fail to assume their own claim to power, they end up reinforcing rather than subverting the master's authority.[16] They don't confront Bush as an equal in political debate. They issue demands that he can accept and reject from the very position of the master their demands presuppose. This issuing of demands, moreover, *installs* Bush into the position of master. Instead of screening a movie and demanding democracy, the protestors could acknowledge the division between their position and that of the government—and at least half of American citizens at the time—and work toward building a militant countermovement or joining with existing movements. They could refuse to play by the apparent rules of American political discourse and eschew the legitimizing shelter of the term *democracy*.

If democracy is missing in the Middle East and Bush is the instrument through which it can be provided, his discourse is perverse and his position of enunciation that of the pervert.[17] Despite the demands of the hysterics, Bush is not a master. Or differently put, the demands of the hysterics demonstrate the way the position of the master is always that of a fraud. His words fail to coincide with his position. And here, to an extent, Gutmann and Thompson are not wrong to emphasize the importance of continued questioning and argument for democracy. Such questions and arguments can expose the fact the master is not a master; his authority is a result of his position. It is relational rather than absolute.

The innovation of democracy is to draw attention to the distinction between the occupant and the place of power. As Claude Lefort argues, the key element of the democratic invention is the assertion that the place must remain empty.[18] Principles of right and law are to guarantee this emptiness, to maintain the gap between the place of power and whoever occupies this place. When Bush speaks, then, he does not fully occupy the place of power. His word is not law. Rather law speaks and Bush carries it out. His position of enunciation is that of an instrument of the law. Thus, he executes the will and desires of others, not himself, in accordance with law. To do so, to carry out the wills and fulfill the desires of others, he has to presuppose that he knows these desires, that he possesses the knowledge of desire. We might think here of Bush's frequent invocations of the Iraqi people and their desires for freedom and democracy. All that he does is for them, to realize their desire for liberty. In helping them realize their desire, he, like America, is a tool in the hands of nature and history. As Bush declared in his State of the Union address in 2006, "We are the nation that saved liberty in Europe, and liberated death camps, and helped raise up democracies, and faced down an evil empire. Once again, we accept the call of history to deliver the oppressed and move this world toward peace."[19]

Read in terms of the discourse of the pervert, Bush's aim to spread democracy around the world relies on an excess of power, on a point of decision. As he said when pressed by reporters to justify retaining Secretary of Defense Donald Rumsfeld after six retired generals called for the secretary's resignation, "I'm the decider."[20] This position is supported by the knowledge he claims to subject himself to as he carries out its mandate to spread democracy.

I can now clarify how Bush's position as an instrument of a future democracy resists the exchange of reasons: insofar as he is merely the executor, he doesn't speak for himself or participate in the exchange of reasons. The reasons, or knowledge, already underpin his decision and are subject to his servicing of them. Bush addresses the subject, the split hysterical subject of democracy, the protestors, from this position of instrument. In this way, their questioning misses the mark. He isn't offering them knowledge; he is offering them action. He therefore reiterates his decisiveness, his conviction, his resolve, the fact that he is acting in the service of a cause, principle, and design of nature that is incommensurate with his will. And as we have seen, this hysterical process produces, but does not depend on, the authority of the master. The pervert doesn't recognize himself in the address of the hysteric because he is merely an instrument.[21]

There is a way, however, that this reading of the protestors and Bush in terms of the discourses of the hysteric and the pervert is too rigid. Their positions are too fixed and thus unable to account for an overlap in their claims regarding democracy's absence. Upon closer analysis, the fact that the two positions share a lack means that they each pass into the other.[22] With respect to the examples of the protestors and Bush, what we have is the passing of questioning into decision, of inclusivity into division, and back again.

Žižek's discussion of Hegel helps clarify this sharing of a lack. Žižek emphasizes that "antithesis" is "what the 'thesis' *lacks* in order to 'concretize' itself."[23] He writes, "The 'thesis' is itself *abstract*: it presupposes its 'mediation' by the 'antithesis'; it can attain its ontological consistency only by means of its opposition to the 'antithesis.' "[24] The protestors lack the power to execute their demands. Their discourse only achieves consistency, then, as a demand for power, for what they lack. They slide into their opposite as they position themselves as vehicles for the realization of a democracy to come, as they make their activities the practices constitutive of democracy, decisively excluding torturers, warmongers, and right-wing Christians from the democratic imaginary they thereby produce. These exclusions need to be emphasized, brought to the fore as exclusions, as the very limits establishing the protestors' political ideal. To avow such exclusion, however, would shoot the fantasy of an inclusive, undivided democracy in the foot. And as its own kind of political violence, such a decisive exclusion would force the protestors to abandon their stance as beautiful souls. Nonetheless, as hysterics, they refuse to acknowledge this element of their discourse, preferring instead to continue questioning the master.

What about Bush? If he is simply the perverse instrument or executor of a larger law beyond himself, or of a greater will, how does his discourse achieve consistency? Via the insertion of questioning, via a hystericization

—but not toward the protestors. Its relation to the protestors is not complementary as in two sides of a synthetic whole. This lack of complementarity is clear when we recall that in neither the discourse of the hysteric nor that of the pervert are claims made to some sort of equal. These discourses are not structured in terms of the exchange of reasons. Rather the Bush discourse is hystericized in relation to a different position, from its point of symbolic identification, the point from which it sees itself.[25] And this point is clearly that of its opponent, "Islamic fundamentalism" or terrorism, which the discourse itself elides. In effect, underlying Bush's position is a challenge to his opponent that both neurotically asks "Are we who you say we are?" and perversely proclaims "We are not soulless, weak, materialist, consumerist, decadent, capitalist, imperialists." *There is more to us than reality television, McDonald's, and net porn. The U.S., too, is resolute, strong, willing to fight to death, able to stay the course in a long, struggle with no end in sight. We are righteous. And I, as President, am the unwavering instrument of the higher law.*

The following chapter considers the willingness to name and confront evil as an indicator of Bush's resolve. For now, what is important is the gaze Bush imagines watching him when he speaks, the other he imagines looking at, judging, the United States. In the 2006 State of the Union address, Bush avows, "By allowing radical Islam to work its will—by leaving an assaulted world to fend for itself—we would signal to all that we no longer believe in our own ideals, or even in our own courage. But our enemies and our friends can be certain: The United States will not retreat from the world, and we will never surrender to evil." Before this imagined gaze—primarily that of the enemy, the terrorist who would receive the signal that the United States is sending—the willingness to die for freedom demonstrates that American freedom is not simply a market freedom, a decadent freedom to shop or choose from a wide array of colors, but something more, something as powerful as the conviction driving the so-called terrorist.

Democratic Theory as the Discourse of the University

The third invocation of democracy, Gutmann's and Thompson's theory of deliberative democracy, is usefully read in terms of the discourse of the university. Recall, in this version of the social link, knowledge is in the position of the speaker or agent. Underlying this speaking knowledge, in what Lacan designates as the position of truth, is the signifier of the master. The knowledge that speaks in university discourse relies on an unstated, underlying power, a master's claim to truth. Two points arise from reading Gutmann and Thompson via university discourse. The first appears when we understand them to be espousing a normative theory and involves their occupation of the position of neutral knowledge. The second appears when we read them as providing a descriptive theory and involves, one, the imaginary character of their synthesis of Bush and those who opposed his march to war as equals in democratic deliberation, and, two, the closure, the loss of a hope for a different future, that accompanies their account of the openness of democracy.

Žižek writes that "in the University discourse, it is Knowledge which occupies the agent's . . . place, turning the subject ($) into that which is 'produced,' into its unassimilable excess-remainder."[26] In the discourse of the university, the facts speak for themselves and when they do there is no proper place for the subject; the subject emerges as an extra, as present but altogether unnecessary. We can understand this point in terms of the exchange of reasons. In university discourse, reason trumps any personal or political claim. Faced with a rational argument, the subject can either accept the argument or view itself as "irrational," "malign," or "duplicitous." In the discourse of the university, then, knowledge is underpinned by an unacknowledged power. Seemingly neutral knowledge is authoritative even as, especially as, it claims and disavows its power at the same time. In Žižek's words, "The 'truth' of the University discourse, hidden beneath the bar, of course, is power, or the Master-Signifier: the constitutive lie of the University discourse is that it disavows its performative dimension, presenting what effectively amounts to a political decision based on power as a simple insight into the factual state of things."[27] The power of the facts is that they speak for themselves. To engage the facts is to accept their authority. (This sheds light on the Bush administration's rejection of "reality-based media"—their point is precisely that the facts *do not* speak for themselves.)

This neutral knowledge speaking for itself even as it rests on the unacknowledged support of power appears in Gutmann's and Thompson's elaboration of the basic moral principles underpinning deliberative democracy. Deliberative democracy, they argue, depends on "the principle of the economy of moral disagreement" which enjoins citizens to "find justifications that minimize their differences with their opponents" (7). They highlight offering reasons "that any citizen who is trying to find fair terms of cooperation could reasonably accept" (53). To emphasize one's differences from one's opponent is thus morally objectionable, a violation of the principle of the economy of moral disagreement. Likewise, failing to accept another's reasons or finding another's reasons unacceptable is to be irrational or possibly duplicitous because one is not working toward fair terms of cooperation.

Gutmann's and Thompson's treatment of Stanley Fish illustrates the way that power underpins university discourse. Selectively rehashing criticisms Fish raises in his contribution to a volume dedicated to discussing Gutmann's and Thompson's *Democracy and Disagreement* (and failing to consider any of Fish's other work), they point out that Fish argues that "the demand for justification is misguided because it presupposes a shared understanding of what counts as a good reason" (46). They then claim that Fish "seems to suggest that there is no way to distinguish between justified and unjustified exercises of political power" and that he "seems to have put democracy on the same moral footing as apartheid, authoritarianism, and fascism" (47).

Accusing Gutmann and Thompson of failing to follow their own principle of the economy of moral disagreement as they morph Fish the critic into Fish the fascist is too easy. More interesting is their failure to recognize Fish's fundamental point that context matters. This is the idea of a shared understanding: what counts as a good reason depends on reason's setting, the context in which a reason is given. Indeed, Fish's argument is even stronger. Meaning requires limits, discursive parameters establishing the conditions of truth and falsity, of adequation and appropriateness. A justification is convincing not when it is independent of power but due to the prior operation of power in securing the context within which it becomes compelling. Gutmann and Thompson don't consider Fish's account of shared understanding this way. Instead, they insert him into their way of thinking, their episteme, accusing him of reducing all argumentation to power politics. In this way, their refusal even to acknowledge the validity of another epistemology, of another way of thinking about meaning, principles, and the practice of reason giving, ends up demonstrating Fish's point: context matters, meaning depends on a prior set of conditions.

Gutmann and Thompson fail to allow for differing conceptions of the Real or differing approaches to truth, preferring instead to install claims of mutual acceptability and general accessibility in a supposition of morality rather than in an epistemic, political, or aesthetic formation. Accordingly they include (only to dismiss) Fish's point that accounts of deliberative democracy "make decisions and policies seem more moral when they are not" (46). Given their use of Bush's march to war as an example of deliberative democracy, Fish's comment hits the mark in advance. How else can one describe their treatment of Bush than as making a decision and a policy seem moral when it is not?

Employing their own rough notion of a performative contradiction, Gutmann and Thompson claim that if Fish is giving reasons while arguing against reason then he "enters willy-nilly into the forums of deliberative democracy, and falls under its obligations of reasonable argument" (48). But Fish's point is that the practice of reason giving that Gutmann and Thompson advocate is part of a specific practice, the academic practice of the university. He is participating in this practice—offering reasons. So the issue is not whether one participates in justificatory practices. Rather, it is whether these practices establish the terms and conditions of *politics* and whether these practices legitimize *political* outcomes. Gutmann and Thompson don't answer these questions. Instead, they present justification as a neutral, fundamental fact of the matter, a fact that transcends the settings in which it could have meaning. They ignore this presentation's dependence on a prior acceptance of the authority of a certain account of knowledge. They fail to consider that the practices of academic debate, practices discussed here in terms of the discourse of the university, do not coincide with the multiplicity of discourses operating in politics.

To be sure, Gutmann and Thompson don't claim that current democracies are perfect or even that theories of deliberative democracy have provided a final account of political legitimacy. Yet in an allowing for the fallibility of accounts of deliberation, they oscillate between different loci of failure or sites of insufficiency. A failure at one point is thus supplemented by the potential of the second point. This process of oscillation and supplementation enables them to produce an imaginary synthesis between proponents and opponents of preemptive war against Iraq. It also encloses hopes for the future into a justification for present injustice. Let's consider these points in more detail.

Gutmann and Thompson are at pains to acknowledge the limits of deliberation. Not only do they allow that deliberation was unlikely to stop the Bush administration's march to war but they admit that the "Bush administration relied to some extent on secret intelligence to defend its decision" (5). They also grant that deliberation has to stop well before a consensus is reached because decisions have to be made. Deliberation, they point out, "must end in a decision" even as deliberative democracy does not specify the procedures "for reaching a final decision" (18). Deliberative democracy requires a supplement that it itself cannot provide. Gutmann and Thompson concede further that citizens will often need to rely on experts, that the "deliberative mandate" should not apply to all governmental institutions, and that deliberation need not always involve giving reasons—"passionate rhetoric can be as justifiable as logical demonstration" (32, 51). These acknowledgments of the practical and institutional conditions of politics make sense—but not as elements of a justification of a theory of deliberation. In the latter setting, they appear as so many exceptions, indeed, as easily allowing for precisely that sort of "state of the exception" a procedural notion of democratic legitimacy was designed to avoid.[28]

The limitations and expectations that sustain Guttman's and Thompson's notion of deliberation rest uneasily against their claims for democracy. Given the gap between discussion and decision, how can the decision be understood in terms of government by the governed? In other words, if democracy is conceptualized in terms of deliberative procedures and practices of justification, in what way are the acts and decisions that evade and supplement these practices democratic? Democracy seems limited to the discussions surrounding a decision, the discursive context of a decision, but forever unable to reach the decision itself. The decision continues to exceed the circulation of reasons. Gutmann and Thompson argue that democracy is an attribute of the inclusivity of the discussion (10). But this doesn't even touch on the problem of the relation of the discussion to the political decision.[29]

In Gutmann's and Thompson's account of deliberative democracy, deliberation is self-justifying. Any problems it might encounter are best solved through more deliberation, in the future, after the decision. The benefits deliberation provides, especially insofar as there remains a gap between deliberation and decision, are reflexive and postponed, the benefits of enhanced deliberative capacity in the future. This inclusion of the future to legitimate present practices, moreover, shields Gutmann's and Thompson's account of deliberative democracy from normative or principled critique. Rather than an outside from which one might criticize the present, the future is already included as a justification for the present, as a way of saying *Let's just get on with it, we can redo it later*. When deliberation only circulates around the decision as a justification of itself, the demos never has to accept responsibility for the decision, much as the democratic theorist need not accept responsibility for a political outcome. The issue becomes the process and keeping the process open to a future it has already imagined in terms of itself.

Gutmann and Thompson characterize the run-up to the United States' commencing of aggressive war against Iraq in terms of deliberative democracy. They imagine that the supporters and opponents of the war are two sides in a debate, a debate that continues after the bombs have fallen and thousands have died. Emphasizing the circulation of reasons (inclusive of passionate rhetoric and secret intelligence), they treat the site of decision as a partner in an exchange of reasons, relieving it of accountability for the decision it makes as they shift political responsibility onto a discursive process where it can be perpetually deferred. *We can always change our minds, reconsider. And, then, we can say now things are different, hindsight is always 20/20, we need to put the past behind us.* But the two sides are not equal: one of them decides. One of them has the power to decide and to execute. Gutmann's and Thompson's imaginary synthesis justifies this power by placing it within the neutral context of a deliberation, by equating it with challenges to it.

Reading Gutmann's and Thompson's version of deliberative democracy in terms of university discourse, a discourse in which the facts speak for themselves, shows how their imaging of democracy fails to account for the power to decide, providing instead the permanent deferral of political responsibility. This deferral incorporates the future into the present as a justification for current failures, thereby shutting it off as a source of utopian energy. When democracy is justified by the very fact of justification, as it is in theories of deliberative democracy, the presence and absence of democracy overlap: our acknowledgment of failures justifies a failed democracy.

Present Democracy

The idea that democracy is present, at least in its notion, took hold in the nineties. Socialism, the only apparent alternative to democracy, seemed barren, exposed as a costly, deadly, failed experiment. Expansions in networked communications technologies seemed to realize in material form the conditions necessary for deliberation. With more and more people able to access more and more information, to register their opinions and participate in deliberation, how could any government but democracy even be possible? Of course, matters are not so simple. Some of the most repressive regimes (e.g., Singapore, Indonesia) are some of the most heavily networked. And as I emphasize throughout this book, extensions in communication have been accompanied by, indeed rooted in, amplifications of capitalism.

As Gutmann and Thompson make clear, the idea that democracy is present justifies Bush's decision. He is acting out a mandate, exercising the people's will, carrying out the law. But what about the sign in the coffee shop? If we say that democracy is present, then the protestors' appeal to democracy makes no sense: why are they fighting for something that they have? Are they saying, "More of the same! More of the same!"? Clearly this is not what they are after and this is why their appeal to democracy is fruitless: it is an appeal to the status quo for more of the same, with an emphasis, however, on more—more information, more participation, more deliberation—as if sheer quantity could bridge the gap and produce a different outcome. To this extent, it falls into the traps of communicative capitalism, strengthening the very structures it ostensibly aims to change.

The protestors (and the left more generally) appeal to democracy because they look at themselves from the position of their opponents, the Bush administration (or the right more generally), just as the Bush administration looks at itself from the position of its opponent, the so-called Islamic fundamentalist or terrorist. And just as the Bush administration adopts the tactics of its opponent to try to fill the lack it sees—political will, moral rectitude, the resolve to name and confront evil—so does the left try to live up to, respond to, right versions of its failures. Avoiding the extremes, it puts itself in the middle. It isn't partisan, one-sided, or politically correct but fair and democratic, not a special interest group but in tune with mainstream American values. It isn't socialist (and really doesn't favor the welfare state) but is instead committed to economic growth and free markets.

Because the appeal to democracy presupposes democracy is the solution to the problems of democracy, because it incorporates in advance any hope things might be otherwise as already the fundamental democratic promise and provision, it is a dead end for left politics. Entrapped by such an appeal, left and progressive contestation remains suspended between the discourse of the hysteric and the discourse of the university. Such suspension fails to break free of the continued workings of the discourse of the pervert as hysterical contestation affirms the position of the master. Moreover, the appeal to democracy remains unable to elaborate a convincing political alternative because it accepts the premise that we already know what is to be done—critique, discuss, include, and revise. Left reliance on democracy thus eschews responsibility not only for current failures (*Look, democracy isn't perfect*) but also for envisioning another politics in the future.

4

Resolve

SPEAKING OF EVIL

In his State of the Union address in 2002, George W. Bush invoked an "axis of evil." What available rhetorical fields enabled *the president* to link together North Korea, Iran, and Iraq and then judge the result as evil? What could hold this unstable train of signification together? How is such a monstrous, bizarre moral geography *even comprehensible*?[1] This chapter shows how "evil" finds a hospitable environment in Bush's presidential addresses because of the speculative identity of two seemingly opposed patterns of belief prominent in the United States under communicative capitalism—pervasive relativism and absolutist conviction.[2] The convergences of neoliberalism and democracy, the materialization of democratic ideals in the information and communication technologies that support and extend global corporate capitalism, establish a matrix wherein each is entitled to her own opinion and incited to protect that precious opinion by voicing it as loudly and resolutely as possible. Bush summoned the axis of evil not to describe three countries and their relationship but to demonstrate his own resolve.

While chapter 5 considers left retreat from a politics of conviction, this one focuses on the conservative embrace and extension of such a politics. Through a retrospective on "evil" in presidential speeches, it locates the current coincidence of relativism and resolve first in the rhetoric of Ronald Reagan, arguably the figure Bush most sought to emulate as president. At work in the words and personae of both the fortieth and the forty-third presidents is a powerful combination of conviction and vacuity such that resolve exists simply for its own sake: the lack of meaning creates the conditions for a certain conviction effect.

In Bush's speeches this resolve culminates in a vision of himself and America as instruments of the will of God. "Evil" could inhabit the 2002 State of the Union address not simply because of Bush's fluency in the language of faith but because of the coincidence of conviction and the broader culture of relativism in which the term *evil* floats so freely. "Evil" is powerful, efficacious, because its very lack of meaning (or the excesses of meaning overdetermining it, which is the same thing) enables the term to produce a conviction effect: no matter what "evil" means, people can be confident in Bush's conviction—*he knows*.[3] Hearing the 2002 State of the Union address, we believed that he was convinced there was an axis of evil.[4]

Many Evils

More obvious explanations for the presence of "evil" in the 2002 State of the Union address are, one, the ready availability of a discourse of fear and terror following the events of September 11, and, two, the prominence of religion in American life. Evil clearly flourishes in these discursive environments.[5] But these quick explanations distract us from the pervasiveness of evil and the multiplicity of its modes of appearance. Hence they fail to account for the evil in Bush's speech.

The first explanation regarding the discourse of fear and terror repeats the familiar (but nonetheless wrong) mantra that September 11 changed everything.[6] It is said 9/11 exposed the pernicious danger of postmodern relativism and the soul-destroying impact of irony. It demonstrated the persistence of evil in the world. And it reconfigured reality by challenging us, the *civilized* (according to Bush and Samuel Huntington), to confront, wage war on, evil.

Accounting for "evil" in the president's speech by appealing to this changed environment, however, fails to acknowledge the setting of these claims—a discursive habitat nourished through the culture wars long preceding 9/11—and grows out of the assumption that over the past forty years Americans have lost their moral sense, their capacity to speak seriously about evil. This loss is said to be significant, a truncating of the moral world insofar as the category "evil" is necessary for evaluating experiences, harms, sufferings, and dangers. Concern with the amputation of Americans' moral sense, moreover, shares its discursive habitat with critical claims regarding the culture of irony, a fecund environment already in the post–World War II era as the presumption of the general secularization of American society took hold.[7]

The discursive environment of the culture wars supports an additional assumption linked to claims that 9/11 changed everything, namely, the assumption that relativists hate America. A number of conservative thinkers contend that the problem with liberals and postmodernists is not that they are relativists but, on the contrary, that their apparent ethical pluralism is in fact ideological. Liberals and their ilk are not really relativist at all. Rather, liberals believe that America itself is evil.[8] For these conservatives, relativism and its multicultural, ecumenical, and ethically pluralist kin serve as the ideological guise of a treasonous anti-Americanism. They take it as a given that a concept of evil remains part of a postmodern worldview, a worldview antithetical to American values that September 11 revealed to be a threat to American unity and security.

The problem with the idea that September 11 provides the conditions of possibility for Bush's use of "evil" because "everything has changed" is that it is too vague to account for the specificity of the rhetoric of evil. Why did the change in "everything" not reconfigure political language in terms of hope, care, and the triumph of the human spirit? Why did support for the police and firefighters not lead to a renewed commitment to the sharing of benefits and burdens, to a more equitable distribution of privilege and prosperity? That contemporary political rhetoric does not provide a hospitable environment for such a political language seems fairly obvious—but why? A plausible account needs to attend to the culture wars, finding there the context delimiting "everything."

Even if there were a plausible link between 9/11 and evil, this link could not extend by itself to North Korea, Iran, and Iraq. What made *this* link possible?[9] What enabled *this* use of "evil"? An appeal to September 11 can't answer these questions—none of these countries had anything to do with September 11.

The second obvious explanation for "evil" in Bush's speech points to the prominence of religion in American life. Surely here we find a readily available reservoir of terms of moral denunciation and outrage. Eighty percent or more of Americans do not doubt the existence of God, pray daily, and believe in a final judgment.[10] The religious right is a powerful political force, one that has strengthened its hold and influence over the past thirty years.[11]

We shouldn't be too quick to jump to this explanation either. The appeal to the ready availability of languages of faith conflicts with the notion that September 11 changed everything. The latter idea presupposes an underlying secularization or falling away from faith, a loss of faith to which the day's events awakened us, not its prominence and ready availability as a language of moral condemnation.[12] So there is an incompatibility between the two explanations.

More important, however, is the rich variation among and within American religious discourse. Religious language inhabits the political register in multiple, changing, and inconsistent ways. There is not a single or constant discourse of religion in American history: evil isn't and never has been "one thing" in American life. President Dwight D. Eisenhower, for example, drew on a language of faith, beginning his first inaugural address with a prayer. Yet his use of "evil" differs significantly from Bush's. Indeed, religious controversy and disagreement is far more prevalent in U.S. history and politics than anything like a unified Christian doctrine. There is even fragmentation and disagreement on the so-called religious right. One of the hardest-hitting critiques of the "evils of Fundamentalism" comes from John F. Baugh, a mainstream Southern Baptist who anchors his arguments firmly in the Bible.[13]

To be sure, that "evil" in the 2002 State of the Union address grew out of a language of faith is uncontroversial. Former Bush speechwriter David Frum reports that "axis of hatred" in the original draft of the speech was changed to "axis of evil" because it resonated better with the theological language Bush had been using since 9/11.[14] To call this theological language "religion," however, consolidates multiple stories, tropes, ethics, and imaginaries. Bush's own salvation experience, his *personal* religious walk, does not stand for "religion" in the singular. In fact, his relation to scripture and experience of conversion are not tied to mainstream denominational religion. Rather, they emerged out of a small-group program of focused reading and discussion called Community Bible Study. The difference between Bush's "faith walk" and his father's Episcopalian upbringing enabled the younger Bush to serve as the liaison to the religious right for the 1988 presidential campaign.[15]

In the face of religious pluralism, the historical changes and variations within and between American religions, Bush's religiosity cannot account for the "axis of evil." Instead, we need to know more about the variety of ways in which religious invocations can be convincing in politics. How, in other words, are these invocations at home in a community larger than a specific community of faith?

The problems that arise with trying to explain "evil" in the State of the Union address as the result of September 11 or religion arise from a unicity of thought. Each account, in inverse ways, formats evil as a singularity as if "evil" were a master signifier capable of stopping shifts in signification. The idea that "everything has changed" obscures its rhetorical habitat, treating as settled values and suppositions contested in the culture wars.[16] The idea that a pervasive American religiosity accounts for "evil" likewise is inattentive to the varieties of religious practice and expression. In short, operating within each idea is a failure to attend to the ways evil stimulates speech, how it opens speech up rather than closes it down.

Evil is not at all uncommon. It's all over the place.[17] Evil is a major literary theme. A quick Google search turns up more than five million websites that contain the word *evil*. Many are satirical. Some involve faux mathematical equations proving that women are the root of all evil. Horror movies often explore the nature of evil, whether in the guise of say, Hannibal Lecter or Austin Powers' nemesis, Dr. Evil. In psychoanalytic terms, *evil* functions not as a master signifier or nodal point but as *objet petit a*, Jacques Lacan's term for that fantastic/Real excess that attracts us and repels us, that we can desire but never reach, that we might flee but can never escape.[18]

So even as Bush may invoke evil as that ultimate threat which cannot be left unaddressed, this invocation does not unleash a repressed language of evil. That language is already there. Evil thrives in various habitats and registers. It adapts to differing practices, uses, and deployments. Journalists emphasize this multiplicity, seemingly stunned by the excesses of evil's free-floating moments even as they ponder the instability of any and all attempts to explain or signify evil.[19] This very multiplicity figures into invocations of evil as that which *must* be confronted as it comes to be embodied and summoned through extreme, unbearable images. Writing in *Time* magazine, Lance Morrow declares, "Even if it's elusive and even if the term is used brainlessly, evil is still there—a mystery, a black hole into which reason and sunshine vanish but nonetheless . . . there. Talk to the children with chopped off hands in Sierra Leone."[20] Armed with horrifying examples, one invokes evil as that which even the most deconstructive postmodernist cannot deny. One might say that in this way "evil" functions as a conservative logic of performative contradiction (by getting the relativist to deny that Hitler or slavery is evil, say, the absolutist thinks he has exposed a fundamental inconsistency that calls into question the place from which the relativist speaks) or a theological diagnosis of relativism's universal symptom (if one accepts that X—or denies that Y—is evil, then one has no way not to accept, ultimately, the extermination of masses of people, the obliteration of humanity, or the destruction of the world).[21]

Detailed, embodied, sexualized bottom-line evil appears in Frum's account of his role in constructing Bush's 2002 State of the Union address. Frum notes his reservations regarding what exactly to say about Saddam Hussein given that children might be watching the television speech with their parents: "Did we really want the president describing how Saddam murdered his enemies by burning them alive in acid baths? Or broke their nerve by forcing them to watch as his soldiers raped their daughters and wives? Or cut off the hands and ears or gouged out the eyes of soldiers he suspected of lack of courage?"[22]

These same reservations did not restrain Bush's 2003 State of the Union address. In this address, Bush mentions children being tortured while their parents are forced to watch. He lists various methods (harsh interrogation techniques?) used in the "torture chambers of Iraq": electric shock, burning with hot irons, dripping acid on skin, mutilation with electric drills, and cutting out tongues. And he concludes his list by saying "If this is not evil, then evil has no meaning."[23]

More needs to be said about the details of evil and the role of these details in creating a habitat for the language of evil in political discourse (the devil is in the details). The matter is not, however, one of uncovering dogmatism. I say this because the interesting and thoughtful account of the modes and genres of political moralizing offered by Jane Bennett and Michael Shapiro overlooks the appeal of moral certainty in politics. For them, moralizing refers to "a style of speaking, writing, and thinking that is too confident about its judgments and thus too punitive in its orientation to others."[24] This overconfidence, they continue, "slips easily into dogmatism." Under communicative capitalism's intensive and extensive circulations of media, though, getting a message to register or holding an alliance together may well require strong, clear positions. There are also times when the political situation requires lines to be drawn and stands to be taken, when partisans cannot welcome every view and should not acknowledge the validity of every opinion. The right knows this—and has used the left's disregard of this crucial fact of politics to dismantle basic social welfare provisions and install a neoliberal regime of greed worse than that of the gilded age's robber barons.

Deployments and incursions of "evil" in political language are resolutely, profoundly, deliberately dogmatic. When Bush uses the term *evil*, he announces that he knows that there are circumstances where dogmatism is necessary. After all, the right has not hesitated to use the word *revolution* —Reagan revolution, Gingrich revolution—to name their triumphs. The excess that dogmatism denotes ("*over* confidence" and a "*too* punitive orientation" in Bennett's and Shapiro's words) is the key to its appeal. For those who find it appealing, or even necessary, dogmatism is a strength, a virtue. What is needed, then, is closer consideration of the settings within which dogmatism becomes attractive and reassuring.

A look back at appearances of the word *evil* in presidential speeches is one way to get a sense of the settings of dogmatism's appeal. The speeches considered here suggest an inverse relation between dogmatism and signification. The stronger the chain of significations articulated with evil, the less dogmatic is the use of the term. More simply put, when "everybody knows" what evil is, when its meaning is clear and seemingly widely accepted, then its use in a presidential speech describes an object. Yet when "evil" is amorphous and unclear, its appearance in a presidential speech says something not about an object but about the (dogmatic) conviction and resolve of the subject willing to name evil.

Presidential Evil

Evil has long been at home in presidential rhetoric, easily adapting to its changing demands. Taking up the Puritan political sermon or jeremiad, Sacvan Bercovitch specifies the role of this rhetoric in producing "America" as a symbol in the country's early decades.[25] My account begins in the Depression and period directly prior to the Cold War. As president, Franklin Delano Roosevelt turns to evil as he leads the country out of the

Depression. He links evil with capitalist excess and the poverty it engenders. His successor, Harry S. Truman, continues to associate evil with poverty even as he worries about the potential for evil linked to technological development. At the same time, his language comes to express the polarities that will structure the Cold War. Evil, however, is not an element in this articulation. Thus, while evil's primary rhetorical host is economic distress, a secondary variant of evil also emerges in the initial years of the Cold War. This evil rides in on complexity and its challenge to power in a democracy.

Roosevelt's 1933 inaugural address is known primarily for its oft-repeated line "the only thing we have to fear is fear itself."[26] Evil, then, is nothing to fear. Government can address and manage evil. Performing this address and management, Roosevelt speaks of evils in the plural and expels these evils to the past. He observes that there are two safeguards against a return of the "evils of the old order:" strict supervision of all banking, credits, and investment and an end to speculation with other people's money. In Roosevelt's second and third inaugural addresses, evil inhabits the same rhetorical environment. Not only does Roosevelt continue to criticize those who "betray for profit the elementary decencies of life" but he also notes that Americans no longer tolerate abuses of power and heedless self-interest, "evil things formerly accepted" but now not so easily condoned. The third inaugural address announces that the country has survived its crisis and "put away evil things."

Even as evil is comfortable in the register of past economic practices no longer threatening America, an evil variant appears in the second inaugural address. Evil remains something to be managed through governance, but its temporality changes. Rather than banished to the past, it is projected into a sort of indefinite future-present, the universal extratemporality of moral engagement. Suggesting that the strength of democracy stems from the power lodged in the people, Roosevelt advises that "as intricacies of human relationships increase, so power to govern them also must increase, power to stop evil; power to do good."

In his first years as president, Truman reiterates Roosevelt's associations of evil with poverty. His 1948 State of the Union address refers to economic distress as a "disease whose evil effects spread far beyond the boundaries of the afflicted nation." The following year, in a general treatment of economic and social problems such as low minimum wage, growing monopolies, prejudice, and intolerance as opportunities for the Congress and the president to work together for the good of the people, he underscores that "our first great opportunity is to protect our economy against the evils of boom and bust."

In addition to linking evil to poverty, Truman also employs the evil variant that appeared in Roosevelt's second inaugural address, positing evil as something in the future, something to be resisted or overcome through the power of the people. His State of the Union address in 1950, alluding to scientific, technological, and, presumably, military developments associated with "opening the secrets of nature," announces, "Man must create the moral and legal framework for the world which will insure that his new powers are used for good and not evil. In shaping the outcome, the people of the United States will play a leading role." Like Roosevelt's speeches, Truman's establish a fitting rhetorical habitat for evil. Poverty, economic inequality, and the unchecked pursuit of profit are matters appropriately designated evil. At the same time, evil also appears as the object of a project for the future, one associated with the moral strength of democratic governance.

Nevertheless, along with the political climate, the discursive environment of the late 1940s was changing. One site where the change can be detected is in a speech Truman gives before a joint session of Congress in 1947. In that speech, Truman requests economic assistance for Greece and Turkey (and elaborates what would become known as the Truman Doctrine).[27] He also uses the term *evil* and suggests a vision of the world as split between freedom and oppression. Rather than explicitly tied to Soviet communism, however, evil remains articulated with poverty. Truman asserts: "At the present moment in world history nearly every nation must choose between alternative ways of life. The choice is too often not a free one." On one side is a way of life based on the will of the majority and "distinguished by free institutions, representative government, free elections, guarantees of individual liberty, freedom of speech and religion, and freedom from political oppression." On the other side is a way of life that "relies upon terror and oppression, a controlled press and radio, fixed elections, and the suppression of personal freedoms."[28] Despite this characterization of Soviet communism, Truman refrains from referring to either the regime or the ideology as evil. Instead, evil retains its link with economic deprivation: "The seeds of totalitarian regimes are nurtured by misery and want. They spread and grow in the evil soil of poverty and strife." Evil flourishes in fetid zones of neediness, brutality, and despair. With this variation in the rhetorical environment established, Truman's image of the conflict in Korea as an "evil war by proxy" in his 1951 State of the Union address is not surprising.[29]

Eisenhower drops from his rhetoric the social and economic sense of evil, embracing instead Truman's opposition between freedom and slavery. Speaking within the symbolic frame of the Cold War, Eisenhower depicts this opposition in terms of a moral struggle between good and evil, although like Truman he refrains from calling the Soviet enemy itself evil. Additionally, even as Eisenhower adopts more religious language than his two immediate predecessors, the link they make between scientific and technological power and the challenge this power poses for future paths toward good or evil nevertheless continues to inhabit his speeches.

Eisenhower's first inaugural address establishes the rhetorical patterns for his presidential speeches.[30] He begins by asking his audience to bow their heads as he utters what he refers to as "a little private prayer of my own." (That Eisenhower refers to a prayer said in a public office-taking ceremony as "private" deeply challenges the notion of private, particularly given that he speaks the prayer aloud and asks the audience to join him in bowing their heads. Still, the very fact that he felt compelled to refer to his prayer as "private" suggests the continued presence of some sort of boundary separating personal expressions of religious faith from public responsibility. In other words, were he to have no sense of the importance of a separation between church and state or faith and politics, Eisenhower would not have paid lip service to the distinction between public and private acts.) He then testifies to the significance of the present moment in American history: "The world and we have passed the midpoint of a century of continuing challenge. We sense with all our faculties that forces of good and evil are massed and armed and opposed as rarely before in history. This fact defines the meaning of this day. We are summoned by this honored and historic ceremony to witness more than the act of one citizen swearing his oath of service, in the presence of God. We are called as a people to give testimony in the sight of the world to our faith that the future shall belong to the free."[31] Having grown in strength and responsibility in the course of confronting wars and economic depression, the United States finds itself calling upon God for guidance and "groping to know the full sense and meaning of these times." Is the world heading toward darkness or nearing the light? This particular time of trial "comes at a moment when man's power to achieve good or to inflict evil surpasses the brightest hopes and the sharpest fears of all ages." Yet the very hopes and promises that mankind's scientific and technological achievements have enabled now imperil life itself. The proper response to science, the only response adequate to the threat of darkness and annihilation facing the world, is faith.

For Eisenhower, it is time for America to reaffirm and proclaim the faith of the free in man's deathless dignity as governed by eternal and natural law. "This faith defines our full view of life," he declares. "It establishes, beyond debate, those gifts of the Creator that are man's inalienable rights, and that make all men equal in His sight." Enemies of this faith worship force and torture truth. America's destiny as the leader of the free world is thus to confront these enemies with confidence, conviction, moral strength, and, again, staunch faith. All Americans must be united as they renew their faith and devote themselves to the nation's fundamental precepts: "No person, no home, no community can be beyond the reach of this call. We are summoned to act in wisdom and in conscience, to work with industry, to teach with persuasion, to preach with conviction, to weigh our every deed with care and with compassion. For this truth must be clear before us: whatever America hopes to bring to pass in the world must first come to pass in the heart of America." The United States stands on a moral precipice facing the ultimate confrontation between good and evil. What Roosevelt and Truman projected into the future as the possible object of a collective project confronts America as a problem now, in the present. Evil is that in opposition to which America can know and realize who it is.[32]

John F. Kennedy's inaugural address ("ask not what your country can do for you . . .") adopts a tone decidedly different from Eisenhower's. Rather than emphasizing a fundamental division in the world, Kennedy appeals to hopes for peace, to civility, to arms control, to scientific wonder (rather than terror), and to shared struggle against common problems of disease, poverty, and war. Kennedy's language is also far less religious than Eisenhower's (likely because religious language from Kennedy would suggest his Catholicism and could occasion anxiety about papal influence).

These changes do not lead to a discursive environment completely inhospitable to evil—but close. In two speeches given in June 1963, Kennedy refers to communism as an evil system. But he qualifies these remarks, noting that "no government or social system is so evil that its people must be considered as lacking in virtue" and bracketing the attribution of evil as words of "a few who say."[33] Such qualification may have enabled the mutated evil that appears in his address on the Nuclear Test Ban Treaty. This speech links evil neither to America's moral destiny nor to economic and social ills. Rather, evil appears as a judgment in non-American eyes, as how others may see America. The president notes: "These tests befoul the air of all men and all nations, the committed and the uncommitted alike, without their knowledge and without their consent. That is why the continuation of atmospheric testing causes so many countries to regard all nuclear powers as equally evil; and we can hope that its prevention will enable all those countries to see the world more clearly, while enabling all the world to breathe more easily."[34] Kennedy's language suggests that if America looks at itself from the perspective of nonaligned nations, it might well recognize a more complex moral world than the one governing its prior assumptions of right.

Lyndon B. Johnson retains this more complex vision, one less suited to a language of "evil." His "Let Us Continue" speech, given soon after Kennedy's assassination, doesn't declare war on evil or attempt to unite Americans in steadfast dedication to evil's eradication. Johnson holds that the challenge is *not* to linger over this "evil moment" but instead to move forward. To this end, he urges Congress to increase taxes and enact a civil rights bill. Johnson concludes: "The time has come for Americans of all races and creeds and political beliefs to understand and respect each other. So let us put an end to the teaching and the preaching of hate and evil and violence. Let us turn away from the fanatics of the far left and the far right, from the apostles of bitterness and bigotry."[35] Finding evil's proper home in the extreme speech of fanatics, Johnson attempts to weed it out of political speech.

Yet he can't eliminate it entirely. Evil sometimes appears in its older form as a social and economic evil, as lack and deprivation.[36] Evil also sprouts up in Johnson's 1967 State of the Union address, albeit sheltered within a quote from Thomas Jefferson: "It is the melancholy law of human societies to be compelled sometimes to choose a great evil in order to ward off a greater evil." Johnson here uses Jefferson's words to justify the choice to fight a limited war in Vietnam.

Perhaps because evil has become, at least in this specific rhetoric, something America chose, that is, an acknowledged although dreaded attribute of American actions, it only rarely occurs in the speeches of the three presidents who follow Johnson. For the most part, these presidents actively and consciously employ a political language designed to lessen political tensions. For example, in his first inaugural address, Richard Nixon reiterates Johnson's attempt to produce a moderate political language even as he distances himself from Johnson's war. Drawing from Quaker belief in simplicity, quietude, and responsive listening, Nixon suggests that answers to America's problems might be found if Americans looked within themselves for "the simple things, the basic things" such as "goodness, decency, love and kindness." To listen responsively, moreover, requires that Americans stop shouting. Nixon notes, "America has suffered from a fever of words; from inflated rhetoric that promises more than it can deliver; from angry rhetoric that fans discontents into hatreds; from bombastic rhetoric that postures instead of persuading." As "we," the American people, learn to speak quietly, government, also identified as "we," will listen: "We will strive to listen in new ways—to the voices of quiet anguish, the voices that speak without words, the voices of the heart—to the injured voices, the anxious voices, the voices that have despaired of being heard."[37] In the environment responsive listening creates, evil has no place.

Gerald Ford also expresses exhaustion with evil, a sense that words like "evil" should not inhabit political discussion. "Evil" is too extreme and dangerous a term for politics. But even as Ford wants the term eliminated, it undergoes an additional mutation in his rhetoric: evil is how others refer to America. In his State of the Union address on January 19, 1976, Ford complains that Americans have for too long "downgraded" themselves as a nation. "The American people have heard too much about how terrible our mistakes, how evil our deeds, and how misguided our purposes. The American people know better. The truth is we are the world's greatest democracy."[38] In his official speeches as president, Jimmy Carter doesn't use "evil" at all, not in connection with the Iranian hostage crisis, the Soviet invasion of Afghanistan, or the economic hardships brought about by the recession and energy crisis. In his famous "Crisis of Confidence" speech given in July 1979, Carter emphasizes the "paralysis, stagnation, and drift" facing the country.[39] Like presidents before him, he positions the United States at a crossroads between two paths of freedom. One path leads to fragmentation, self-assertion, chaos, and immobility. The other is the path to true freedom, one that entails common purpose and the restoration of American values. Evil appears on neither path, but struggle and even sacrifice accompany both.

Ontological Evil

Ronald Reagan's presidential speeches employ a radically different rhetoric from those of his immediate predecessors. On the one hand, the stark divisions of his cold warrior stance create, as did Eisenhower's, a fertile environment for the oppositions of good and evil, free and totalitarian, us and them. On the other hand, Reagan's speeches provide such a fertile political habitat for evil that the term rapidly reproduces and spreads far beyond the initial binary of American and Soviet. Among those items Reagan identifies as evil are dim economic prospects, inflation, stagflation, terrorism, deaths of American soldiers in El Salvador, international drug trafficking, "more and more government intervention," segregation, discrimination based on race, religion, and sex, racism, anti-Semitism, ethnic and religious intolerance, Hitler, and the Holocaust.[40] In Reagan's speeches, multiple issues are matters of intense moral conflict. Michael Rogin thus misreads the specificity of evil in Reagan's rhetoric when he views Reagan's associative lists of evil in the world as confusing communism with terrorism and political opposition with crime and disease.[41] *Contra* Rogin, Reagan does not locate evil in a central cause or place. Nor does he project all that is evil outside the United States and threatening to violate its borders, again as Rogin argues.[42] Rather, for Reagan evil is in the very nature of things; it's the setting of humanity's moral struggle.

For Reagan, this condition of struggle is ontological. The world itself consists of great good and great evil. Such an establishing of evil as a fact of existence changes the character of the moral judgment. When evil is a basic aspect of the world, failing to recognize it indicates moral weakness, an unwillingness or inability to face honestly the truth of our situation. Correspondingly, naming evil demonstrates moral strength, courage, and resolve. Reagan's presidential language thus blends two approaches to evil, moral and ontological. This blending transforms political struggles between winners and losers into moral struggles between saints and sinners or, worse, the forces of God and the forces of Satan.[43]

Ontological evil pervades Reagan's "evil empire" speech. Reagan delivered it before the National Association of Evangelicals in Orlando, Florida, on March 8, 1983.[44] The first half of the speech emphasizes policies dear to the Christian right: restrictions on abortion and a constitutional amendment to restore prayer to public schools. Although this part of the speech appeals to religious tenets with a long history in American political rhetoric (with cites to William Penn, Thomas Jefferson, and George Washington), it is not itself expressed in the language of religious conviction. That mode of expression appears in the second half of the speech. As Reagan concludes his discussion of every child's right to life, he observes "a great spiritual awakening in America." Shortly thereafter, he repeats, "America is in the midst of a spiritual awakening." He then repeats the biblical keynote of the evangelical association's meeting, "Yes, let justice roll on like a river." These repetitions provide a bridge to a more religious mode of speaking, the transition to a language of faith. Indeed, as Reagan moves to the last two issues of his speech, he calls on philosophy and theology to ground his claims about ontological evil: "We must never forget that no government schemes are going to perfect man. We know that living in this world means dealing with what philosophers would call the phenomenology of evil or, as theologians would put it, the doctrine of sin. There is sin and evil in the world, and we're enjoined by Scripture and the Lord Jesus to oppose it with all our might." The world is a moral battlefield, the site of the epochal struggle between good and evil, right and wrong. God commands his people not to turn the other way or shield themselves from evil, not to appease or accommodate their adversaries but to struggle with all their might against evil in this world.

Humanity's fundamental struggle against evil is the setting for the last two issues in Reagan's speech. The first enacts the purification of the soul or the putting in order of one's house that prepares the chosen for spiritual warfare. Reagan tells his evangelical audience that America, too, has "a legacy of evil with which it must deal." This legacy involves racism, anti-Semitism, bigotry, and prejudice.[45] He enjoins his audience to transcend these evils: "Use the mighty voice of your pulpits and the powerful standing of your churches to denounce and isolate these hate groups in our midst. The commandment given us is clear and simple: 'Thou shalt love thy neighbor as thyself.' " Cleansed of past sins and girded in moral rectitude, America will have the strength for the ultimate battle, a spiritual battle, against the "aggressive impulses of an evil empire."

The stakes are high—people's very souls. After he urges his audience to stand with him in opposing "the so-called nuclear freeze solutions proposed by some," Reagan shifts, dramatically, to the story of a young father, a father who loves his two little girls so much that he would rather see his "little girls die now, still believing in God, than have them grow up under communism and one day die no longer believing in God." The fight against the Soviets is a fight for salvation, eternal life. Reagan declares: "Yes, let us pray for the salvation of all of those who live in totalitarian darkness—pray that they will discover the joy of knowing God. But until they do, let us be aware that while they preach the supremacy of the state, declare its omnipotence over individual man, and predict its eventual domination of all peoples on the earth, they are the focus of evil in the modern world." Like the serpent in the garden, an image Reagan also invokes, Marxism-Leninism tempts humanity with false promises of power and omnipotence. But these are not promises any government can keep: true strength is spiritual. America, although it needs strong defense, cannot rely simply on bombs and rockets: "The real crisis we face today is a spiritual one; at root, it is a test of moral will and faith."

Evil is alive in Reagan's speech. It permeates the world in which Americans find themselves and establishes the very conditions that give meaning to their lives. These conditions are uncertain and opaque: insofar as there are so many evils—totalitarianism and intolerance, intrusive government and sexual and racial discrimination—it becomes difficult to see what, precisely, the attribution "evil" signifies. How can Reagan invoke a Christian God, claim that the Soviets are evil because they do not believe in God, *and* urge tolerance? Reagan's emphasis on tolerance introduces an uncertainty as to what, exactly, is evil. The American legacy of evil he invokes is rife with division on precisely this point: is what was once understood as the evil of miscegenation now to be recognized as an instance of the evil of discrimination? What about the right to abortion? Might that right be important in ending sex discrimination, another evil that Reagan urges his evangelical audience to address?

The ambiguity here is crucial: it produces the space for moral will, for decisiveness and action. Reagan knows what evil is. When he calls evil by name, he locates himself in a prophetic tradition dear to evangelicals and rooted in American history. He places himself in the position of someone with an ontological knowledge of the truth and with the moral courage to speak the truth. Evil's ambiguity thus enables the import and weight of the term, its efficacy, to shift to the one willing to invoke it.

In a later interview, Reagan emphasizes that in this speech the term *evil* was important not because it rightly characterized the Soviets (although it did), but because it explicitly acknowledged real differences between the United States and the USSR. Responding to the interviewer's observation that the speech made it seem that reconciliation between the two powers was impossible since a confrontation between good and evil was at stake, Reagan explains: "I think it is somehow lifting that out of context—of this line and this description as the focus of evil and so forth. Certainly their entire beliefs, beginning with the disbelief in God—their beliefs are so contrary to what we accept as morality. Witness a Kampuchea and an Afghanistan and so forth. But no, what I was pointing out there, and I still believe is time-tested and proven, is not the inevitability of war, but a recognition and a willingness to face up to what these differences are in our views and between us, to be realistic about it."[46] Realism, for Reagan, involves recognizing the existence of evil in the world and willingly accepting the fact that the world is not a perfect place and never will be. Reagan is a realist because he knows what the world is like and is strong enough to face this world without blinders.

This conviction, this willingness to acknowledge and name evil in the world, does not depend on or require the discursive environment sustained by the Cold War. In fact, the Cold War's end releases evil from the already weak constraints of the confrontation between the United States and the USSR. This spreading, flourishing evil, and the resolve to name it, is an additional aspect of Reagan's speeches flourishing in the rhetoric of George W. Bush. It appears most strongly in a speech Reagan gave in England after he was president and after the end of the Cold War.

On December 4, 1992, Reagan delivered the address, "Democracy's Next Battle," at the Oxford Union Society.[47] Noting that the fight against totalitarianism "was a grand and noble cause, one that united the entire civilized world," Reagan finds that its end has "robbed much of the west of its uplifting, common purpose." "Will we turn inward, lulled by a dangerous complacency and the short-sighted view that the end of one Evil Empire means the permanent banishment of evil in all its forms?" he asks. To answer, and in answering restore a sense of mission to the "civilized world," Reagan returns to ontological evil: "Evil still stalks the planet."

Although this evil is not identical to the evil of Marxism-Leninism, although it is not systematic, coherent, or localized, it continues, inevitably, to permeate the world. Reagan declares, "Its ideology may be nothing more than bloodlust; no program more complex than economic plunder or military aggrandizement. But it is evil all the same. And wherever there are forces in the world that would destroy the human spirit and diminish human potential, they must be recognized and they must be countered." The mission Reagan envisions is for "civilized nations" to stand "in unison" against "immoral and deadly excesses" around the globe such as those undertaken by Saddam Hussein and in places like Bosnia, Somalia, and Sudan.

Fighting these evils will require imposing "civilized standards" of international conduct and enforcing those standards with a fully equipped United Nations force—"an army of conscience." Thus, Reagan challenges his Oxford audience to contribute to the "age-old battle for individual freedom and human dignity." The next generations, like the ones before them, have a cause, and service to this cause will give their lives meaning. They should not forget the victims of suffering and violence. As Reagan enjoins, "Do not abandon them to the evils of totalitarian rule or democratic neglect." In this late speech, then, democratic neglect, failure to name and act, is itself an evil, one that Reagan is continuing to fight.

Since Reagan's presidency ended, conservatives have continued to praise his resolve. Crediting him with bringing down the Soviet Union and, echoing his 1984 campaign theme, restoring morning to America after the "malaise" of the Carter years, those on America's political right celebrate Reagan for the realism and moral strength of his political message. But what is realism? Does "realism" refer to the emphasis on security characteristic of the realist school of international relations? If so, why are a bifurcated worldview and disdain for arms control realistic responses to a nuclear standoff?

A better way to conceive Reagan's realism focuses on his supposition of ontological evil. For Reagan, evil is Real. It flows throughout the world, threatening and subverting the civilized order. Its pervasive, excessive nature, moreover, makes evil slippery, deceptive. Recognizing it, naming it, thus requires resolve—the will to break with conventional wisdom, to stop paying lip service to the order of appearances, and to reject established political norms (this rejection of norms is a key feature of realist international relations). Insofar as conventional wisdom, the order of appearances, and established norms are not to be recognized, insofar as the symbolic order is violated or denied, strength of will is a necessity. Evil cannot just be named. Once named, it must be met, confronted, countered. Responding to evil demands a willingness to "do what is necessary," to engage in acts and practices that, from the perspective of the symbolic, may themselves seem to be evil.

Lacanian psychoanalysis holds that the decline of the symbolic leads to a powerful alliance of the imaginary with the Real. Such an alliance is clearly at work in the Reagan presidency. Fantasy images of Reagan as a cowboy and explicit acknowledgments of his work as an actor accompany the ontological evil he identifies in the nature of things.[48] The realism of Reagan's political will, in other words, is supported by fantasies of figures of strength. Reagan played these roles and, indeed, gestured to them by repeating lines from his movies, perhaps most memorably "Win one for the Gipper."

American presidents have long found political inspiration in religious language. Twentieth-century presidents have, like those who came before them, used the term *evil*. But the term means different things in different settings—and sometimes it doesn't mean anything at all. Sometimes it points to the will of the one who speaks it, not the object to which it is applied. The discursive environment supplied by Reagan's speeches differs significantly from that of his immediate predecessors—Kennedy, Johnson, Nixon, Ford, and Carter. Superficially, it resembles Eisenhower's, but this resemblance is misleading. Eisenhower refers to his inaugural prayer as "private" and refrains from attempting to convert the Soviets from their atheism. He also treats the forces of good and evil as elements within the symbolic order of the Cold War: freedom is good and totalitarian slavery is evil. Eisenhower invokes a symbolically consistent moral world, one where the ambiguities and tensions always subverting attributions of good and evil are repressed, contained. In that moment of history when the world faces a choice between good and evil, America must not give way on its faith in human freedom and dignity. These inalienable rights are gifts of the Creator; the struggle to secure them takes place in the presence of the Creator, and America turns to the Creator for guidance in these times. But Eisenhower does not say that he or America is an instrument of the Creator. He does not say that God has instructed the United States to fight His battle against the forces of evil. In short, Eisenhower's language works within the symbolic order of the Cold War as it presents Americans as subjects with choices and responsibilities. Reagan depicts evil as Real and says that God commands us to fight against it.

The difference between Reagan's language and that of Truman and Roosevelt is also misleading. Like them, he links evil to technological complexity, diminished human potential, and that which is to be fought through the moral strength of democratic governance. Yet what is most striking is what happens to governance in the face of Reagan's ontologization of evil: a radical fusion of previously separate fields and practices. Recall, Reagan finds evil in dim economic prospects, deaths of American soldiers in El Salvador, terrorism, drug trafficking, "excessive" government intervention, intolerance, segregation, discrimination, racism, and anti-Semitism. In the Oxford Union speech, moreover, he urges that all such forces must be recognized and countered wherever they arise. He envisions a UN–backed "army of conscience." Ontological evil thus overflows already unstable distinctions between war and policing, religion and politics, justice and administration. In the face of the Real of evil, these divisions fall apart.

Vacuous Resolve

Just as Reagan prays for the salvation of those living in totalitarian darkness, so does George W. Bush find in religion the best response to political troubles. As Howard Fineman observes, "The Bush administration is dedicated to the idea that there is an answer to societal problems here and to terrorism abroad: give everyone, everywhere, the freedom to find God, too."[49] Moreover, like the vision in Reagan's Oxford Union address, so is the world depicted in Bush's speeches the site of a cosmic battle between good and evil (typically formatted through a racial logic of civilized versus barbarian). Yet Bush expands and intensifies ontological evil as he speaks within the discourse of the pervert.[50] The pervert has no doubts; he

"brings to light, stages, practices the secret fantasies that sustain the dominant public discourse."[51] The pervert knows what is required and makes
himself into that instrument that does what is required. So not only does
"evil" inhabit Bush's speeches as an ontological given and thus highlight
his resolve in naming it but it works further to designate the subject
confronting evil as an instrument of God. Because conviction comes from
God, the one who names evil serves as an extension or embodiment of
divine will. More strongly put, the only way Bush can guarantee that he is
chosen by God is by demonstrating the power God gives him to name and
confront evil without wavering, with complete and utter conviction (in
the face of criticism, facts, and alternatives). For the responsible will of
fallible and uncertain political subjects, then, ontological evil substitutes
confrontations between objects in accordance with the inevitabilities of
the will of God.

Accounts of the presidential campaign of 2000 emphasize the emptiness, if not downright stupidity, of George W. Bush. Bush exhibited little
interest in policy specifics and little knowledge of political issues. Frank
Bruni, the *New York Times* reporter assigned to the Bush campaign and
White House, notes that polls taken during the primaries "showed that
support for Bush was less firmly grounded in anything real than support
for some other candidate was."[52] Respondents found it difficult to give
specific reasons for their support for Bush. Yet Bush's vagueness was
useful. Bush was a candidate "whose very lack of bold definition—whose
spongy failure to make an emphatic mark—allowed him to assume the
attributes of the scenery around him. It enabled him to be whatever
people were inclined or wanted to see, a Rorschach running for president."[53] A key element of the Republican campaign was thus to rely on
images that would affect voters viscerally. The Bush campaign demonstrated, Bruni writes, "how much could be fixed with powder and puffery,
how thoroughly a candidate could be transformed from the outside in,
how little he had to do but stand on the right set, under the right lighting,
and say the right lines. If it was hard to figure out exactly what Bush was
made of—and if, by September 11, 2001, it was not a whole lot easier—this
was a good part of the reason."[54]

Bush's vagueness persisted into the early months of his presidency.
Again, he demonstrated little patience with the details of governance or
the complexities of public policy. His few public statements were vapid

sound bites; anything more he tended to bungle with the sort of malapropisms one associates with young children.[55] As his former speechwriter, David Frum, emphasizes, "Bush's political vision was unclear." Bush had political instincts and general beliefs, but in the first half of 2001 it was nearly impossible to tell what, if any, ideas Bush actually had.[56]

Bush's vacuity was coupled with conviction. His personal faith, the salvation experience that led him to quit drinking and get serious about his life, was his most distinct feature. Voters may not have known what compassionate conservatism entailed, but they did know that Bush was a man of convictions, that he was decisive and relied on his gut instincts. The fact of this conviction dominated Bush's speeches and the message his administration sought to impart after 9/11. The terms *evil* and *evildoers* frequent this rhetoric, as do deeper and more significant religious allusions.[57]

Yet the confused and scattered initial reactions of the Bush administration to the attacks of September 11 should not be forgotten. Speaking in an elementary school in Florida when the planes hit the Twin Towers, Bush didn't return to Washington for over nine hours, flying instead to air bases in Louisiana and Nebraska. To many, his initial speeches seemed ill-suited to the magnitude of the moment. Early polls suggested that barely half the country was "highly confident" in Bush's ability to handle the crisis.[58] The White House staff worked to control the situation by repeating, at every possible moment, that the president was "focused" and "resolute." According to Bruni, "The efficacy of even such transparent tactics soon became clear. By using this vocabulary over and over, aides lodged it so deeply in the minds of reporters that these reporters began adopting it without even realizing it. On the morning after Bush's address to Congress, stories in both the *Washington Post* and the *Times* that analyzed his demeanor used the word 'resolute,' without quotation marks, in the first paragraphs."[59]

Not surprisingly, the term *resolute* and its kin, *resolve* and *resolution*, feature prominently in Bush's address to Congress on September 20, 2001. They characterize what Bush asks of the American people as they enter into "civilization's war," a war that divides the world into those who stand with America and those who stand with America's murderous enemies. They also characterize Bush's own rhetoric: he is certain. He knows—the rightness of the war, even the end of the war. As he testifies, "The course of this conflict is not known, yet its outcome is certain. Freedom and fear, justice and cruelty, have always been at war, and we know that God is not neutral between them."[60] Bush doesn't know the course of the war, but that sort of detail doesn't matter. What matters is Bush's certainty that God is on America's side and that God's side always wins. After the speech, confidence in Bush jumped to 86 percent (an extraordinary number for an American president) and remained over 80 percent during the next several months.[61]

Such confidence in Bush results from the combination of vacuity and resolve. The content of Bush's speech registers less than the fact that he demonstrates resolve, strength, command. This is not surprising: as the media said over and over, Americans were looking for leadership—or perhaps someone through whom they could enact revenge for the attacks. Nevertheless, the emptiness of Bush's expectations for Americans is notable. Americans were to show resolve, too, but in what? In going about their everyday lives, returning to business, loving their families, hugging their children, and shopping. Bush gave Americans permission to do what they want to do. Doing what they want became their patriotic duty.

Media emphasis on Bush as presidential produced a weird split. Insofar as news media in the first months following the September 11 attacks emphasized how *presidential* Bush was, they inadvertently voiced an anxiety that he was not quite presidential or that there was at least a risk of him not being presidential enough. *Shouldn't resolve be demonstrated by more than going back to our everyday activities? Shouldn't someone be made to suffer? To die?* Differently put, attention to the appropriateness of his resolve or demeanor underscores the gap between the man and his office. As the war on terror continued, this gap was covered over by the fantasy of a second, evil, more powerful leader, one less constrained by goodness or compassion, one willing to exact the necessary, awful revenge—Vice President Dick Cheney at work in his secret underground bunker, heading the shadow government.

Slavoj Žižek's account of two figures of the master helps to explain the importance of this doubling of authority. The invisible master, Žižek writes, "is a kind of uncanny double of public authority: he has to act in shadow, invisible to the public eye, irradiating a phantomlike, spectral omnipotence."[62] If Bush was the visible voice of justice, resolute but vague nevertheless, then fantasies of Cheney provided the obscene supplement underpinning this resolve. After 9/11, Bush relied on "evil" as a nodal point holding together the discourse that would establish the meaning of the war on terror. Bush and Cheney were two sides of an image of the master momentarily securing this meaning. Bush could give people what they wanted, and the very vagueness of what he was giving could be masked by the fantasy of the repulsive Cheney at work behind the scenes, a fantasy of people *really* getting what they wanted. Cheney provided the fantasy of secret power, of actions so unbecoming to the president, to America, that they best not see the light of day.

The war on terror is the appropriate background for Bush's axis-of-evil speech not because Saddam Hussein had any connection with September 11 but because Bush's ontological evil fuses all violence, crimes, threats, and the *potential or possibility* of any violence, crime, or threat into the theater of absolute struggle. As he said in his address on September 20, 2001, anyone not on the side of America was on the side of the terrorists, that is, on the side of evil. This ontological evil makes clear why the facts and details and justifications for war against Iraq had so little to do with the actual invasion. Bush knows—he doesn't need to be bogged down by policies and inspections. Bush is certain—he doesn't need the support or consent of other nations. His certainty comes from God. Precisely because Bush doesn't think so much as feel and pray and rely on his gut, he can know and be certain. Naming evil enacts this certainty. The war against Iraq made sense because it was part of the struggle against evil.

The imaginary axis of evil says nothing about Iraq, North Korea, and Iran. It says something about Bush. Secretary of State Colin Powell admitted as much as he defended the speech by emphasizing "the president's very powerful and clear and honest statement."[63] The statement is powerful, clear, and honest—the president spoke from his heart. The actual facts are not the issue. Bush's conviction empowers him to see among the excesses of evil flowing throughout the world that evil that must be directly confronted and named. He can do more than fight a vague war on terrorism. He can locate in the present those evils that might threaten us in the future. "Evil" thus designates that "special something" (*objet petit a*), that extra beyond brutal, repressive, very bad, that Bush takes as his call to eliminate. (And, conveniently, considering evil as *objet petit a* highlights the impossibility of its eradication. Evil is an aspect of the drive to eradicate as such. Bush's notorious landing of a small Viking jet onto the USS *Abraham Lincoln* aircraft carrier in May 2003 to announce the victory of

U.S. forces in Iraq is a good example here. Criticism of this publicity stunt misses the way the warrior image enacted not Bush's fantasy of U.S. militarism but the reality of U.S. militarism—the staged fantasy didn't cover up the truth of ongoing military conflict. On the contrary, it performed it and in so doing expressed the truth of Bush's intentions to continue in his fight to eliminate evil from the world.)

One last aspect of the way "evil" inhabits Bush's language is crucial to understanding how Bush could invoke an axis of evil. This last aspect, moreover, points less toward Bush's serving as some kind of a master who knows than it does to Bush's functioning perversely as a kind of object or instrument of knowledge. Bush sees himself as chosen by God. He sees America as duty bound to ensure the establishment of God-given rights all over the world. To this extent, fighting evil is a false choice: we have no choice; or the only response to this choice is to accept it, *bring it on!*—anything else is damned from the outset. The falseness of this choice is clear when we try to introduce it into the field of politics and debate it: *Okay, we can end world poverty, find a cure for cancer, or eradicate evil in the world*—whoever "votes" against eradicating evil must secretly support it! Perhaps the proper response to Bush's ontological evil is to take the choice of fighting evil seriously—yes, there is evil in the world, but there are other challenges as well.

Once the United States is God's chosen instrument for removing evil from the world, we confront the truth of democracy in communicative capitalism: it's a perverse form of governance protecting raw power while immunizing it from substantive change since all change has already been coded in terms of democracy. Any mistake, problem, or excess is always already captured as demanding democracy as its solution. The invocation of evil as Real, however, belies the fetishistic denial driving such appeals to democracy. Ontological evil subverts and exceeds the symbolic order of language, rules, and norms on which democracy has been premised. Bush can barely speak. His administration uses language as a mantra, meme, or slogan to affect people directly and viscerally. His invasion of Iraq broke explicitly with previous U.S. foreign policy and the norms of the international community. How far this has gone might be seen in the attacks on Howard Dean during the 2004 presidential campaign. Dean was widely mocked for suggesting that Osama bin Laden should receive a fair trial. The rule of law, it seems, is now a joke, a joke preventing the United States from eradicating evil from the world, its God-given mission as a democracy.

Absolute Relativism

While evil has long flourished in the fecund discursive habitats of Americanized religiosity, it has inhabited political speech as well, evolving as it adapts to changes in political climate. Evil is at home in George W. Bush's presidential rhetoric not because of his own personal faith but because of a larger coincidence of relativism and absolutist conviction, of the instability of signification and the resolve to signify in the face of this instability. Rather than two warring ethical or epistemological attitudes, relativism and absolutist conviction are two sides of the same coin, part of the same ideological matrix. On the one hand, this coincidence of opposites involves the way that each position limits and conditions the other—relativists understand their position against absolutists and vice versa. To this extent, neither position is fully identical with itself; each is internally split, possible only through the other. But more important is the way that the speculative identity between relativism and absolutism can be expressed as internal to relativism: relativism denotes an attitude toward absolutes. Far from negating or even taking issue with these absolutes, relativism requires the acceptance of particularized convictions, the acknowledgment that each is entitled to her own beliefs and opinions. Differing positions or beliefs are not to be engaged, compared, analyzed, or brought into critical dialogue with one another. They are to be accepted as wholes, as essences, unique to the self-identity of another. Absolute conviction appears in and through relativism. Relativism encourages certainty in one's own convictions because it accepts that others have their own convictions: *My convictions make me who I am.*

Given the rich variability in evil's discursive habitats, the multiple registers in which it thrives, determining the fields of reference informing a specific invocation of "evil" is difficult, potentially unending. Much easier is the registration of affect: an invocation of evil expresses an intensity of judgment and belief. The efficacy or weight of the term *evil* thus shifts from the signified to the signifying subject. The subject is convinced, certain. He knows the truth. He feels it deep in his soul. Moreover, as hearers join the speaker in filling in evil with content, they become invested in the struggle against evil. Insofar as they have suppressed uncertainties and installed their own unacknowledged fantasy of evil into the empty place the term occupies, they identify all the more deeply, libidinally, with the battle against it. Evil might thus be usefully analogized to obscenity in First Amendment jurisprudence: giving a clear, principled, definition of obscenity is too difficult; nevertheless, "we know it when we see it." The emphasis shifts from the object to those who know, to those brave and forthright enough to look evil in the face. Were the terms *obscenity* and *evil* clear and unambiguous, using them, applying them to their proper objects, would be no great feat. In the United States of George W. Bush, as in the United States of Ronald Reagan, this shift of the efficacy of the term *evil* from its object to the signifying subject suggests will, courage, and faith; indeed, it points to the resolve and conviction of a subject who knows.

This chapter's retrospective on "evil" in presidential speeches indicates how Reagan's invocation of evil differs markedly from that of his predecessors as evil becomes an ontological fact. Ontological evil permeates the world, establishing the conditions of existence even as its specificity as an attribute or judgment remains elusive. This elusiveness, in turn, reflects on the moral character of the one willing to confront the truth of evil. Likewise, Bush's invocation of an "axis of evil" is not an empirical claim regarding a political or military alliance among Iran, North Korea, and Iraq. It is also not a statement about September 11. Rather, it marks Bush's attempt to tell the United States and the world just what kind of man he is. He is a man of conviction, he is certain, and he knows. Armed with certainty, Bush is resolved to fight evil in all its myriad, shifting, evolving manifestations. He will fight it as possibility, as potential, before its pernicious effects can even be felt. In the face of Bush's knowledge of ontological evil, reasons are at best signs of weakness, lapses in certainty. At worst, they are hosts for pernicious evil, a mutant form of liberalism or leftism in which evil hides.

5

Ethics

LEFT RESPONSIVENESS AND RETREAT

As conservatives have resolved to fight any and all opponents to the death and neoliberals have been ever more emboldened in their grotesque grabs for greater and greater shares of the world's wealth, many on the academic and typing left have urged peace, love, and understanding. These influential voices advocate a turn to ethics, a generosity to difference and awareness of mutual vulnerability. They respond to the religious, nationalist, and market fundamentalisms dominating contemporary social and political life by rejecting dogmatism and conviction, advocating instead micropolitical and ethical practices that work on the self in its immediate reactions and relations. They are likely right that engaging others with affirmation and generosity is a nice thing to do. But it's politically suicidal. The more the left refrains from divisive political engagement, the more the right advances.

Some on the left share my concern about the futility of a politics based on making sure that nobody is offended. An editorial in *The Nation* on June 26, 2006, for example, urged progressives in the United States to recognize that now is the time for conviction, not caution. This editorial might be thought of as a direct counter to Judith Butler, who argues against conviction and for responsiveness in *Giving an Account of Oneself* (2005). There she portrays conviction in terms of an ethics that "takes the self to be the ground and measure of moral judgment."[1] Butler admits that there might be times for condemnation and denunciation. But she warns against these modes of judgment insofar as they carry with them a certainty and opacity that disallow connections to others. Left politics, Butler suggests, is ultimately incompatible with conviction, condemnation, and denunciation.

Butler's recent work is emblematic of the ethical turn in left political theory, one that seems to embrace ethics out of a kind of political despair. For her, ostensible barriers to justice can become opportunities for responsibility, recognition, and resignification.[2] Opacity, vulnerability, exposure, and grief provide potential openings to others and to ourselves, resources that might enable us to understand how our human being is necessarily and unavoidably a being together. The cost of this ethical sensitivity, however, is politics. Butler presents ethical resources as available only under conditions of the denial of politics. Should we make political choices or act politically we will cut ourselves off from the insights and capacities arising out of vulnerability and grief. Thus, Butler offers a set of responses to contemporary fundamentalisms that eschew condemnation and conviction and present openness and critique not only as ethically preferable to decisions for or against but as necessarily incompatible with the division necessary for politics.

To be sure, Butler's ethical turn need not displace politics. Rather, as this chapter explains, such displacement results from her constrained conception of sovereignty, wherein sovereignty functions less as a political arrangement than as a kind of master capable not only of holding together diffuse meanings and effects by the force of its word, a word with power to initiate and end, but also of fully determining the words that it utters and the effects of these words. I show how Butler's critique of sovereignty misfires as it shoots at fantastic returns of a master rather than attending to the more complex reformatting of sovereignty in globalized communicative capitalism. Because she aims at the wrong target, left political conviction ends up a casualty of friendly fire, a result that contributes to neoliberalism's advance.

Governmentality and Fantasy

Butler's *Excitable Speech*, published in 1997, explores power and agency against the background of Michel Foucault's notion of governmentality. Foucault argues that state power from the eighteenth century on has formed an ensemble of "institutions, procedures, analyses and reflections . . . calculations and tactics . . . which has as its target population, as its principal form of knowledge, political economy, and as its essential technical means apparatuses of security."[3] Butler takes this notion of governmentality to mean that contemporary power is not "constrained by the parameters of sovereignty" but "diffused throughout disparate and competing domains of the state apparatus, and through civil society in diffuse forms."[4] In contrast to Foucault, who asserts the continued centrality of the problem of sovereignty even as he recognizes that the governmentalized state is lacking in unity, individuality, and functionality, Butler reads governmentality as *replacing* sovereignty. She writes that "contemporary power is no longer sovereign in character" and power is "no longer constrained within the sovereign form of the state"—as if there were some time when it had been (*ES*, 74, 78).

The claim that governmentality has replaced sovereignty is crucial to Butler's critique of critical legal studies arguments in favor of regulating hate speech. She argues that a "particular historical anxiety" accompanies the dispersion of power characteristic of governmentality, and she links this anxiety to problems in locating injury and finding the origin of specific acts. The historical loss of the sovereign organization of power gives rise to the fantasy of its return (*ES*, 78). Butler finds evidence of such fantastic returns in idealizations of speech acts as sovereign actions coupled with idealizations of sovereign state power. These idealizations, she claims, underpin arguments for hate-speech codes. Fantasies of sovereign power emerge to compensate for a prior loss of sovereign power. The fantasies that in speaking one wields sovereign power and that state speech takes a sovereign form compensate for the absence of such a sovereign.

Although one might do well to note the Nietzschean resonances in Butler's reading of legal theorists' efforts to produce a subject capable of being responsible, such an approach misses the way sovereignty in Butler's account functions as a master signifier linking together an unstable chain of significations. Butler's criticism presumes that holding a person legally accountable for her words requires viewing that person as a sovereign speaker, as an originator of words, a controller of words, a user of words who remains unbound and unconditioned by them. For Butler, hate-speech codes overdetermine "the scene of utterance" as they reduce racism to a single linguistic site. This reduction, she explains, presupposes the efficacy of the speaker in injuring and subordinating another through the force of her speech. It presupposes, in other words, the fantasy of a *sovereign* speaker, of a speaker capable of consolidating at a single site the structures, practices, and harms of racism.

Butler rightly rejects this fantastic figure of sovereignty. But why should we accept that such a figure inhabits the writings of critical legal theorists or hate-speech codes at all? Two aspects of Butler's own account make her figure of a fantastic sovereign returning to haunt the law unconvincing.

First, given her focus in *Excitable Speech* on American law and the place of free speech in American jurisprudence, it is difficult to make sense of the phrase *no longer* when Butler claims that "contemporary power is *no longer* sovereign in character." If the notion of sovereignty she has in mind is one invested in a single sovereign body or locus of authority, then the American framework of separation of powers eludes from the start a simple notion of sovereignty. The innovation of the American Constitution was its investment of sovereignty in the people and its provisions for enabling the people to exercise sovereignty not only through laws but through necessarily separated powers.[5] The federal system relies on separating and distributing the means of governance, again, so as to ensure that the people remain sovereign. If sovereignty in the United States has been thought as a sovereignty of the people, then what could it mean to say that the figure of a unified, powerful, sovereign master returns in legal discourse?

Second, given Butler's reliance on Foucault's notion of governmentality, why should we not consider hate codes and the discourse around hate codes likewise in terms of the decentered structure of the state? Interventions into the constitution and management of a population, regulations on hate speech are typically pursued at campus, local, and state levels rather than as federal laws. We might say, then, that such codes are tools or instruments that the people use in governing themselves, in arranging their interactions with one another. And we might well recognize that these instruments will be contested, open to interpretation, and implicated in other practices through which the people attempt to change their collective modes of being. Yet Butler treats these legal codes as somehow resistant to interpretation and resignification, insisting instead that they are attempts to isolate accountability in the words of a single sovereign speaker.

Perhaps my reading of governmentality misses what is actually at stake in Butler's emphasis on a "particular historical anxiety." She is attending to the setting of what Lacanian psychoanalysis theorizes as a change in the discourse of the master. As chapter 2 explains, in his later work, Lacan moves away from his earlier notion of a symbolic order held in place by a master signifier to emphasize the instability of signification and the absence of guaranteed meaning. Understood in terms of this setting, Butler's account of the change in sovereignty appears not simply as an analysis of legal arrangements of power but also as a discussion of changes in subjectivity and the character of the social link. The speaking subject is not sovereign. Speech is out of its control. This subject is called into being in and through speech and necessarily remains vulnerable to and dependent upon these linguistic arrangements. Just as sovereignty is not concentrated in a single extrasocial location but penetrates society as a whole, relying on various state and nonstate apparatuses, so does the subject persist in and through language, wielding the very terms that produce and sustain it. For Butler, the "contemporary scene of cultural translation emerges with the presupposition that the utterance does not have the same meaning everywhere, indeed, that the utterance has become a scene of conflict" (ES, 91). Chapter 2 introduces Žižek's notion of the decline of symbolic efficiency as a tag for this setting of instability and conflict. While Butler views this setting as opening up opportunities for resignification and new experiences of freedom, Žižek emphasizes the closure and domination that accompany our inability to know what to trust or on whom we might rely.[6]

In *Excitable Speech*, Butler argues that conflict over an utterance enables subversive resignification. Law, though, neither provides an opportunity for such resignification nor can itself be subversively resignified. Nonetheless, Butler looks optimistically to new meanings that offer "an unanticipated political future for deconstructive thinking" (ES, 161). She juxtaposes the willingness to remain open to the futures opened up by the "insurrectionary effects" of the reappropriation of terms like *freedom* and *justice* to a dogmatism that opposes the destabilization of reality (ES, 162).

In contrast, Žižek notes the suffocating closure effected by the decline of symbolic norms. The undecideability of basic questions, the ready availability of multiple, conflicting interpretations, turns decisions into risky gambles. The decline of symbolic efficiency thus results in a combination of impotent interpretations and raw violence. For example, Žižek points to the rise of "ethical committees" that issue instructions and recommendations, noting that these suggestions are unable to orient the subject in a world. Instead, the subject clings to imaginary spectacles and simulacra, while both striving for and being impacted by experiences in the Real.[7] Unprotected by symbolic norms, the subject feels threatened by all sorts of imaginary figures, at the mercy of the superego injunction to enjoy even as these figures threaten its enjoyment—*Why does everyone else seem to be having more fun, wilder sex, cooler vacations, fitter bodies, and better jobs than I?* In sum, the decline of symbolic efficiency introduces new opportunities for guilt and anxiety as well as new attachments to domination as subjects seek relief from the endless injunctions to enjoy— and do so properly.

I return to these injunctions below. At this point, I simply want to emphasize Butler's account of the conditions of resignification as openings to a political future, openings that the return of the fantastic figure of a sovereign risks closing off.

Sovereignty and Resignification

In *Precarious Life* (2003), Butler confronts the resignifications that followed the attacks on the World Trade Center and the Pentagon on September 11, 2001. The unanticipated future installed by the insurrectionary effects of this resignification has unfolded as one of preemptive war, indefinite detention, and ever increasing threats to civil liberties. In the name of freedom and democracy, the United States attacked a country that not only had not attacked it but presented no imminent danger. Given that resignification worked to advance militarism, what role does Butler assign it in this later work?

Assign is likely the wrong term here. Butler does not speak of resignification. She enacts it, though, as she reworks vulnerability and mourning into opportunities for connecting with others rather than occasions for securing violated borders. Yet the very sensitivity Butler brings to these moments of vulnerability and mourning exceeds a notion of resignification. After all, she is not saying mourning means that one has not undergone a loss. Rather she takes awareness of this loss to be an opportunity to appreciate the way we are given over to others. Feeling loss we are reminded of our deep interconnections. Vulnerability and loss, as she puts it, might thus provide new bases for "reimagining the possibility of community."[8] So it is rather inapt to read Butler's method in terms of resignification.

This is particularly true with respect to Butler's argument against former Harvard president Lawrence Summers's charge that criticism of Israel
is effectively anti-Semitic. For rather than resignifying that charge and
identity, rather than noting the ways that Summers's speech might misfire,
might open up opportunities for insurrection, rather than attending to the
repetitions and citations enabling Summers's speech, as one might expect
from her arguments in *Excitable Speech*, Butler criticizes Summers for
identifying Israel with the Jewish people and for attempting to stifle critical debate (*PL*, 111, 126). I agree with Butler's criticisms. Yet I am surprised
she attributes to Summers's words "a chilling effect on political discourse"
that stokes "the fear that to criticize Israel during this time is to expose
oneself to the charge of anti-Semitism" (*PL*, 102). Butler imbues Summers's speech with the very sovereignty she criticizes critical legal studies
scholars for attributing to hate speech (is this a fantasy of sovereign return
occasioned by the loss of U.S. sovereignty on 9/11?). Her arguments in
Excitable Speech tell us we should recognize how Summers's words do not
have the power to determine the limits of what can and cannot be said.

Butler's move away from resignification unfolds against a refining of her
account of the relationship of governmentality and sovereignty. Whereas
her concern in *Excitable Speech* is with the encroachment of law via the
fantasy of a sovereign power attributed to speech, in *Precarious Life* she attends to the way law's suspension itself produces sovereignty. In this later
book, sovereignty appears where law is not. Sovereignty is unbounded by
law, "outside the law," in excess of law (*PL*, 51). Butler continues to assert
that governmentality operates through law as a "set of tactics" (*PL*, 52). Yet
she focuses on sovereignty's "resurgence within the field of governmentality" (*PL*, 53). She argues that in this new formation, sovereignty is
exercised through acts that "suspend and limit the jurisdiction of law
itself" (*PL*, 53). So while *Excitable Speech* analyzes the way a fantasy of
sovereign power accompanies extensions of the law, *Precarious Life* confronts situations wherein an anachronistic sovereignty is "reintroduced in
the very acts by which the state suspends law, or contorts law to its own
uses" (*PL*, 54). In each case, the resurgence of sovereignty is compensatory, compensating for sovereignty's loss (*PL*, 56).

The cases differ insofar as resignification is a contestory practice opposed to sovereignty in *Excitable Speech* and an aspect of the very operation of sovereignty in *Precarious Life*. In the earlier book, Butler treats

resignification as a practice external to law, a practice she links to the subversion of authority. In the later one, resignification is figured as a means of consolidating authority as sovereign power. Thus, discussing U.S. assertions that it treats the prisoners held in the camp at Guantánamo "humanely" and in a way consistent with the Geneva Conventions, Butler writes: "When the U.S. says, then, that it is treating these prisoners humanely, it uses the word in its own way and for its own purpose, but it does not accept that the Geneva Accords stipulate how the term might legitimately be applied. In effect, it takes the word back from the accords at the very moment that it claims to be acting consistently with the accords. In the moment that it claims to be acting consistently with the accords, the U.S. effectively maintains that the accords have no power over it" (PL, 82). As it takes the word back and applies it in its own fashion, the United States resignifies "humanely," denying the Geneva Accords the power to determine the condition of the term's use. In so doing, the United States asserts its singular sovereignty over and against international norms.

To be sure, Butler herself does not emphasize resignification here, although she notes that sovereign power extends itself by producing equivocation (PL, 80). For her, the crucial aspect of this extension is the way it is bound up with the "extra legal status of these official acts of speech" (PL, 80). Governmentality extends power throughout the population, using law tactically and instrumentally and relying on various nonstate bureaucracies and arrangements. With regard to the indefinite detention of so-called enemy combatants, Butler argues that decisions to detain "are already outside the sphere of law" (PL 58, 67). She refers repeatedly to the extralegal status of various decisions, decisions which, precisely because of their externality to the law, animate a resurgent sovereignty. Sovereignty appears as and through the emergence of an unaccountable power dispersed throughout the diffuse operations and tactics of governmentality and concentrated in specific sites of illegitimate decision.

I disagree with Butler's account of the compensatory emergence of a lost sovereignty within the field of governmentality, and I think she misdescribes contemporary changes in the structure of the contemporary state when she finds this sovereignty at work outside of law. Butler, in keeping with the limited view of law she presents in Excitable Speech, fails to attend to conflicts and changes within law. After all, the Bush administration's policies with regard to trying so-called enemy combatants in special military commissions had to be affirmed by the Supreme Court—which, fortunately, rejected such a grab for power out of hand. When law is itself a site of contestation (as well as a contested site), the very idea of a division between inside and outside makes no sense. Conflict over the limits, extension, and terrain of law persists throughout various legal apparatuses, including the writings and opinions of multiple lawyers and judges, journalists, and politicians, in the setting, in other words, of a governmentalized legal regime.

Butler's constrained account of law is linked to her general avoidance of the economy and the ways the nonstate bureaucracies and arrangements crucial to governmentality are private sector, corporate, financial, and market enterprises. She abstracts the actions of the Bush administration from the legal and economic settings that enable them. Paul A. Passavant attends to these settings, explicating changes in governance from the Keynesian welfare state to the contemporary post-Fordist state.[9] He writes: "Consumer capitalism has made extensive and intensive systems of surveillance, which, through a process of articulation, have vastly extended state surveillance powers. We are also governed by the state through a logic of consumerism whereby the state zones subjects as security risks for differential treatment based on one's consumer profile compiled from commercial data bases. And we are governed by a homeland security regime that is becoming increasingly resistant to change as more and more elements become financially invested in this state's projects and projections."[10] Passavant situates the policies of so-called preventative detention within criminology's "zero tolerance" approach to crime, imprisonment, and security. He emphasizes the legal precedents for the USA Patriot Act, particularly the Anti-Terrorism and Effective Death Penalty Act of 1996. And he draws out the economic dimensions of the current "strong neoliberal state," the way that the combination of consumerism and communicative capitalism produces new opportunities for extensions of state power via the emergence of massive commercial databases, the securitization of places of consumption, and the commodification of security.

Like Passavant, Saskia Sassen emphasizes the fundamental importance of the global capitalist economy in understanding changes to the institutions and practices of sovereignty. She theorizes sovereignty as decentered, its elements "unbundled" from earlier constellations, displaced from national to international territories and reconstituted for the benefit of financial capital.[11] Both scholars thus alert us to the emergence of a new legal regime that strengthens the power and reach of the state by securing and protecting corporate, financial, and market interests. For example, contracting for services, outsourcing, and competitive bidding are practices through which public agencies make use of private enterprises legally to extend their reach and sidestep the regulations and oversight that typically govern public projects. To describe these developments in terms of the resurgence of sovereignty, as Butler does, condenses the larger economic setting into singular loci of decisions, displacing attention from the state's imbrications in the globalized neoliberalism of communicative capitalism. Law is not suspended. Laws are introduced, changed, and applied in ways that alter and extend state power in some directions (surveillance, detention, military force) rather than others (education, health, social welfare).

As mentioned above, the decline of symbolic efficiency ushers in new anxieties and experiences of domination. Capitalism contributes to this disintegration, its deterritorializing impulses fragmenting and recombining previous meanings and practices. Arguing that capitalism relies on the circulation of enjoyment, on an inescapable injunction to enjoy, Žižek highlights the link between Lacan's notion of *jouissance* or surplus enjoyment and the Marxian notion of surplus value. He writes: "Because it is focused on the surplus of *objet petit a*, capitalism is no longer the domain of the discourse of the Master. This is where Lacan takes over and paraphrases in his own terms the old Marxian theme, from the *Manifesto*, of how capitalism dissolves all stable links and traditions; how, at its onslaught, 'all that is solid melts into air.' Marx himself made it clear that this 'all that is solid' does not concern only and primarily material products, but also the stability of the symbolic order that provides a definitive identification for subjects."[12] In late capitalism, nuggets of enjoyment (*objet petit a*) providing momentary, fleeting sites of attachment take the place of the master signifier. This diminution of the master's discourse has specific repercussions for neoliberal hegemony. As chapter 2 explains, unlike the welfare state formation associated with Keynesianism, contemporary neoliberalism offers not symbolic identities but multiple, imaginary identities. Subjects under communicative capitalism are encouraged to remake themselves, to see themselves as mutable projects ever available to improvement and refashioning. We are bombarded with messages telling us that the purchase of a given item will deliver that extra special something missing in our lives. Yet even as no item ever really has that "extra something," capitalist subjects continue to shop and strive, and capitalism continues to intensify and expand, subjecting ever more aspects of life to its inexorable processes. Communicative capitalism is thus characterized by the prevalence of the superego injunction to enjoy. Rather than constrained by a master, contemporary subjects are told they can have it all, they must have it all, and something is deeply wrong *with them* if they don't have it all.

These injunctions are a trap: not only do contemporary subjects know full well that they cannot have it all but they know that actually having it would be completely dangerous. Fully losing oneself in sexual delirium could lead to the transmission of disease. Taking fabulous party drugs or drinking large quantities of alcohol could result in death. Eating loads of expensive chocolate could invite obesity and diabetes. Moreover, all the regulations associated with enjoyment return us to the regulations suggested by experts and ethical committees. These regulations do not provide subjects with symbolic identities grounded in norms. Instead, they provide advice, advice that is ultimately contested and ungroundable and therefore experienced as illegitimate constraint. The shift away from the discourse of the master, then, does result in the emergence of authorities and regulations, as Butler notes. But these authorities are not signs of a resurgent sovereignty. Instead, they are part of a capitalism's incessant self-revolutionizing, its generation of and reliance on excess, wherein supereogistic injunctions to enjoy overlap with contested regulations to suffocate the subject in a situation of unbearable closure.[13]

Žižek's emphasis on the superego injunction to enjoy also helps explain the obscene underside of power accompanying public law, thereby accounting for the lawlessness Butler links to sovereignty.[14] Recall, Butler argues that sovereignty reappears through the suspension of law in an extralegal operation of power. To call specific practices of the Bush administration resurgences of sovereignty—practices that include the use of signing statements to limit the scope of legislative acts, as well as surveillance activities undertaken with the knowledge of congressional leaders—mistakenly covers over the split already within law, the criminality supporting public power. Not only does it treat as something new the lawless irrationality already pervading law as law but it unnecessarily consolidates and strengthens this lawlessness into the figure of a sovereign. We should not forget that the U.S. president is in no way a sovereign.

In a more persuasive account of the irrational violence accompanying law, Žižek demonstrates how law is split between its public letter and its obscene superego supplement.[15] At the basis of all law is a violent, irrational element, the tautological force inextricable from law's command, from law's claim that it must be obeyed because it is the law. This violent, irrational, superegoistic side appears as the obscene, nightly or underground, dimension of law sustaining the public ideological edifice, attaching members to a community as it unites them in a shared, dirty secret. For example, the Bush regime denies that it tortures prisoners in Abu Ghraib or anywhere else. At the same time, it is more than clear from its evasions, from public discussion of the conditions under which torture might be permissible, and from published photographs of victims of torture that, yes, the United States is permitting and performing torture. Far from a new development, this sort of obscene violence has long suffused American prisons and persisted as an aspect of covert U.S. operations abroad. Obscene violence is widespread as the set of officially disavowed transgressions conditioning and staining the law. We might also think of sexual abuse within the Catholic Church and the traditional nuclear family, the everyday harassment of women, sexual, and ethnic minorities, and the brutal rituals of fraternities, secret societies, and sports teams, in short, those unmentionable acts the practice of which differentiates members from nonmembers. As Žižek makes clear, this obscene underside "forms the necessary supplement to the public values of personal dignity, democracy, and freedom."[16] To speak, then, of a resurgence of sovereignty ignores the obscene supplement of violence that accompanies law, the split in law between its public letter and the unacknowledged practices that must be disavowed for law to remain in force.

Nonetheless, Butler speaks of sovereignty, of the resurgence of arbitrary, exploitative, and instrumental power through the suspension of law. Governmentality enables this resurgence, this state power that is not of the state, this legal power that is, paradoxically, outside the law. This focus on a sovereignty that operates through the tactics of governmentality might suggest a variety of sites from which to intervene politically (PL, 98). That is, coherence of the argument aside, the left could find political advantage in focusing on a sovereignty operating through governmentality. Butler thinks one such advantage comes from the possibility of recognizing and focusing on the stateless. I would add that any such advantage is lost to the extent that it is not tied to a critical politicization of globalized neoliberal capitalism. Yet Butler, albeit rightly attuned to the complexities of rights claims in international law, not only forgoes the opportunity to condemn U.S. militarism and imperialism as specific governmental tactics but also moves from the issue of political intervention to the ethical question of the "human." That is, she takes a key benefit of the notion of governmentality to be the way it opens up "those discourses that shape and deform what we mean by 'the human'" (*PL*, 99).

Butler's shift in focus to "the human" is ill-conceived. The religious, imperialist, and militarist terms of the so-called war on terror (or, more specifically, indefinite detention) do not challenge the human status of either the enemy or the imprisoned (*contra* Butler, *PL* 89). George W. Bush, Dick Cheney, and their conservative supporters are explicit about their entitlement to take *human* life. Their self-understanding of their power is premised on precisely this entitlement: they are the ones who know which *humans* can be killed—they do not need to exclude some from the category. Additionally, it may well be that the ethical command is toward not just the human but the *inhuman*, toward those that I cannot see as like me in any way, who remain monstrous to me, completely different, completely other. Thus Žižek, criticizing Butler for ignoring the status of the inhuman in Kant's ethics, argues that the inhuman marks "a terrifying excess which, although it negates what we understand as 'humanity', is inherent to being human."[17] A key exemplar of such an inhuman, Žižek notes, is "the terrifying figure of the *Muselmann*, the 'living dead' in the concentration camps."[18]

Butler's discussions of governmentality seem to back her into a corner. Resignification under conditions of governmentality is not simply a progressive, democratic, or liberating practice available to those unbound by law. It is also available to those in power, to those using law instrumentally, to those who have led the country into the horrifying future of indefinite and preemptive war. Likewise, sovereign power, a power to effect a closure, to cut off, to decide, operates both as law and lawlessly, through law and through law's suspension. Perhaps Butler moves to ethics so as to escape this deadlock.

A passage in *Precarious Life* suggests this might be the case. Butler describes participating in a discussion about the current situation of the humanities. She notes a confusion in the discussion, an uncertainty regarding whether people were willing to stand by their words, "whether anyone really was willing to own a view" (PL, 129). She concedes that her work has tried to "cut the tether" of author to words, an effort linked to her critique of sovereign speech. She admits as well that it would be a "paradox" were she now to try to tether discourse to authors. To avoid this paradox, Butler offers another move, "a consideration of the structure of address itself" (129). As she explains:

> The structure of address is important for understanding how moral authority is introduced and sustained if we accept not just that we address others when we speak, but that in some way we come to exist, as it were, in the moment of being addressed, and something about our existence proves precarious when that address fails. More emphatically, however, what binds us morally has to do with how we are addressed by others in ways that we cannot avert or avoid; this impingement by the other's address constitutes us first and foremost against our will or, perhaps put more appropriately, prior to the formation of our will. So if we think that moral authority is about finding one's will and standing by it, stamping one's name upon one's will, it may be that we miss the very mode by which moral demands are relayed. (PL, 130)

Morality, then, is less a matter of a will than of relations prior to that will, relations that Butler considers in terms of the structure of address. We come to exist by being addressed. This address, and consequently our own existence, can fail or misfire. Hence, we need to attend to this structure. If we move too quickly to willing, Butler suggests, we may fail, harm, or do violence to our relation to the other who addresses us, a relation on which depend.

Address and Condemnation

Butler's sustained consideration of the scene of address appears in *Giving an Account of Oneself*. She takes up the limits that condition our ability to give an account of ourselves, limits that include exposure, or our condition of corporeality before others (as opposed to pure interiority, say); normativity, or the way that we come into being within a set of norms that precedes us and remains indifferent to us; and the structure of address in which any account of ourselves takes place. She elaborates, moreover, the way our very foreignness to ourselves is the source of our ethical connections to others (*Giving*, 84). And she offers a conception of ethics "based on our shared, and invariable, partial blindnesses about ourselves. The recognition that one is, at every turn, not quite the same as how one presents oneself in the available discourse might imply, in turn, a certain patience with others that would suspend the demand that they be self-same at every moment" (*Giving*, 42–43). Insofar as we remain opaque to ourselves, we cannot demand an impossible transparency or self-knowledge from the other. We cannot expect others to know fully why they do what they do, what their motives are, and why these are their motives. The lack in what we can know about ourselves thus might be understood as the lack in what others know about themselves. Although I may often be tempted to fill in this gap with an always impossible certainty, my ability to cultivate an awareness of this lack could enable me to be more forgiving of others and perhaps even of myself. Allowing for openness, not demanding an impossible accounting from another, thereby provides a necessary emendation to theories of recognition insofar as it attends to an underlying desire to persist (*Giving*, 44).

The exposure and normativity conditioning us also condition the other. Our relation to each other, the mutual dependence through which we impinge upon one other, condenses into a kind of irreducible, enigmatic stress, an excessive unknowability which addresses us and which we cannot avoid. Describing this "signifying stress" immanent to our relations with others, Eric Santner writes: "To use a Heideggerian locution, our *thrownness* into the world does not simply mean that we always find ourselves in the midst of a social formation that we did not choose . . . it means, more importantly, that this social formation in which we find ourselves immersed is itself permeated by inconsistency and incompleteness, is itself haunted by a lack by which we are, in some peculiar way, addressed, 'excited', to which we are in some fashion answerable . . . reality is never fully identical with itself, is fissured by lack."[19] Santner adds to Butler's account of the conditions of address an emphasis on how a certain lack within these very conditions addresses us as well. Our conditions are inconsistent and incomplete, exposed to potentials unfulfilled, harms unrecognized and unredressed.

For Butler, living as a subject split between the norms through which we emerge and the corporeal, finite life that we lead means we must become critical. She develops this idea as she rethinks responsibility, arguing that insofar as we remain strangers to ourselves responsibility cannot rest on a myth of transparency but must instead be understood as dependent on the unknowable, the limit, the trauma within and necessary to me. In making this argument, she draws from Adorno's account of the inhuman as necessary for the human, as well as from Foucault's telling the truth about himself. Crucial to each account is a limit that conditions the becoming of subjects and reminds us how ethical norms not only guide conduct but decide who and what is human. Persisting in a poorly arranged world poses ethical dilemmas: our own desires to persist have consequences for others. Although we do not choose the norms through which we emerge, insofar as we speak within them, or recognize another in the way that they frame, we transmit these norms and thus bear a responsibility for their consequences. To this extent, an ethics that does not involve critique, that does not call into question these norms and their consequences, is itself unethical, culpable, unresponsive as it disavows the relations of power on which it depends.

The ethical disposition Butler finds in the context of address may arise. Or it may not. It may well be the case that sometimes something more is called for—judgment or perhaps even condemnation. Butler allows for this when she observes that judgment does not "exhaust the sphere of ethics" and when she says that judgments are necessary for political life (*Giving*, 45). Yet Butler holds back, refusing to condemn those persons and practices, those norms and ·desires upon which our poorly arranged world depends. She writes:

> Condemnation, denunciation, and excoriation work as quick ways to posit an ontological difference between judge and judged, even to purge oneself of another. Condemnation becomes the way in which we establish the other as nonrecognizable or jettison some aspect of ourselves that we lodge in the other, whom we then condemn. In this sense, condemnation can work against self-knowledge, inasmuch as it moralizes a self by disavowing commonality with the judged. Although self-knowledge is surely limited, that is not a reason to turn against it as a project. Condemnation tends to do precisely this, to purge and exter-

nalize one's own opacity. In this sense, judgment can be a way to fail to own one's limitations and thus provides no felicitous basis for a reciprocal recognition of human beings as opaque to themselves, partially blind, constitutively limited. (*Giving*, 46)

That condemnation *can* work against self-knowledge does not mean that condemnation everywhere and always *does* so. Condemnation does not always moralize a self through disavowal, seeking to purge and externalize opacity and necessarily failing to own its limitations. Can we not imagine a condemnation capable of acknowledging its own limits? Can we not imagine a condemnation born of past failures, indeed, a condemnation indebted and responsible to failure? Butler, in opposing condemnation to connection and the acknowledgment of opacity, blocks from view the political possibility of drawing a line, of saying "this, not that" and in so doing transforming our connections, connections which condemnation itself may forge.

If I condemn racism, homophobia, or cruelty in another, I am not necessarily disavowing racism, homophobia, or cruelty in myself. I may be addressing it in myself as I confront these tendencies in another. More importantly, I may be calling into question, condemning, practices in which I, too, am implicated such that I recognize this condemnation as a self-condemnation, a condemnation of *us* and of *our* practices. Such condemnation may well be my ethical as well as political responsibility insofar as I seek to transform the set of norms in which I find myself, thereby changing the contexts in which others are addressed.

If I condemn someone for pursuing preventive war or for defending a notion of preventive war, I need not base this condemnation on a sense that my knowledge is more certain. I can base it on the sense that the pursuer of preventive war aims to produce a future I reject, or even if these are not his aims, that I fear will arise in the course of this war's pursuit. My condemnation may be a way of grappling with, of confronting, additional elements of the contexts of address, elements that involve power, hierarchy, and responsibility for other futures, other contexts, other beings. Failure to condemn risks disavowing relations of power and one's complicity in these relations. Rather than indicating an ethical responsiveness, such failure retreats from the political demand to refuse to remain within a certain structure of address and to challenge its terms, to acknowledge the

way these terms block from view those who remain incapable of addressing us at all. Refusing the address, denouncing the presumption of relations an address may endeavor to reinforce, could well be necessary if we
are to attend to the peculiar lack that addresses us and to which we are
responsible. As Santner argues, responsibility to the excluded and for
opportunities missed in the past may require radical acts that *suspend* the
social bond.[20]

Butler does not always avoid condemnation. Important to my argument is the fact that her ethics need not preclude condemnation and that
it can and should be sharpened so as to account for such divisive, political
moments. When Butler does condemn, though, it is as if she finds herself
in that moment trapped within a discourse she rejects, to which she can
only gain access through a condemnation. In *Precarious Life*, she condemns "on several bases the violence done against the United States and
do[es] not see it as 'just punishment' for prior sins'" (*PL*, 40). Butler
seems to find herself compelled to condemn those who attacked the
United States on September 11, 2001, *before* she criticizes the U.S. government, as if this condemnation gives her permission to argue. Yet in her
analyses of U.S. policies of indefinite detention in Guantánamo Bay, U.S.
violence against Afghanistan, the "shock and awe" attacks on Iraq, and the
Bush administration's hegemonization of political discourse after 9/11 in
terms of its own position as victim, she does not condemn. Rather, she
analyzes, explains, contextualizes, interprets, interrogates, and, in so doing,
critiques. This raises the question of Butler's separation of condemnation
and critique and the political place and function of each.

Butler presumes that condemnation involves closure and that closure
entails finality and disconnection. That is, she treats condemnation as an
act of sovereignty bent on effacing its own supporting conditions, its own
vulnerability and dependence. So even as she recognizes judging as a
mode of address premised on the context of address that "can and should
provide a sustaining condition of ethical deliberation, judgment, and conduct," she reads condemnation as violently eroding "the capacity of the
subject addressed for both self-reflection and social-recognition" and denunciation as working to "paralyze and deratify the critical capacities of
the subject to whom it is addressed" (*PL*, 49). If the one who is condemned and denounced is already positioned in a prior relation of subor-
dination, such erosion and paralysis may result. But not necessarily. The

condemned may reject the bases, the terms, of condemnation—*I am not who you say I am* or *Because I am who you say I am, you are the one who ultimately suffers, who is left shattered and bereft in condemning me.* The denounced may accept the words of the denunciation, but challenge the suppositions supporting these words, the suppositions that give it an ethical valence beyond a mere statement of fact—*Yes, I am a godless communist, so?*

Condemnation and denunciation may not succeed. Their effects on the addressee as well as their relation to other acts and interpretations cannot be determined in advance. If the condemned is powerful, at the head of a mighty military machine, then to associate condemnation with paralysis and deratification surely overstates the power of the address. One could wish that condemnation had such effects, and with respect to Bush's unconscionable, immoral, unjustified, illegal, and imperialist war against Iraq, I certainly do. Bush's persistence in his preemptive war against Iraq in the face of the condemnation of millions throughout the world, however, points to the weakness and inefficacy of condemnation unbacked by force.

At the same time, condemnation may work in a different direction. Weakness in one respect may enable another sort of strength, a capacity to form new alliances and connections, to open a space wherein to imagine the possibility of another world. So condemnation and denunciation may produce new links. When I condemn, I may do so in the context of addressing another, one whom I am not condemning. If in a political gathering I condemn the president of the United States, I will be addressing others, attempting to politicize and change the scene in which we find ourselves. Such politicization, moreover, may well be called for by the very inconsistency and lack in this scene that excites us, as Santner suggests.

Condemnation is not as powerful and efficacious as Butler implies. And insofar as it occurs within a context of address, condemnation is citational, relying for its efficacy on a set of prior norms that it reiterates, a set of prior practices and values to which it connects. Condemnation does not occur ex nihilo but is based on something, something shared, something that will be unavoidable, incomplete, and fissured. As with other utterances, condemnation is "uncontrollable, appropriable, and able to signify otherwise and in excess of its animating intentions" (*ES*, 98). To condemn, then, is to appeal to a prior set of connections at its basis and thereby to open up this basis for critique and politicization. It is also, and more importantly, to be excited by the lacks fissuring our social formation and to take responsibility for the past harms and omissions that enable it.

Politics and Unknowingness

Butler argues for an ethics that stems from an irresolvable unknowability, a trauma that limits and makes possible our need and capacity for response. Attunement to this unknowingness, this limit within each of us, calls up the ways we are each given over to another. Butler rejects moralizing responses to vulnerability, trauma, and opacity that seek to shield the subject from pain through appeals to self-defense and recourse to violence. Yet her rejection remains *ethical*. She offers an alternative response to vulnerability that emphasizes our common place, our common risks, and our common limits.

What can be said about a *political* response to those who reject this ethics? What about those who prioritize preservation of a narrowly conceived self and nation over acknowledgment of common vulnerability? Should they not be condemned, denounced, opposed? Butler's account of the context of address seems to presume an other who shares this context or who can and will accept her account of it, as if the other answers the call to give an account in necessarily the same way, without a fundamentally different ethics of his own. If the subject's self-crafting takes place in relation to the norms in which he finds himself, then differing sets of norms will condition differing senses of oneself and others and differing ways of conceiving this relation.

In light of the decline of symbolic efficiency and the inconsistency of any ideological formation, moreover, the risks to which we find ourselves vulnerable, the experiences of embodiment inflecting our senses of exposure, will necessarily be *uncommon*. For you, to be in my presence as a menstruating woman may risk defilement. For me, to confront your *jouissance* may be unbearable. Once we emphasize these fundamental gaps and conflicts, politics cannot be avoided. Not only are we called by inconsistencies in our social formations, by the past harms and omissions that make them what they are, but we are responsible for the arrangements of power in which we encounter each other. In the face of these inconsistencies and responsibilities, we make decisions, political decisions for and against, decisions of which we may remain unaware (insofar as we fail to attend to how in our daily practices we repeat and reinforce given arrangements) but which are no less political for this unawareness. Butler, however, displaces attention from the political matter of decision as she presents an ethics animated by an appreciation for the opacity and unknowingness rupturing any expectation to complete coherence or fully transparent self-identity.

If unknowingness conditions ethics then it necessarily conditions politics as well. Our political choices to condemn and denounce, the connections we pursue through what we exclude, take place under traumatic conditions of unknowability and unpredictability. Our decision for this rather than that will necessarily involve a kind of violence, a foreclosure of the possibility of the future that would have resulted had we decided otherwise. When we intervene politically, we act within situations not of our own making, often in terms of representations and practices we might otherwise trouble or critique. Through our actions, we affect these representations and practices, changing them and ourselves in ways we cannot predict.

Associating condemnation and denunciation with sovereignty, Butler eschews a politics of conviction as necessarily incompatible with the ethical conditions sustaining the scene of address. Yet condemnation and denunciation need not be associated with a notion of mastery or unconditionality. Instead, they can be necessary and proper political responses to the violence that informs the scenes in which we find ourselves and the inconsistencies that attempt to cover over past omissions and harms, responses necessary for emboldening left politics. As mentioned above, despite the way she opposes conviction to responsibility, Butler also condemns: she condemns the attacks made on the United States on September 11, 2001. She does so as a way to enter into a certain conversation, enacting thereby the way that condemnation may provide not closure and detachment but an opening to new relationships, a possibility of political alternatives. Condemnation of one may be the way we address another, answering the lack that excites us, and forming a new, militant connection.

6

Certainty

9/11 CONSPIRACY THEORIES AND PSYCHOSIS

In a poll conducted in 2004 by Zogby International, 49.3 percent of New York City residents said that some U.S. leaders "knew in advance that attacks were planned on or around September 11, 2001 and that they consciously failed to act."[1] According to a *New York Times*–CBS News poll carried out in October 2006, only 16 percent of those surveyed thought the Bush administration was telling the truth about what it knew prior to September 11 about possible terrorist attacks on the United States.[2] Fifty-three percent of respondents said that they thought the administration was hiding something. Twenty-eight percent thought the administration was mostly lying. A Scripps Survey Research Center–Ohio University poll carried out in July 2006 asked the more pointed question as to whether respondents thought 9/11 was an "inside job." Thirty-six percent of respondents found it very or somewhat likely that "federal officials either participated in the attacks on the World Trade Center and the Pentagon or took no action to stop them 'because they wanted the United States to go to war in the Middle East.'"[3] The press release for the poll notes that this 36 percent is slightly less than the 40 percent convinced that a lone gunman was not responsible for the death of President John F. Kennedy and the 38 percent who believe the government is withholding proof of the existence of extraterrestrial life. It also reports that those suspecting 9/11 was an inside job are more likely to get their news from the Internet than from mainstream media sources, which is hardly surprising given the hundreds of websites devoted to investigating the day's events, criticizing the official account, and finding patterns in facts scattered throughout and virtually ignored by the mainstream media.

What, if anything, might these numbers mean for left politics in the United States? Does the movement loosely organized around 9/11 truth involve dynamic political struggle? Is the movement an essential site of resistance against the policies of the Bush administration, its illegal wars, and its attempt to increase executive power and stifle civil liberties? Insofar as information at odds with the official story of 9/11 circulates primarily on the Internet, do we find in the truth movement an example of the power of alternative and participatory media over the corporate-controlled mainstream media?

The conflict over 9/11 truth is a battle over facts, knowledge, who knew, who knows, and who has a right to know. Pervasive skepticism renders every fact, every claim, suspect. So does the push to uncover the truth of September 11 continue the democratic project of undermining the sovereign privilege of secrecy by making hidden knowledge public?

Most mainstream discussions of the 9/11 truth movement, even those challenging the adequacy of the administration's account of the events of September 11, dismiss truth activists as a lunatic fringe, as paranoid conspiracy theorists with a fragile hold on reality. This gap between official and alternative accounts raises the question of the possibility of facts credible both to those convinced by the official account and to those who reject it. Could any information exist that would disprove the suspicions of the MIHOP or made-it-happen-on-purpose segment of the 9/11 truth movement (the other segment is LIHOP, let it happen on purpose)? Conversely, could any facts be revealed that would firmly establish the Bush administration's complicity in the attacks on the World Trade Center and the Pentagon? Differently put, is the matter simply one of revelation and disconcealment such that a smoking gun could emerge that all would agree is definitive proof of the truth of the event? Or is something else at stake, something that concerns the conditions of possibility for knowledge and credibility?

Confronting this dilemma is crucial for thinking through the role of media—old and new—as well as for grasping the setting of contemporary politics. If facts and information are introduced into a media environment wherein they are rejected or suspected in advance, that is to say, if facts are immediately presumed to be either lies in the service of ideology or the irrelevant factoids of the reality-based community, and if they circulate primarily as eyeball bait in communicative capitalism's endless circuits, then are they necessary for or relevant to left political projects? What if the so-called facts circulate tribally, consolidating communities of the like-minded even as they fail to impress—or even register to—anyone else?

Building movements, particularly of those alienated from the main-stream, is no trivial task. It has been a key tactic in the culture wars—as the success of the previously discredited school of neoliberal economics as well as of Christian fundamentalism indicates. Each has benefited from contestations over truth and the pluralizing of facts and values, from the relativism toward absolutes that construes each as entitled to her own opinion. Nonetheless, new media advocates often fetishistically proceed as if networked and participatory media—blogging, the introduction of videos onto the Web, the independent journalism associated with indy media—are necessarily progressive, as if radical left politics is somehow built into the technology. They presume their introduction of information into the media stream is a crucial element of left opposition or anticapital-ist resistance. Not only do they carry on as if the information and images they produce are visible and known, as if this information registers within the massive circulation of contributions within communicative capitalism, but these content providers also take it for granted that the information they provide is meaningful. They act as if those who come into contact with this new information will find it credible, as if common standards for the assessment and evaluation of this information exist and are widely, rather than tribally, shared.

Most political discussion (as well as democratic theory) takes for granted the existence of a consensus regarding the rules and conditions for establishing truth and falsity, not to mention a shared notion of reality. Quickly formatting "the conversation" via the exclusion of myriad views and positions as crazy or not serious, such discussion is premised on the fantasy that there is no fundamental disagreement over the basic character of the world (or that such disagreement has no bearing on politics).[4] This presumption is misplaced. Our present political-medialogical setting is one of dissensus, incredulity, and competing conceptions of reality. Commu-nicative capitalism thrives under these conditions—but can left politics?

In *Publicity's Secret* (2002), I discuss the deep imbrications of conspiracy thinking and the hope for an American public, imbrications that demonstrate the ways democracy relies on publicity as a "system of distrust," to use the words of Jeremy Bentham. Crucial to democracy's triumph over absolutism was the power of revelation, a power claimed for the people over and against the arcane mysteries of monarchy. As Carl Schmitt explained over eighty years ago, belief in openness as a value for its own sake is a product of this time, a product ill-suited to the practicalities of party politics under mass democracy where electoral victories and defeats depend on much more than a revelation here or there. In the present setting, moreover, openness, publicity, and the power of revelation further the expansion of networked information technologies to consolidate communicative capitalism. Materializing democratic aspirations and suspicions, the adoption, expansion, and intensification of communicative technologies is urged—on all sides, by left and right, privileged and disadvantaged—as vital to increasing democratic participation (as if a deficit in participation were the primary problem confronting democracy today). The ideal of publicity functions ideologically, serving global capitalism's reliance on networked information technologies and consumers convinced that their every blog post, virtual march, or YouTube upload is a radical act rather than an entertaining diversion. Communicative capitalism mobilizes the faith in exposure animating democracy as the perfect lure. Subjects feel themselves to be active even as their every activity reinforces the status quo. Revelation can be celebrated because it is ineffectual. Its results are medialogical, just another contribution to the circulation of content with little impact on power or policy.

Is the 9/11 truth movement, then, another instance of the convergence of conspiracy thinking and the Internet, another manifestation of the desire to make the links, to enact the fantasy of publicity by revealing the secrets? No. Something different is going on. The movement associated with 9/11 truth manifests a shift in conspiracy thinking, a shift from questioning to certainty and from a logic of desire to a logic of drive. And this shift isn't confined to the conspiratorial fringes. On the contrary, it is symptomatic of a larger sociocultural development that involves a new constellation of questioning, doubt, credibility, and certainty.

To make this argument, I turn again to Lacan, Žižek, and Santner. I explain the shift as one from the discourse of the hysteric to a new form of psychotic discourse, a shift that replaces a logic or economy of desire with one of drive. As chapter 3 explains, the discourse of the hysteric is one of four kinds of social link. Its primary characteristic is questioning. The hysteric constantly asks the master, "Am I what you say I am? What are you saying and why are you saying that?" The discourse of the hysteric can thus be understood as providing the basic form of democratic discourse— which reminds us that these Lacanian terms are offered as analytical categories, not means of pathologization. Like the hysteric, democracy challenges claims coming from a master. It is motivated by desire, a desire enabled by the very law that seems to block its fulfillment. By way of an example, we might note how various Democrats and journalists contested the Bush administration's classifying of previously public knowledge, its removal of all sorts of documents from the Internet after 9/11. It's unlikely that these Democrats and journalists knew or even cared about this infor- mation while it was public. After it was secretized, however, then they desired it.

Some conspiracy theorists echo democratic assumptions insofar as they don't provide theories but instead ask questions. They desire the truth; they want to know. They endeavor to reveal secrets and thereby call into being a public that will get rid of the corrupt conspirators and restore legitimate government. In so doing, they situate themselves firmly in the democratic, anti-absolutist tradition (a tradition in which the American Declaration of Independence also belongs). Asking questions, making links, such conspiracy theorists try to persuade readers and hearers to think, to find out for themselves. Yet under contemporary conditions of communicative capitalism, this desire to reveal is a trap. For all its aspira- tions to democracy it remains caught in a pseudo-activity that reduces politics to a single operation—revelation.

Appeals to "find out for yourself" appear in the videos, books, and websites of those involved in 9/11 truth. But frequently accompanying these injunctions to ask questions and challenge authority is another sort of claim, a claim to certainty. This introduction of certainty changes the mode of the injunction to "find out for yourself." It now indicates less the openness of desire, a desire to know, than the closed circuit of drive. *The facts are already there, we can be certain of that. There's no need to accept anything on the basis of belief.* Commemorating the first anniversary of the group Scholars for 9/11 Truth, its founder James Fetzer writes: "We have established beyond reasonable doubt that the Twin Towers were destroyed by a novel form of controlled demolition from the top down, that WTC-7 was brought down by a classic form of controlled demolition from the bottom up, and that, whatever may have hit the Pentagon, multiple lines of argument support the conclusion that it was not a Boeing 757."[5] Fetzer, a university professor, doesn't adopt the discourse of the hysteric. He is certain. The Scholars for 9/11 Truth know some things to be true. They don't need to persuade people to consider the evidence. The facts speak for themselves.

Žižek explains that, unlike in desire, where the object emerges at the moment of its loss, in drive loss itself is an object.[6] September 11 names such a loss. The very term designates not just a day but a trauma. September 11 has become a meme for loss, repeated endlessly in official accounts and reiterated in unofficial ones. In all these accounts, moreover, 9/11 marks the loss resulting from excessive, impersonal, obscene power, power with little regard for life, power permeated with the *jouissance* of its conviction. Explanations for what happened on September 11, official and unofficial alike, circle around this knot of obscenity and loss, albeit in different circuits. Žižek further links drive to constituent anxiety, to pure confrontation with the void (*objet petit a*).[7] Theories of the events of 9/11 rely on and reinforce this constituent anxiety as they confront the specific horror of the disintegration of the social link, the destruction of the symbolic pact promising security and holding society together.

In much of the production of the 9/11 truth movement, this confrontation with a hole in the symbolic order is accompanied by *jouissance*—repetition, intensity, affect. The *jouissance* connecting each fact to another produces certainty as an effect—*it feels true (we can feel it in our gut)*. Indeed, *jouissance* arises through connectivity, through the specificity and systematicity of the facts circling the hole of loss. Connections are excessive, nearly impossibly interlinked. Every specific fact—exact times and temperatures, flight schedules and passenger manifests, military exercises and official communiqués—is linked. Everything is meaningful by virtue of pointing to something else. Enjoyment is produced by the very drive to link, connect, and document, by the intensity of detail and specificity. Because the most central component of the explanation remains unknown —who did it?—the evidence accumulates in extreme and specific detail, establishing connections without ever reaching its goal.

The 9/11 truth movement combines its intense certainty with an over-

whelming skepticism. Explanations are doubted: why does the administration's story change over several years? Why are there differences in the
official times of the planes crashing and the towers following? Why is a
close associate of Condoleezza Rice, Philip Zelikow, appointed to head the
commission investigating 9/11? A volatile mix of certainty and skepticism
occupies the place of the lack of belief in the official story.

This combination of certainty and skepticism takes the form of the
discourse of the university. We saw in chapter 3 that in university discourse
the facts speak for themselves. Experts claim objectivity even as they
attempt to overlook the institutional power that supports their claims to
expertise. Scientific socialism, the press, and economics are all instances of
university discourse. Each emphasizes facts. Facts are supposed to determine outcomes independent of power. Purporting to let the facts speak for
themselves, the 9/11 truth movement is structured in accordance with
university discourse. Yet it lacks its authorizing support (the institutional
power we saw Gutmann and Thompson assuming yet ignoring). Accordingly, I view the movement for 9/11 truth as a clone of university discourse, a psychotic clone.[8]

Why psychotic? Because of Lacanian psychoanalysis's account of psychosis as a missing signifier, an absence and a foreclosure. The loss of
authority on September 11 produced a hole in the already fragile, declining
U.S. symbolic order. The Bush administration attempted to fill in that hole
by explaining the events of the day in terms of terrorism. The 9/11 truth
movement rejects this explanation and builds a discourse around the hole
that is left, a response that is psychotic in its formal structure. To hold its
speculations together, this psychotic discourse models itself on other,
more conventional discourses such as university discourse (hardly a surprise given both the present ubiquity of university discourse and the role
of actual university professors in the movement).

While the 9/11 truth movement is exemplary of the psychotic cloning of
university discourse, the fragile discursive habitats of communicative capitalism increase the likely proliferation of such psychotic clones. Characterized by the circuit of drive, by an intensity, certainty, and skepticism that
circles around a fundamental loss, psychotic discourse perpetuates anxiety. It renders all that comes into contact with it suspect, uncertain,
permeated with possible meaning. The gap between the official story of
9/11 and the 9/11 truth movement (and reappearing within the movement

itself) thus suggests less an engaged political struggle than it does a more debilitating political deadlock that displaces action onto impossible subjects, futures, and terrains. What sort of politics is possible when there is knowledge without belief, when certainty and skepticism persist in tandem, each supporting but immune to the other? And what does any answer to this question entail for aspirations to collective approaches to equity and justice?

Conspiracy Theory

Conspiracy theory is typically considered a vernacular discourse, one that speaks and thinks outside the official institutions of power about power's excess, about the crimes and obscenities hidden from and by power's public face. Critics fault conspiracy theorists for their amateurishness, considering them dabblers in a realm of expert knowledge who try to know what they cannot know, what they should accept on faith. They dismiss conspiracy theorists as autodidacts unschooled in rules of evidence and rational argumentation. They deride conspiracy theorists for their extra-institutional position, their lack of conventional expertise. These critics emphasize as well the absence of the credentials necessary to speak in what is upheld as the public sphere. A language of infection tends to follow as the critic worries about the health of the public, the vitality of public reason. For critics, the overall unauthorized character of conspiracy theory signifies the illegitimacy of the theories produced by those who look for and find evidence of conspiracies. They treat conspiracy theorists in all their questions and suspicions, accumulations of facts and amassings of evidence, as extremists, deluded denizens of the lunatic fringe so alienated from general society that they are compelled to resort to the most outlandish explanations to make sense of the world and their lives in this world.

Some critics find conspiracy theorists to be so outside the mainstream that they mar or insult true political memory. Accusing those involved in the 9/11 truth movement of insulting the police officers and firefighters who raced into the burning towers of the World Trade Center (a strange, displaced insult that fails to grasp how the alternative explanations of September 11 hardly insult these workers but instead the government who allegedly caused their deaths and now covers its crimes in their heroism),

Senator John McCain finds 9/11 conspiracy theories "a distraction from the proper lessons of 9/11, from what is truly important to this country."[9] McCain reiterates the accepted critique of conspiracy theories: "They ignore the methods of science, the protocols of investigation, and the dictates of logic. The conspiracy theorists chase any bit of information, no matter how flimsy, and use it to fit their preordained conclusions. They ascribe to the government, or to some secretive group, powers wholly out of proportion to what the evidence suggests. And they ignore the facts that are present in plain sight."[10]

The stigma attached to the "outsider-y-ness" of the conspiracy theorist enables the very term *conspiracy theorist* to be wielded so as to exclude a view in advance. For example, the *New York Times* columnist David Brooks dismissed Kevin Phillips's book *American Theocracy* as crude conspiracy mongering.[11] The book is a critical account of the conservative coalition in American politics, a coalition that Phillips, as a young Republican strategist, helped build. Similarly, Senator James Inhofe sought to discredit attributions of global warming to human factors as "the greatest hoax ever perpetrated on the American people."[12] In each case, the critic attempts to render a book or an issue as so outrageous that no sensible person could possibly find it worth any serious attention.

The stigmatizing effect of labeling someone a conspiracy theorist is so great that allegations of conspiracy brought by governmental officials seem somehow not themselves to be conspiracy theories. Theorizing a conspiracy, then, is not what makes a conspiracy theorist; thinking or positing something that mainstream common sense (what Lacan calls "the big Other") deems paranoid nonsense is. Thus, we find ourselves in the weird situation where some conspiracy theories have a presumed legitimacy in part because they cannot be called conspiracy theories. Around the time the Bush administration was asserting that a conspiring group of Islamic fundamentalists armed with box cutters hijacked four planes, brought down the World Trade Center, smashed through the west wall of the Pentagon, and crashed in a field in Pennsylvania, U.S. government officials and the mainstream media publicized the proliferation of conspiracy theories in the Arab world, conspiracy theories that blamed the attacks on the World Trade Center and the Pentagon on the Mossad or the U.S. government itself. In a speech to the United Nations General Assembly on November 10, 2001, George W. Bush declared, "We must speak the

truth about terror. Let us never tolerate outrageous conspiracy theories concerning the attacks of September the 11th; malicious lies that attempt to shift the blame away from the terrorists, themselves, away from
the guilty."[13]

As part of this effort not to tolerate conspiracy theories, the State
Department posted several articles "debunking" the top September 11
conspiracy theories on its website.[14] Part of the problem with its debunking, however, is that it cites evidence many in the 9/11 truth movement
find suspect, evidence like the video of a plane crashing into the Pentagon
(many viewers, I among them, don't see a plane in this allegedly definitive
proof) or tapes of Osama bin Laden taking responsibility for the attacks
(some conspiracy theorists argue that the translation is wrong or that the
tapes are fakes). The State Department site also refers to a book put out
by *Popular Mechanics, Debunking 9/11 Myths: Why Conspiracy Theories
Can't Stand Up To The Facts*, as well as the *9/11 Commission Report*, texts
which the 9/11 truth movement has already heavily criticized. And with
respect to the *9/11 Commission Report*, the truth movement is not alone:
immersed in controversy from the beginning—the Bush administration
attempted to block the formation of a commission and, after it conceded,
persistently failed to fund the commission's work or supply it with the
requested information—the commission's report was widely viewed as
bland and disappointing at best. In the words of a *Harper's Magazine* essay
by Benjamin DeMott, the report is "a cheat and a fraud. It stands as a
series of evasive maneuvers that infantilize the audience, transform candor
into iniquity, and conceal realities that demand immediate inspection and
confrontation."[15]

Some self-proclaimed conspiracy theorists celebrate their outsider status, finding that it establishes the authenticity of their work. Precisely
because they have refused to be bought by the system, refused the privi-
leges of the mainstream, they can be trusted. Their views are in no way
compromised by the conflicts of interest typical of those working in the
interstices of government, big corporations, the military, and the universities.[16] To establish their credibility, then, conspiracy theorists often describe the danger, exclusion, and hardship they've undergone for the sake
of the truth.

Many conspiracy theorists prize their ability to cut through the government's and mainstream media's conceits and dissimulation. They often

manifest their rejection of the mainstream aesthetically. Conspiracy-oriented websites tend to be visually complicated and messy, crowded with links, facts, evidence, and information. The sites are confusing, hard to navigate. One is never quite sure where one is. And not surprisingly, they heavily interconnect, mutually citing and reinforcing each other even as they may disagree, furiously, over whether the World Trade Center was taken down by planted explosives made of thermite or remote-controlled drones. Among conspiracy researchers, the complexity of images and multiple fonts, the visual enactment of confusion and connection, affirms their position as outsiders. Their books, their sites, aren't slick, with slick denoting a mindset and aesthetic overattuned to the deceptions of the mainstream.

9/11 Truth

Two factors contributing to the production and circulation of alternative claims for what happened in the United States on September 11 distinguish the 9/11 truth movement from other assemblages associated with conspiracy theories: one, the way the ideas circulate on the Internet as videos and, two, the participation of a variety of highly regarded academics. These same factors also make 9/11 truth a central site for examining contemporary problems around credibility and certainty.

"LOOSE CHANGE"

Most people who doubt the official story of the events of 9/11 get their information from the Internet. Particularly interesting in this regard is the way 9/11 conspiracy theories circulate not simply through websites and blogs but as full-length videos. I can compare this with alien abduction—in the nineties, as accounts of alien abduction became more visible in American popular culture, those involved in the abduction community relied in part on email and websites.[17] Nevertheless, the circulation of knowledge of abduction took place primarily through books, conventions, and made-for-television investigative reports. The television specials—while exploiting the trash value of abduction—included heavy doses of skepticism; they gave a lot of air time to debunkers. The 9/11 truth movement differs in that people make and distribute their own videos.

The most prominent video associated with 9/11 truth is *Loose Change*, an eighty-minute documentary made by Dylan Avery, a twenty-two-year-old from Oneonta, New York. It first appeared on the Web in the summer of 2005. Since then it has had at least ten million viewings. The magazine *Vanity Fair* calls *Loose Change* "the first Internet blockbuster."[18]

A striking aspect of the video is its production of certainty through repetition, intensity, and affect, in other words, the way it performs the shift from the questioning of the hysteric toward a certainty more characteristic of psychosis. Here is its version of "find out for yourself" in the film's final voice-over:

> I'll say it again: why are they hiding from us? What are they hiding from us? And what's it going to take until people in this country give a damn and do something about it? Now that the evidence has been presented, what will you do about it? Will you find comfort in the official version of events? Or will you go out and investigate for yourselves? Will you share this information or will you ignore it? Will you be at ground zero on September 11th? America has been hijacked. Is it more likely by Osama bin Laden and his ragtag group of Arabs with box cutters or by a group of tyrants within our own government, ready and willing to do whatever it takes to keep their stranglehold on this country? It's up to you. Ask questions. Demand answers.

To whom is this demand raised? To the tyrants, the all-powerful obscene tyrants supposed/produced through the operation of the theory. So the same tyrants who allegedly committed the crime are here demanded to expose themselves, to admit to it, to come clean. There is a strangeness to this demand, an incompatibility between it and the crime and criminals it is raised to expose.

More interesting is the attitude of certainty: the viewer is enjoined to investigate. Yet the film presents itself as already knowing what the subject will find out. It's certain and it manifests this certainty straightforwardly in the evidence presented, the information shared, the America hijacked. Even if "it's up to you," the film already knows what you will discover, as long, that is, as you are brave enough to leave the comfort of the official version of events. Overlaying the final credits is an austere hip-hop piece with a strong base line. The vocals begin: "We all know where you're goin,' we know that you're out there."

The effective and affective success of *Loose Change* stems from its use of music, from the way music provides the connections between different images, screens, and facts. A compelling drumbeat, strong base line, and repetitive samples bypass the mediation of argument to establish a feeling of certainty. The first eight minutes of the film, for example, feature images and a voice-over enumeration of various sorts of items: contradictory quotes from Condoleezza Rice, Donald Rumsfeld, Ari Fleischer, and Richard Clarke; a description of Operation Northwoods, a 1962 plan involving a faked hijacking submitted by the head of the Joint Chiefs of Staff to the Secretary of Defense; the 1984 test of a remote-controlled Boeing aircraft; and, so on up through news reports in early September 2001. The reports mention the significant increase in put options placed on United Airlines, Boeing, and American Airlines; Larry Silverstein's purchase of the World Trade Center and the accompanying 3.5 billion-dollar insurance policy; and Attorney General John Ashcroft's shift to traveling by private rather than commercial aircraft. The items are presented chronologically, events on a timeline leading up to September 11. Because the underlying music establishes continuity among the images, particularly through its repetitions and driving base line, the viewer gets the sense that events are already connected to one another in the Real. Taking the connections between the events for granted, surrendering to the hypnotic rhythm, is easier than disrupting one's enjoyment in the music.

The remainder of the film follows the pattern of voice-over, segment from news media and interviews, and repetition of ambient/chill/lounge/techno samples. Most often, the samples reemerge at those moments when the voice-over is mentioning particularly telling facts, facts that need to be linked to other facts, facts the connection together of which produces the knowledge of a conspiracy within the U.S. government. A segment on Hani Hanjour, the alleged pilot of American Airlines flight 77, the one presumed to have crashed into the Pentagon, features an interview with a staff member from Hanjour's training school. The hypnotic beat and repetitive sampling come in just after the staff member finishes describing how inept Hanjour was as a pilot and the voice-over mentions that air-traffic controllers at Dulles presumed the plane was flown by a military pilot.

The satisfying repetitions of the ambient/chill/lounge/techno tracks reinforce the pleasures of conspiracy theory. They provide the film with an edginess, a trangressive allure that reiterates the transgressions the film purports to reveal. It's a soundtrack of revelation and disconcealment inviting viewers and hearers to share in the secret, the secret knowledge of political violence and obscenity. As mainstream a magazine as *Time* gets it. In a page-one article from the September 11, 2006, issue, the columnist Lev Grossman writes: "Watching *Loose Change*, you feel as if you are participating in the great American tradition of self-reliance and nonconformist, antiauthoritarian dissent. You're fighting the power. You're thinking different."[19] We don't need to believe the Bush administration's lies when we can see the evidence and know what really happened.

One of the final clips featured in the film provides a bridge to the academics credentialing the larger 9/11 truth movement. The clip is from *Hannity and Colmes*, a nightly program on the Fox News Channel. Hannity and Colmes are interviewing Kevin Barrett, an adjunct professor teaching an introductory course on Islam at the University of Wisconsin-Madison. Asking about Barrett's "opinion" and whether he "believes" 9/11 was an inside job, Hannity attempts to browbeat and stigmatize Barrett as a crazed conspiracy theorist. Barrett responds that he *knows*, he doesn't "believe"; he *knows*. He has studied the evidence for two and a half years and he knows.

SCHOLARS FOR 9/11 TRUTH

As an academic, Barrett is a key point of overlap between *Loose Change* and the second aspect of the 9/11 truth movement that distinguishes it from other conspiracy theories, the emergence of the group Scholars for 9/11 Truth. The group was founded on December 15, 2005, by James H. Fetzer, Distinguished McKnight Professor of Philosophy at the University of Minnesota, Duluth, and Steven E. Jones, professor of physics at Brigham Young University.[20] Affiliated with the group is the peer-reviewed *Journal of 9/11 Studies*. Fetzer is the author and editor of a number of books on the assassination of President John F. Kennedy, including *Murder in Dealey Plaza: What We Know Now That We Didn't Know Then*, *The Great Zapruder Film Hoax: Deceit and Deception in the Death of JFK*, and *Assassination Science: Experts Speak Out on the Death of JFK*.

In November 2005, Jones posted a paper on the Web in which he argued that the World Trade Center towers fell as a result of a controlled demolition.[21] As John Gravois notes in the *Chronicle of Higher Education*, "His paper—written by an actual professor who works at an actual research university—has made him a celebrity in the conspiracy universe."[22] ABC News picked up an AP wire feature on Scholars for 9/11 Truth citing a Canadian chemist critical of Jones's account of the collapse of the Twin Towers. According to the chemist, members of the conspiracy community "practically worship the ground [Jones] walks on because he's seen as a scientist who's preaching to their side." So even as the ABC feature notes that few mainstream scientists will engage the work of Scholars for 9/11 Truth so as not to lend it "unwarranted credibility," it recognizes that the academic credentials of the group "could do that anyway."[23] More importantly, the feature alludes to a fundamental characteristic of the group: they already know that the official story of 9/11 is wrong; their effort is expended so as to prove it.

The 9/11 truth movement gained in momentum because of the involvement of credentialed academics. For those in the movement, these scholars provide the expert knowledge, the credibility, they need to fight their battle for truth in the public sphere. Among the most important and influential is David Ray Griffin, a well-established theology professor. Not only did Griffin synthesize in a clear, systematic study many of the criticisms of the official account circulating on the Internet and published in European presses but his book *The New Pearl Harbor* was endorsed by the renowned history professor Howard Zinn and provided with a foreword by Richard Falk, an emeritus professor of international law at Princeton.

The combination of Scholars for 9/11 Truth and the popularity of videos like *Loose Change* make the 9/11 truth movement an interesting site for thinking about problems of credibility. For some in the movement, the slickness of *Loose Change* is propagandistic, making the film into an instrument of disinformation instead of scientific inquiry. Writing for the 9/11 Research website, Victoria Ashley, in an article praising the contribution of Steven Jones, criticizes *Loose Change*: "Propaganda techniques, such as repeating an emotionally charged scene over and over, or approaching the unanswered questions of 9/11 in the manner of a ghost story telling, keep viewers transfixed by the presentation without any involvement of a rational evaluation of evidence."[24] The very aspects of the film that make it powerful and popular seem to some to undermine the movement's efforts toward challenging the Bush administration's version of events.

The scholars whose work rejects the official story have had to defend their academic freedom and scholarly credentials. In October 2006, Brigham Young University announced Jones's retirement. This announcement followed a month after Jones had been relieved of his teaching responsibilities and placed on leave. Lawmakers have challenged the academic integrity, not to mention the intellectual honesty and overall sanity, of scholars working in the area of 9/11 truth. During the summer of 2006, Wisconsin legislators pressured the University of Wisconsin-Madison to fire Kevin Barrett for his view that September 11 was an inside job. The provost, Patrick Farrell, defended Barrett, although he warned Barrett that should he continue to "illustrate an inability to control" his interest in garnering publicity for his ideals, he would have less confidence in Barrett's ability to teach the course.[25] The same academic credentials providing credibility to the 9/11 truth movement are being called into question and, to some extent, revoked.

In yet a further twist, challenges to scholars' credibility arise from within the ranks of those working on 9/11 truth. In late November 2006, Jones and others split from Scholars for 9/11 Truth. The following month, they formed a new group, Scholars for 9/11 Truth and Justice. Some lamented the infighting among the Scholars, recognizing the link between this fighting and the larger struggle for credibility even as they displaced the fundamental problem. In the words of "Lividlarry": "I've been somewhat 'torn' on this infighting issue for quite some time and can see some truth in at least two positions with regard to what information is 'credible.' It comes as no surprise that disinformation agents are busy sowing confusion anywhere that they can when such a horrible reality is at stake."[26] Aware of the problem of credibility, Lividlarry subsumes it under conviction and suspicion. A horrible reality is at stake, a certain horror and a certain reality. Confusion is thus a matter not of this reality but of disinformation, of those who want to cast doubt on what he and others already know for certain. In fact, Lividlarry is particularly skeptical regarding efforts to establish credibility. He continues, "When those interested in accumulating whatever information and/or insights are out there fall into the trap of determining 'credibility' based on their interpretation of plausibility there is a danger that a piece of the puzzle might go unnoticed." What happened on September 11 was incredible, implausible. Limiting oneself to plausibility avoids encountering what is already certain.

Factions among the Scholars offer different explanations for the split. Fetzer claims Jones was blocking people from posting on the Scholars' website and trying to take over the group.[27] He also charges Jones with attempting to keep controversial theories about 9/11 out of the public eye. The theories in question were proposed by Judy Wood, a former assistant professor at Clemson University with a Ph.D. in materials engineering science, and Morgan Reynolds, emeritus professor of economics at Texas A & M. Reynolds and Wood had posted a number of critiques of Jones's work on the Internet.[28] Challenging Jones's claim that "nano-enhanced thermite or thermate" was used to bring down the WTC in a controlled demolition, they point out that Jones does not establish that thermite or thermate has ever been used to bring down large buildings much less pulverize them. They note as well that Jones doesn't account for how much thermite or thermate would need to have been used, where it would need to have been placed, and how it would have been ignited.[29]

Additionally, Reynolds and Wood accuse Jones of failing to credit the work of others on 9/11 truth, ignoring the fact that "no Boeing 757 went into the Pentagon was proven years ago," and upholding too many components of the official government conspiracy theory.[30] Wood suggests that space-based laser beams perhaps in connection with very large mirrors brought down the WTC.[31] Jones both rejects the "no planes hit the Towers" theory and charges Wood and Reynolds with engaging in ad hominem attacks, in part because they mention his previous work on cold fusion. In a broadcast in January 2007 of Fetzer's radio show *The Dynamic Duo*, on which Reynolds and Wood appeared as guests, Fetzer, in what he claims is not an ad hominem, mentions a paper written by Jones wherein Jones uses archaeological evidence to prove the Mormon claim that Jesus visited the Americas.[32] For much of the remaining portion of the show, Fetzer, Jones, and Wood discuss problems in Jones's claims to follow the scientific method and suggest that his work has more in common with pseudoscience.

In yet a more fundamental critique, Gerard Holmgren criticizes the entire community of Scholars for 9/11 Truth (including Fetzer and Jones by name) for plagiarizing the earlier work of Internet researchers. In Holmgren's words: "The scholars make their presence in the media felt not through original research (they haven't done any), nor through quality of presentation (they make frequent factual errors—if indeed they are 'errors'). They make their presence felt purely by swagger in parading that Jones and a number of his associates are professors. . . . Not only do the scholars plagiarize their 'research' articles, but their press statements are calculated to reinforce the false notion that their work is original, that the revelations are new, and also to play the hero card by claiming personal risk in unveiling these shocking new revelations."[33] On his website, Holmgren explains that the so-called 9/11 truth movement is actually controlled by the very people who perpetrated the crimes of September 11. Their control relies on carefully placed disinformation and on the careerism and opportunism of those who want to profit from the 9/11 truth industry.[34] Disinformation keeps the myth that planes actually crashed into the Pentagon and World Trade Center alive. Holmgren knows that these are fabrications. American Airlines flights 77 and 11 (the ones allegedly hitting the Pentagon and the North Tower) never existed. The well-known footage of the plane striking the South Tower is an animated cartoon. Holmgren is convinced that the events of 9/11 are like a giant snuff film consisting of real explosions and fake planes and hijackers.

Skepticism and Certainty

Žižek's account of the decline of symbolic efficiency, Santner's discussion of the crisis of investiture, and Lacan's teaching on psychosis can help sort through these layers of credibility, incredibility, and certainty. Together, these ideas help us understand the problem posed by 9/11 truth not as one of credibility but of its absence, that is to say, the absence of conditions of possibility for something like belief or credibility.

As chapter 2 details, the decline of symbolic efficiency refers to a breakdown in signification. Identities, arguments, or signs that are clear and compelling in some settings carry little weight in others. One might imagine Nicole Richie and Jürgen Habermas in an airport waiting area. Neither would recognize the other's symbolic weight or be able to assess the other's cultural capital.

That identities, arguments, and signs are limited in their power and range, that they fail to be thoroughly compelling in a variety of contexts, has repercussions for contemporary subjects. We are often skeptical about what we hear. To approach this from the other side, Žižek frequently describes symbolic efficiency with the question, "What do you believe, your eyes or my words?" In a functioning symbolic order, we believe the words, no matter what our eyes tell us. We recognize that the judge is not just the man we see but the office he holds. We recognize the doctor is more than the woman before us. She is also the trained, experienced expert on whom we depend. In the mediated networks of communicative capitalism, though, we don't believe their words. We believe our eyes. Present subjects accept very little on face value. We don't believe what we hear. If a doctor gives us bad news, we get a second or third opinion and then reject Western medicine in favor of more authentic folk remedies. If the judge makes a ruling we reject, we suspect he was paid off, corrupt, or invested in an opposing ideology. And even when we concede that another is likely using her best judgment in as fair a way as possible, we find ourselves emphasizing the plurality of possible views: everyone has her own opinion. Experts disagree.

So we are skeptical. But often our skepticism is combined with a kind of certainty or conviction. We don't challenge or reject everything all the time. To keep going, we have to keep some aspects of our lives stable and secure. We need base points from which to navigate. Skepticism toward the mainstream news, then, is combined with an increased division between who watches what and who trusts whom. Some sources can be trusted. Republicans in the United States are more likely to watch Fox News and report that they trust what they hear on Fox. Vice President Dick Cheney has said he only watches Fox. The idea of the decline of symbolic efficiency clicks on this fragmentation, on the inability of elements that flourish in one discursive habitat to take root and thrive in another.

As Žižek points out, Donald Davidson designates the background assumption that everything another says is not completely wrong the "principle of charity." It's a presumption of underlying agreement on which disagreement rests. Davidson argues that "charity is not an option . . . charity is forced on us; whether we like it or not, if we want to understand others, we must count them right in most matters."[35] The decline of symbolic efficiency points to the withering away of this principle of charity—less and less are people today forced to presume charity. There are strong material-technological explanations for this withering away. Not only are communication technologies charitable in our stead, making connections with other machines, but the interconnecting of ever more people lets us find enough of those who share our convictions that we don't have to believe. In a previous age, we may have been isolated in our views, village idiots roaming the streets, madwomen in the attics, or psychotic judges driven to document our illness and our discoveries. Now we're part of a discourse, community, or movement.

Santner's discussion of the memoirs of Judge Daniel Paul Schreber provides a second element useful for thinking about contemporary problems around credibility and certainty.[36] Whereas Freud's reading of Schreber was central to his understanding of paranoia (particularly with regard to its presumed link with homosexuality), Santner underscores the similarity between the crises leading to Schreber's psychotic breakdown and those facing modernity more generally. He understands these crises as crises of symbolic investiture.

Symbolic investiture refers to the way a person becomes endowed with a new social status that informs her identity in the community (xii). Examples include the ordination of a priest, a marriage ceremony, graduation and the conferral of a degree, or winning a prestigious prize. In modernity, Santner argues, symbolic identities become ever more fragile, less able to "seize" the subject at the core of her self-understanding. Modern subjects, then, understand themselves as never fully occupying their identities. I am not just a mommy, professor, woman, Caucasian, American. There is always more to the modern subject than her role or position. And this means that the roles themselves are less than they had been. They carry less meaning and weight. They are less impressive, less efficacious. Fully aware of the distance between the person and her role, we are inclined to see the role as a sham, a ruse, a cover for corruption or abuse. We sense the tautological character of symbolic roles and social institutions. The judge is a judge because we treat him as a judge. People become married in a marriage ceremony because that's what a marriage ceremony does.

The crisis of symbolic investiture reveals the violence and compulsion, the "vicious circularity," underlying social order (a point Santner explores with reference to Walter Benjamin's "Critique of Violence," 43). Typically, subjects forget or repress their knowledge of violence. This forgetting and repressing is necessary for the continued function of the social field and the credibility of symbolic identities. At points of crisis, however, knowledge of the dependence of the social function on coercion and repetition becomes difficult to repress (139). At these points, Santner tells us, "we are at the threshold of a psychotic universe where the subject has become unable to forget, unable (primordially) to repress the drive dimension of the symbolic function, which expands into a general state of rottenness and decay" (43). The force underlying knowledge fails to authorize facts but instead infuses them with the pervasive, irrational violence of coexistence.

Santner's crisis of symbolic investiture deepens and extends Žižek's account of the decline of symbolic efficiency by connecting the crisis of symbolic investiture to paranoid psychosis. A central lesson of the Schreber case is that a generalized loss of symbolic power can generate feelings of overproximity, in Santner's words, "loss of distance to some obscene and malevolent presence that appears to have a direct hold on one's inner parts" (xii). Confronted with the excessive proximity of authority, the subject can't continue to play the game of everyday life, a game that requires it to deny the "impasses and dilemmas of symbolic power and authority" (144). The traumatic loss of symbolic authority thus impacts the subject such that he feels this now-missing authority to be all the closer, more powerful, and intrusive. He confronts the irrationality and violence underpinning authority per se—the tautological way we obey law because it is law and accept the judgments of a judge because she is the judge. Santner's psychotic, then, is not delusional because he accepts as certain what is necessarily false but because he denies the falsity, the fiction, the lie necessary for the functioning of the symbolic order. The psychotic doesn't fall for the performative magic of utterances backed by symbolic authority. He focuses instead on the "rottenness and decay" that underlies them.

What are the implications of the decline of symbolic efficiency and the crisis of symbolic investiture for thinking through the problems posed by the 9/11 truth movement? The decline of symbolic efficiency tags the movement's setting in profound skepticism. Contemporary subjects don't have to believe. They can find out. This skepticism is coupled with a sense of certainty or confidence. Not everything is called into question at the same time, and some sources are more reliable than others. So contemporary Americans might claim media cannot be trusted and support that claim with evidence taken from media they trust. Their trust, however, doesn't travel from one setting to another. What they find to be authoritative, to count as expert knowledge, is similarly limited. The crisis of symbolic investiture highlights the loss of a powerful authority or authorizing power. Subjects respond to this loss by positing an all the more intrusive, invasive, and proximate power, by failing to believe the fiction of the symbolic order and suppress the sense in which it covers over arbitrary power.

Those who view September 11 in terms of the U. S. government's failure to secure its citizens and its territory might respond to this loss by positing another power and by tracing the workings of this other power throughout the sociopolitical terrain. For them, the lost sense of American invincibility is accompanied by the loss of a signifying authority, one capable of providing meaning, of authorizing an explanation for the events of 9/11. They don't accept the authority of the administration's signification of the event. Instead, they focus on the "rottenness and decay" underlying political and state power.

Lacan's teachings on psychosis help specify this site of crisis and loss. In *Seminar III*, he distinguishes between the psychotic and the normal subject: "What characterizes a normal subject is precisely that he never takes seriously certain realities that he recognizes exist. You are surrounded by all sorts of realities about which you are in doubt, some of which are particularly threatening, but you don't take them fully seriously, for you think . . . that *the worst is not always certain*, and maintain yourselves in an average, basic—in the sense of relation to the base—state of blissful uncertainty, which makes possible for you a sufficiently relaxed existence. Surely, certainty is the rarest of things for the normal subject."[37] The normal person has a lot of doubt, but he doesn't let these doubts get in the way of his everyday functioning. There are many things he doesn't know for sure, but this doesn't bother him. He doesn't worry about it. In fact, his happy persistence requires him not to ask questions or look too closely at things. The normal subject carries on in an uncertain world where many things are unknown and lies are pervasive. Indeed, Lacan says, "the normal subject spontaneously rejects certainty"; he may deny the truth that is right before his eyes just so he can keep on going (76).

In contrast, for the psychotic, Lacan explains, "reality is not the issue," certainty is (75). What he is certain of may well be ambiguous, unclear, opaque. But the psychotic is certain, nonetheless. And this certainty does not correspond directly with reality. Reality isn't at stake. After all, normal subjects persist in a terrain of reality filled with uncertainty and falsity. The psychotic rejects this ambiguity, the ambiguity of the everyday, of language, replacing it with certainty. Lacan notes that the psychotic's certainty is often expressed through writing. The paranoid write, they produce "sheets of paper covered with writing." Schreber, for example, published his writings on his psychosis, which raises the question for Lacan of what the need for recognition might mean (78). Perhaps it might be a need for acknowledgment or community as a way of lessening the unbearable and direct confrontation with power alone. Perhaps Schreber's desire for recognition is a desire for conversation and camaraderie, for others with whom he might discuss and compare his findings such that he might escape the isolation of his certainty. Networked communication technologies provide ways of meeting this need.

Lacan defines psychosis in terms of the foreclosure of the Name-of-the-Father and the hole this creates in the chain of significations. As he puts it, "Something primordial regarding the subject's being does not enter into symbolization and is not repressed, but rejected" (81). Because the Name-of-the-Father or master signifier stabilizes and makes possible language and signification as such, in its absence there is chaos. The psychotic responds to this hole, this chaos, in various ways. He may affirm, emphatically, another other. Most of us are familiar with paranoia as positing an other behind the scenes, pulling the strings. Often, this other remains mysterious, enigmatic (194). This comes as no surprise given the absence of a way to hold the signifying chain together. The lack of such an anchoring point perpetually stimulates the effort to find meaning.

To compensate for the hole in the symbolic, the psychotic turns to the imaginary. Lacan refers to a "captivating image" (204). The psychotic fastens on this image, positioning himself in relation to it. Insofar as this relation remains at the level of the imaginary, it is not a symbolic relation capable of anchoring meaning or offering a clear degree of separation between the subject and the other. On the contrary, precisely because the relation is on the imaginary plane, it is characterized by fear, rivalry, and aggression (205). The psychotic enters into a rivalrous game with the imaginary other, a game of deception and deceit that turns his world into a kind of phantasmagoria, an uncertain terrain where nothing is as it seems and everything is permeated by meaning and significance (69). The psychotic may try to mimic the conformist behaviors of those around him as he grapples with the intensity of his fears and of this rivalry. He may seek to avoid confronting his awareness of the power and aggression, but as his psychosis becomes more acute, he will be less able to deny the obscene intrusions of power that surround him.

Thus far I've emphasized several aspects of the Lacanian account of psychosis: that psychosis is a reaction to a hole or absence, that this reaction takes place on the level of the imaginary, and that it involves certainty, fear, distrust, and a sense of permeating meaning that may be expressed through writing and publication. One additional aspect of Lacan's discussion, an aspect that returns us to the setting of psychosis, is necessary for thinking about 9/11 truth as the psychotic clone of university discourse. Lacan writes: "To be more or less captivated, captured, by a meaning is not the same thing as to express that meaning in a discourse designed to communicate it and reconcile it with other variously received meanings. In this term *received* lies the driving force of what makes discourse a common discourse, a commonly admitted discourse" (63). The hole to which the psychotic responds, the hole constitutive of psychosis, is a gap or absence in the "commonly admitted discourse." Normal subjects don't perceive the hole. For them, the symbolic order is intact and they ignore, as best they can, the ruptures of the Real. The psychotic perceives the hole and reacts to it, but he reacts in a way that he can't fully communicate. The image that covers over or takes the place of the hole doesn't function in the same way for him as it does for normal subjects because for them its place is already occupied. Thus, they can't reconcile the psychotic's image, no matter how certain it may be, with the other meanings constitutive of reality. It is simply not part of a common discourse.

But what if discourse is not common? What if our conditions are characterized by the decline of symbolic efficiency and the presence of a variety of differentiated discursive habitats? What, in other words, if the words of the government are already greeted with skepticism and doubt? Under the intensely mediated conditions of communicative capitalism, texts that might once have remained solitary, like Schreber's, can become part of a group, a scene, a genre, a movement, a community. One can discover that one is not alone, that others feel the same way, have the same doubts and suspicions. Schreber's psychotic writings don't establish a social link. Even as he narrates his experience, his writings remain an object within psychoanalytic discourse. Networked information and communication technologies end this isolation, allowing for the emergence of a discourse of the psychotic, a discourse that reacts to a hole with certainty, fear, distrust, and a permeating sense of meaning.

Because it is built around a hole, an absence, this discourse has trouble communicating its findings, its discoveries, to other discourses, to discourses that have already integrated a signifier in the place of the hole. So even as the psychotic discourse may adopt the patterns of other discourses, the hole which generates its investigations remains unrecognized, disallowed. What it finds meaningful cannot be reconciled in their terms.

As it tries to find acceptance, to be recognized, confirmed, as it tries to transmit its findings, the psychotic discourse tends to hold itself together by mimicking other discourses. It forms itself in their image, as their clone, attempting thereby to attract to itself their already established credibility. Particularly compelling in this psychotic attempt is its reliance on fundamental aspects of language and sociality. Psychotic discourse accentuates the truth that, as Lacan says, "language entirely operates within ambiguity, and most of the time you know absolutely nothing about what you are saying" (115–16). The psychotic confronts us with the lack in language, with indeterminacies we normally overlook. More fundamentally, he reminds us of the violence and irrationality underlying the symbolic order, the way law "is sustained not by reason alone but also by the force / violence of a tautological enunciation, 'The law is the law,' " as Santner explains.[38] The psychotic discourse tries to prevent us from repressing what we already know, undermining thereby the conditions of possibility for credibility.

The Truth of 9 / 11

Accounts of the events of September 11 confront the specific horror of the disintegration of the social link, of the symbolic pact holding society together.[39] The official story emphasizes the incompetence of the U.S. government, its failure to deliver on its trillion dollar defense budget and actually defend. In the face of this overwhelming display of the broken promise of security, Bush repeated, almost daily, his promise to protect the American people, to secure freedom and the American way of life. This repetition reminds us of the loss that compels it.

Part of what gives the administration's account of 9 / 11 its force is the way it hammers home a fact of which we are all secretly aware, namely, that of our underlying passivity, how we are "helplessly thrown around by forces out of our control."[40] Rooted in this passivity, the logic of the incompetence theory is a drive for more power, more security, more surveillance. As it reiterates the meme of loss, the Bush administration seems almost to enjoy its own passivity, its own failure, finding therein a way to ask for, and get, more power.

Fortified by the efforts of the FBI, the CIA, the Department of Defense, and various foreign intelligence agencies, the Bush administration is certain it knows who did it and why. Initially, the administration didn't feel the need to back up its certainty with proof and only reluctantly supplied evidence for its claims. It failed adequately to fund the 9/11 Commission, fought over the release of documents, and resisted testifying before the commission. Bush and Cheney ultimately testified, but in the Oval Office and not under oath. Any notes the commissioners made during the meeting were confiscated. Even as the administration claims to know who did it, it emphasizes that it did not know who was going to do it or when they were going to do it. It didn't have advance warning or information. Its incompetence is thereby rendered as its failure to function properly as a subject supposed to know. It didn't know, but now it does and it will continue to know. And it doesn't matter if anyone believes it. Bush's conviction doesn't depend on polls, on what people think. He acts on what he knows—in his gut, a clear pervert in the Lacanian sense as chapters 3 and 4 explore.

The 9/11 conspiracy theories follow a different circuit. Although certain, their certainty is not, like Bush's, that of the pervert who makes himself an instrument of "the big Other." Rather, it is a psychotic certainty, a certainty that something horrible happened and that the evidence for this horror is clearly before us, if we only know how to see it. They know that some in the administration are not victims but criminals, powerful, wicked, evil criminals able to carry out a conspiracy that took the lives of nearly three thousand Americans, sent the economy into a tailspin, and led to two wars. Countering the official story of passivity, here the government acts, ruthlessly. It's organized, efficient, able to execute its plans without a hitch. Those arguing that 9/11 was an inside job challenge the Bush administration's efforts to reinforce its power by drawing attention to the already excessive obscene power on which the administration rests.

It can already do whatever it wants, whenever it wants, and get away with it. It has the means, the capability, and, most of all, the will. The underlying conviction effect that this view generates, then, lies in its expression of our fundamental unfreedom—an unfreedom the awareness of which we normally repress.

One might wonder why, if the government or a subgroup within it already has this sort of power, would it go to the trouble of taking down the World Trade Center, particularly in the redoubled fashion that appears in emphases on both controlled demolition and airplanes. If the Bush administration, Cheney, or some secret cabal wanted war (and some advocates of alternative explanations point out that plans to invade Afghanistan were already in place as early as June 2001), why would they orchestrate an elaborate attack on U.S. office buildings rather than just go to war? If Bush and Cheney are so powerful, do they really need permission, consent, legitimation? If they wanted to attack Iraq, why didn't they just blame the Iraqis for the destruction of the World Trade Center? Why did they say the hijackers were Saudi and Yemeni—particularly given the close relationship between the Bush family and the House of Saud—instead of saying the hijackers were Iraqi? Why didn't they simply attack Iraq on trumped-up intelligence of an imminent nuclear threat? Given power's demonstrable excess—which is what the 9/11 conspiracy theories demonstrate, what they can't repress—why would power need to display this excess? For whom is it staged?

In the psychotic discourse of 9/11 truth, power is staged for itself. It's the way that power is trying to produce itself as a new world order, a new "big Other" at the site of loss. September 11, in other words, was power's attempt to found a world through the massive expenditure of *jouissance* and the institution of the law. From the standpoint of the conspiracy theories, 9/11 is the founding obscenity or crime that initiates a new order. The primary political task is dissolving this order. Yet at this point, the 9/11 conspiracy theories come up against the passivity underlying their fundamental fantasy—the subjects or, in their words, "sheeple," who fail to share their certainty. And here they overlap with the official discourse on 9/11.

The problem passivity poses is twofold. First, the excess of obscene power is so overwhelming that one is rendered powerless in its presence. In the official discourse, this appears in the impossibility of being able to prevent another attack, in guaranteeing safety. Measures like taking off our shoes and belts and putting liquids in tiny bottles in clear plastic bags accentuate this pervasive helplessness. Anything could happen. Everything is dangerous. Cheney relied on the meme of inevitable attack, accentuating this unavoidable future whenever he could. In the psychotic discourse of 9/11 truth, passivity before power appears in the way that, if the government or a secret cabal of insiders could carry out so effectively the incredible conspiracy of 9/11, then it can do anything. We can do nothing to stop it. Its control is everywhere, an octopus with eye-covered tentacles. Second, insofar as psychotic certainty displaces belief, it comes under the pressure of its own drive. On the one hand, its knowledge persists despite disproof of certain claims. As David Ray Griffin argues, the knowledge of 9/11 is cumulative, not deductive. On the other, such certainty tends to demand uniformity: we can't necessarily believe those in our own movement. Thus, members of the 9/11 truth movement accuse one another of spreading disinformation or producing unreliable and unverifiable studies. We know government is all powerful—and if it's all powerful, how can we trust anything we know? *How do I know I'm not being manipulated?*

This is where the conflict over the truth of September 11 comes up against the hard rock of the Real. And not surprisingly, this doesn't provide us with a way out, with a way through the radically incommensurable perspectives on 9/11. The gap between the official and unofficial accounts of events can't be filled in with a set of facts. It's more fundamental, an indication of the larger decline of symbolic efficiency, diminution of conditions of credibility, and change in the status of knowing and knowledge. As an event that can be signified, it's "never fully verified precisely because . . . there is no external limit to it."[41] The official and unofficial accounts thus perpetually circle around a void that cannot be filled, deriving their enjoyment from the circuit of drive.

Psychotic Media?

What is the role of alternative or progressive media in this environment? My discussion of 9/11 truth shows that new media can be vitally and virally effective. They help build movements and communities. They provide alternative sources of knowledge and information. The counterknowledge they produce enables the emergence, and the flourishing, of epistemologically differentiated spaces. Networked communications—particularly in their continued entanglements with the mainstream media—format the terrain of battle between competing conceptions of the Real.

The subjects navigating these spaces cannot be understood as modernity's typically rational individuals. It's not the case that they simply evaluate the available alternatives, choosing among them on the basis of the best evidence. Far from it. Present subjects have no basis for evaluation, particularly insofar as they confront competing alternatives daily, alternatives about which some are certain, others skeptical, and few actually believe, because of the persistent undermining of belief under conditions of the decline of symbolic efficiency.

The proliferation of contents and voices, sources and alternatives, links and possibilities so vital a counter to corporate media's investments in and support of global capitalism—particularly in its neoliberal form—creates conditions amenable to the flourishing of psychotic discourses. Does it make sense to try to learn from them? Is it possible that endless confrontation with skepticism combined with an inability to repress our knowledge of power's obscene underpinnings could potentially release people from acceptance of the status quo, from the law, from the powers that be? Or does constituent anxiety render us passive, fearful, vulnerable to the lure of the more powerful, the more authoritative? Is the left somehow doomed to a false choice between the embrace of unlimited possible truths and the singular truth of right-wing dogmatism?

While I am pessimistic with regard to the potential of progressive media, seeing it as trapped within and furthering the very suppositions it attempts to combat, my wager is nonetheless for the possibility of breaking out of deadlock around 9/11 that so constrains contemporary left politics in the United States. Confronting our desire for 9/11 is a step in this direction. I don't mean that collectively some group called the American people longed for the destruction of the World Trade Center or hoped for an attack on the Pentagon. Rather, the United States produced the situation within the disintegrated spectacles of communicative capitalism. It desired shock, horror, rupture, some kind of break with the neoliberal confidence, dot-com euphoria, and consumer-oriented cultivation of unique identities characteristic of the Clinton years. Perhaps it is more accurate to say that the events, meanings, and affects linked together and captured by the term 9/11 were an object of intense (and productive) desire.

The Bush administration's appropriation of 9/11 put this desire to work. Rather than presenting the events of September 11 in their complexity—with regard, say, to Europe's past decades of terrorism, the global economic and geopolitical position of the United States, the history of American foreign policy in the Middle East, the repercussions of the Soviet war in Afghanistan and covert U.S. participation in this war, the worldwide market in arms and munitions—the administration locked 9/11 into a simple binary: good versus evil. And for all its preoccupation with the details of the design of the World Trade Center, the training of the 9/11 pilots, the exercises and war games the U.S. military planned for September 11, the truth movement accepts and intensifies this binary. Even as it may seem to deny this desire, projecting it instead onto a malevolent government or faction therein, 9/11 conspiracy theories embrace it. The event is the irrational nugget holding it together, a symptom (or, in Lacanese, *sinthome*) invested with violence and obscenity—rockets, missiles, bombs, explosives, planes filled with passengers taken to secret locations and executed. In each case, the seduction of the opposition between good and evil tells people who they are. It gives them a place in the world, one larger than the ever-fragile and mutable imaginary identities hawked in communicative capitalism.

Without our desire for 9/11, the Bush administration would not have been able to mobilize support for its version of the event. Even as the work of the truth movement raises doubts about the administration's account and even though support for Bush and his so-called war on terror plummeted to new depths in the last year of his administration, most continue to speak in hushed tones about 9/11, to sacralize it, to retain not just respect for the dead but a kind of awe before the event. Among leftists, this awe seems to condition and constrain action, making many wary of being labeled un-American or antipatriotic. At the same time, however, for many of us on the left, the years subsequent to the attacks on the World Trade Center and Pentagon have been invigorating. Just as right-wing righteousness drives what is for all intents and purposes a religious war, a crusade, against Islam, so was left outrage under Bush so much more satisfying than during the cultural wars. But for all our hatred of Bush and his wars, for all the protests and petitions, for all the energy our anger provided, we remained unable or unwilling to take the next steps of imagining, organizing, and creating another world.

The eight years of the Bush administration were a diversion. Intoxicated with a sense of purpose, we could oppose war, torture, indefinite detention, warrantless wiretapping, a seemingly endless series of real crimes. These crimes need to be opposed. Yet such opposition keeps us feeling like we matter while neoliberal capitalism continues to enrich the very, very few and threaten the survival of the planet. We have an ethical sense. But we lack a coherent politics, primarily because we remain attached to our present values.

Introduction

1 Particularly indicative of this tendency was the popularity among left intellectuals of Thomas Frank's *What's the Matter With Kansas?*

2 According to the Pew Research Center, in 2000 the Democratic Party had 33 percent party identification to the Republicans' 28 percent. That is, more people identified as Democrats than as Republicans. In 1999, when leaners (independents leaning one way rather than another) were included, the Democratic advantage was 48 percent to the Republicans' 40 percent. My point is not that Americans had left political views. Rather, it is that leftists overstated the Republicans' advantage as well as the conservatism of the country. See "Democrats Gain Edge in Party Identification," released by the Pew Research Center for the People and the Press, released July 16, 2004. Available at http://people-press.org (accessed July 28, 2008).

3 For an initial elaboration of the notion of communicative capitalism, see my *Publicity's Secret*.

4 An especially compelling discussion is provided in Bauman, *The Individualized Society*.

5 Lenhart, Madden, Macgill, and Smith, "Teens and Social Media."

6 There are important exceptions here. One is Goodin, *Reasons for Welfare*.

7 See my discussion in *Solidarity of Strangers*.

8 In *Publicity's Secret*, I emphasize, *contra* this notion of the victim, the conspiracy and celebrity modes of subjectivization. The conspiracy theorist and the celebrity offer ways for one to subjectivize one's position so as to escape the constraints of the position of the victim. We can think about these options as criticisms in advance, as the ways the dominant culture works to rein in political action by rendering it suspect, illegitimate, and banal or, conversely, the ways that political resistance gets pushed/polarized into paranoid or pseudo-transgressive practices.

9 See Wendy Brown's analysis of the importance of ressentiment and woundedness in identity politics in *States of Injury*.

10   See Connolly, *The Ethos of Pluralization*.

11   For a compelling account of the breast-cancer awareness movement, see King, *Pink Ribbons, Inc.*

12   See his introduction to *Slavoj Žižek Presents Mao*, 17.

13   Rich, *The Greatest Story Ever Sold*, 167–71.

14   Ibid., 163.

15   Žižek, *Organs without Bodies*, 184.

16   An even more compelling example appears in the following account of a company called "Spotrunner" on the blog Edge-generation: strategies for a discontinuous future. According to a post titled "Plasticity and Post-Branding Mini Case Study—Spotrunner": "On Spotrunner, you choose a generic ad, and rebundle it with minor personalized info—your company's name, contact address, etc. The indivisibility of ads has suddenly been vaporized. It's not just that anyone can buy them—when you buy an ad on Spotrunner, you're really buying several rebundled, microchunked goods—so it's that the ad itself has been redefined. This is a perfect example of the way in which microchunking unlocks distributed scale economies—through the reuse and recombination of microchunks. Spotrunner can be hyperefficient not just because it allows access to buying distribution online, but because it microchunks ads, letting them be rebundled—and so reused—making Spotrunner a far more efficient economic solution to buying ads than anything else in its strategic group" (posted January 23, 2006). Multiplicity and variability, the divisibility of what previously seemed indivisible, characterizes the product as well as the strategy behind it. Available at http://www.bubblegeneration.com (accessed October 28, 2008).

17   Frank, *One Market under God*, 305–6.

18   Žižek in *Slavoj Žižek Presents Mao*, 24.

19   Mouffe, *The Democratic Paradox*; Žižek, *The Ticklish Subject*; Ranciere, *Disagreement*; and Brown, "American Nightmare." For a persuasive development of the notion of postdemocracy, see Crouch, *Post-Democracy*.

20   Bauman, *The Individualized Society*, 106.

21   Mouffe, *The Democratic Paradox*, 105. See also Mouffe, *On the Political*.

22   Schmitt, *The Concept of the Political*, 61.

23   Ibid., 38; my emphasis.

24   Ranciere's argument is further complicated by his reading of disruption as the essence of politics and of Plato as a seminal step toward depoliticization. If disruption is the essence of politics, then governance is necessarily depoliticizing. This view of governance allows for a kind of permanent contestation without any responsibility for actual decisions and implementation. The resulting left politics is reduced to a politics of resistance. Additionally, if the problems of depoliticization start with Plato, then how does the term contribute to a diagnosis of the contemporary situation? How is it nothing but the inevitable failure of order?

25   Ranciere, *Disagreement*, 108.

26 Ibid., 110.

27 Žižek, *The Ticklish Subject*, 198–205.

28 Ibid., 209.

29 For elaboration of this point, see my *Žižek's Politics*.

30 Žižek, *The Ticklish Subject*, 204.

31 Ibid., 353.

32 There are of course others. Herbert Marcuse's analysis of "the unification of opposites" that occurs as political and commercial languages merge remains prescient and compelling; see *One Dimensional Man* (1964). Yet insofar as his critique targets the welfare state, technocracy, and the conformity of mass culture, it cannot simply be patched and upgraded as an application to the current setting. For a discussion of the shift from technocracy to technoculture, see chapter 3 of Dean, *Publicity's Secret*.

33 For elaborations of a left ethos of generosity, see Connolly, *The Ethos of Pluralization*; Coles, *Rethinking Generosity*; and White, *Sustaining Affirmation*. See also the debate over postfoundationalism in *Hedgehog Review* 7, no. 2 (Summer 2005).

34 In 2004, 55.3 percent of the voting-age population of the United States turned out for the election. "National Voter Turnout in Federal Elections: 1960–2008," http://www.infoplease.com/ipa/A0781453.html (accessed October 30, 2008). The census bureau reports that 64 percent of U.S. citizens eighteen years of age and older turned out. "Voting and Registration in the Election of November 2004," March 2006, http://www.census.gov (accessed October 30, 2008).

ONE Technology

1 See Dean, *Publicity's Secret*, and "The Networked Empire."

2 Frank, *One Market under God*, 151.

3 I set out the notion of ideology in *Publicity's Secret*.

4 Sassen, *Losing Control?*

5 Harvey, *A Brief History of Neoliberalism*, 3.

6 Colin Crouch identifies similar processes in Europe (primarily Italy and the Netherlands) and Great Britain in his *Post-Democracy*.

7 See Eva Illouz's discussion of the insertion of "communication" as a therapeutic ideal in the heart of corporate culture, in *Cold Intimacies*.

8 Matic and Pantic, "War of Words."

9 My account of antagonism draws from Ernesto Laclau and Slavoj Žižek. For a more thorough elaboration, see Dean, *Žižek's Politics*.

10 For a discussion of the role of speed under neoliberalism, see Armitage and Roberts, "Chronotopia."

11 Actually, one doesn't need to be optimistic or pessimistic to emphasize abundance. Critical analysts of the Internet observe that, contrary to capitalism's supposition that scarcity determines value, the value of the Internet is premised

on abundance. Mark Poster writes, "With the Internet, as with other networked media, a counterposition is installed in which a communication has greater value the more individuals it reaches, the more it multiplies itself, the more common or universal it is," *What's the Matter with the Internet?*, 46. Poster also points out that television advertising is an exception to the idea of scarcity—a television program is more valuable (and hence ad time more expensive) the more popular it is. Contemporary public relations and advertising practices rely on intensifying and expanding brand presence. And here they reassemble other modes of functioning in the capitalist market—the establishment of ubiquity rather than scarcity (McDonald's and Coke come to mind). So rather than indicating that abundance is what makes networked communications so seemingly transformative of capitalist laws of supply and demand, Poster's point reminds us of the limits of those laws—not everything follows the logic of scarcity, ideas and practices (those connected with public health or religious faith, say) perhaps least of all. For an alternative approach to surplus, one that views scarcity as an ideological delusion, see Wark, *A Hacker Manifesto*.

12   See Dean, *Publicity's Secret*, 72–73.

13   A thorough historical analysis of the contribution would spell out the steps involved in the uncoupling of messages from responses. Such an analysis would draw out the ways that responses to the broadly cast messages of television programs were configured as attention and measured in terms of ratings. Nielsen families, in other words, responded for the rest of us. Yet as work in cultural studies, media, and communications has repeatedly emphasized, ratings are not responses and provide little insight into the actual responses of viewers. These actual responses, we can say, are uncoupled from the broadcast message and incorporated into other circuits of communication.

14   Habermas, *The Theory of Communicative Action*, vol. 1: *Reason and the Rationalization of Society*.

15   See Žižek, *The Sublime Object of Ideology*.

16   Barabási, *Linked*, 63. Subsequent page references are given parenthetically in the text.

17   Galloway, *Protocol*, 33.

18   Žižek, *The Plague of Fantasies*, 21.

19   This is one of my primary disagreements with Guy Debord. In addition to relying on a notion of spectacle more suited to mass than personal media, he views the spectacle as supported by an underlying secrecy. See his *Comments on the Society of the Spectacle*.

20   For example, the conservative CATO Institute held a conference in 2004 titled "The Republican Revolution Ten Years Later: Smaller Government or Business as Usual?"

21   Harvey, *A Brief History of Neoliberalism*, 49.

22   Ibid., 42–43.

23   Describing the failure of mainstream feminism to fight for welfare guarantees

for poor mothers, Gwendolyn Mink writes, "A white and middle-class solipsism enforced a general feminist silence about the stakes of welfare provisions for poor women, and that silence gave permission to policy-makers to treat punitive welfare reform as a no-lose situation. Welfare reform did not bear directly on the lives of most white middle-class feminists, and so they did not mobilize their networks and raise their voices as they have in defending abortion rights or protesting domestic violence," *Welfare's End*, 7.

24 American leftists were not wrong in their critique of the welfare state. Historically, its minimal provisions, trapped within states' discretionary powers, were highly moralistic, biased toward the deserving poor, a category which excluded unwed, nonwhite mothers. The struggle to establish that welfare benefits were owed to poor women—and that states could not impose eligibility restrictions —was a long one, fought through the courts (and sometimes through direct action) by groups united into the National Welfare Rights Organization. In fact, it had been in place barely thirty years when Clinton ended even that minimal entitlement to economic assistance. See Mink, *Welfare's End*, chapter 2.

25 Among the key texts in political theory representative of this shift are Laclau and Mouffe, *Hegemony and Socialist Strategy* and Cohen, *Class and Civil Society*.

26 Perelman, *The Confiscation of American Prosperity*, 56.

27 For a recent version of this retreat from the state, see Critchley, *Infinitely Demanding*. Critchley writes, "I think politics should be conceived at a *distance* from the state," 112. Thus, it should come as no surprise that Critchley celebrates the humorous approaches of some contemporary anarchists: "Groups like Pink Bloc or Billionaires for Bush are performing their *powerlessness* in the face of power in a profoundly powerful way," 124. This mindset clearly exemplifies the contemporary failure of the left—a failure to take responsibility for power, in fact, a celebration of powerlessness. It also misreads the performance of the Billionaires in particular: participants dress as the very rich and carry signs such as "More Blood for Oil" and "Save our Gated Communities" in order to take the system at its word; they occupy the position of enunciation of the privileged thereby making it visible as such. For a discussion of "taking the system at its word," see Žižek, *Tarrying with the Negative*, 237.

28 For a longer discussion, see Dean, *Publicity's Secret*.

29 Focusing on Stewart Brand, Fred Turner gives a detailed account of this process in *From Counterculture to Cyberculture*. He writes, "As they turned away from agonistic politics and toward technology, consciousness, and entrepreneurship as the principle of a new society, the communards of the 1960s developed a utopian vision that was in many ways quite congenial to the insurgent Republicans of the 1990s," 8.

30 These bills made explicit a convergence of democracy and capitalism. As the 1996 bill affirmed: "The market will drive both the Internet and the information highway," Dyer-Witheford, *Cyber-Marx*, 34–35.

31 For example, Cass R. Sunstein looks to blogs, wikis, and open-source software

projects as "important supplements to, or substitutes for, ordinary deliberation," *Infotopia*, 148.

32 Dyer-Witheford, "E-Capital and the Many-Headed Hydra," 142.

33 The answer to Mark Poster's question, "Can capitalism still justify itself when the consumer is already a producer?" is thus yes; capitalism has always relied on extracting value from and through consumption. See Poster, *What's the Matter with the Internet?*, 48.

34 Gamson, "Gay Media, Inc.," 259.

35 Ibid., 260.

36 Ibid., 270–71.

37 Sunstein condenses deliberation into a simple matter of information in *Infotopia*.

38 Graham, *Democracy by Disclosure*, 140.

39 Shirky, "Is Social Software Bad for the Dean Campaign?"

40 Freud, "Fetishism," 152–58.

41 I draw from Žižek's elucidation of a concept introduced by Claude Lévi-Strauss. See Žižek, *Enjoy Your Symptom!*, 221–23.

42 See Žižek, "Afterword: Lenin's Choice," 181.

43 Laclau, *Emancipations*, 38.

44 Rogers, "The Issue Has Left the Building."

45 Patelis, "E-Mediation by America Online."

46 See, for example, Sunstein, *Republic.com 2.0*.

47 Wark's vision of two great hostile classes of hackers and vectoralists is an important exception to this tendency. See *A Hacker Manifesto*.

48 For example, see Kahn and Kellner, "Oppositional Politics and the Internet."

49 Boyd, "The Web Rewires the Movement," 14.

50 Ibid., 16.

TWO Free Trade

1 As Wendy Brown argues, neoliberalism "is a constructivist project: it does not presume the ontological givenness of a thoroughgoing economic rationality for all domains of society but rather takes as its task the development, dissemination, and institutionalization of such a rationality," "Neoliberalism and the End of Liberal Democracy," n.p.

2 For a detailed account, see Dean, *Žižek's Politics*, chapter 1.

3 Žižek discusses enjoyment as an ideological factor throughout his work. For a summary, see *Žižek's Politics*, chapter 1.

4 On neoliberalism and corporations, see Pollin, *Contours of Descent*. On neoliberalism and globalization and imperialism, see Colás, "Neoliberalism, Globalisation and International Relations," and Radice, "Neoliberal Globalization: Imperialism without Empires?" On neoliberalism and class power, see Duménil and Lévy, *Capital Resurgent*, and Harvey, *A Brief History of Neoliberalism*. On neoliberalism and governmentality, see Lemke, " 'The Birth of Biopolitics,' " and

Brown, "Neoliberalism and the End of Liberal Democracy." On liberalism and forms of the state, see Passavant, "The Strong Neoliberal State."

5   Lemke," 'The Birth of Biopolitics,' " 10.

6   Ibid., 12.

7   See Harvey, *A Brief History of Neoliberalism*, for a general overview. While nearly all discussions of neoliberalism mention the role of Hayek, some commentators emphasize earlier thinkers and movements as well. Thomas Palley locates the intellectual lineage of contemporary neoliberalism in the laissez-faire economics of nineteenth-century Manchester and the repeal of England's Corn Laws ("From Keynesianism to Neoliberalism"). Simon Clarke locates the foundations of neoliberalism in the work of Adam Smith ("The Neoliberal Theory of Society"). Conversely, Paul Treanor accentuates the differences between Smith's emphasis on property and neoliberalism's emphasis on contract as well as the expansions of the temporal space of the market under neoliberalism ("Neoliberalism"). Lemke, in his reading of unpublished lectures by Foucault, draws attention to Foucault's analysis of German economic liberalism in 1928–30, the Freiburg School or *Ordoliberals*, in relation to the Chicago School. Key to the approach of the *Ordoliberals* was the idea that markets need to be constituted and maintained through political interventions. The Chicago School differs in that rather than endorsing governance in the name and interest of the economy, it treated the social and political spheres themselves as economic domains. In their hands, the state itself is a kind of enterprise. Government practices are thus to be evaluated on the basis of market concepts.

8   George, "A Short History of Neoliberalism."

9   Ronaldo Munck identifies the Pinochet military coup in Chile in 1973 and corresponding restructuring of the economy in accordance with the economic theories of the Chicago School as the first phase of neoliberalism, "Neoliberalism and Politics, and the Politics of Neoliberalism." See also Harvey, *A Short History of Neoliberalism*, 7–9. Harvey, in addition to noting the importance of the Chilean case, finds the management of the New York City fiscal crisis of 1975 crucial to the solidification of neoliberal policies. He writes: "It established the principle that in the event of a conflict between the integrity of financial institutions and bondholders' returns, on the one hand, and the well-being of the citizens on the other, the former was to be privileged. It emphasized that the role of government was to create a good business climate rather than look to the needs and well-being of the population at large," 48.

10 Lebowitz, "Ideology and Economic Development."

11 Duménil and Lévy, "The Neoliberal (Counter-)Revolution."

12 Duménil and Lévy, *Capital Resurgent*.

13 On Bretton Woods, see Lapavitsas, "Mainstream Economics in the Neoliberal Era"; on OPEC, see Lapavitsas and see Pollin, *Contours of Descent*; and on the failure of Keynesianism, see Palley, "From Keynesianism to Neoliberalism," 21.

14 Needless to say, there are exceptions here. My point, however, is that these

exceptions got drowned out, displaced, by left acceptance of the story that capitalism defeated communism, that politics cannot be reduced to class struggle, and that markets are ultimately preferable to state-centered approaches to the economy.

15   See Arestis and Sawyer, "The Neoliberal Experience of the United Kingdom"; and Campbell, "The Birth of Neoliberalism in the United States."

16   Cohen, *A Consumers' Republic*, 393.

17   For a thorough discussion of the ways in which consent to neoliberalism was constructed, see Harvey, *A Short History of Neoliberalism*, chapter 2.

18   Pollin, *Contours of Descent*, 173.

19   Lebowitz, "Ideology and Economic Development," 15–16.

20   Shaikh, "The Economic Mythology of Neoliberalism." See also Perelman, *The Confiscation of American Prosperity*.

21   Žižek, *The Plague of Fantasies*, 6.

22   Ibid., 8.

23   Ibid., 10.

24   Žižek, *The Ticklish Subject*, 4.

25   See Derber, *People before Profit*, 37–38.

26   Global Report on Human Settlements, *The Challenge of Slums*, 40.

27   Žižek, *The Plague of Fantasies*, 32.

28   For an elaboration of the notion of anxiety here, see Copjec, "May '68, the Emotional Month." In the experience of anxiety, Copjec writes, "One has the sense not only of being chained to an enjoyment that outstrips and precedes one, but also of the opacity of this enjoyment, its incomprehensibility and unassumability," 105.

29   Gordon Bigelow describes the early popularity of the notion of the free market among evangelical Christians in England. They believed the free market carried out the will of God, rewarding the good and punishing sinners. Because all are born in sin, "the sweat of hard labor, the fear of poverty, the self-denial involved in saving" provided means of atonement. Helping the poor would deny them this opportunity to atone, and thus damn their immortal souls. See Bigelow, "Let There Be Markets."

30   A fuller account would need to address the importance of global Christian television networks such as the Trinity Broadcasting Company, televangelism, and the growth of Christian publishing, bookstores, and rock music, the emergence, in other words, of an alternative Christian society alongside and within secular civil society. It would also need to consider the Word-Faith or Name It and Claim It thread of charismatic Christianity (an outgrowth of the doctrine of the power of positive thinking) that urges adherents to choose prosperity. Among the more well-known advocates of the gospel of gaining wealth through Jesus are Kenneth Hagin and Kenneth Copeland.

31   Goldberg, *Kingdom Coming*, 58.

32   See http://www.enjoyinggodministries.com (accessed November 10, 2008); http://www.missionmanitou.com (accessed November 10, 2008).

33   For a more thorough elaboration of the superegoic injunction to enjoy, see Žižek, *The Ticklish Subject*, chapter 6, as well as my *Žižek's Politics*.

34   Žižek, *The Plague of Fantasies*, 21.

35   The notion of the obscene supplement comes from Žižek. For elaboration, see Dean, *Žižek's Politics*.

36   Žižek, *The Ticklish Subject*, 315.

37   I explore the fantasies involved in the complex of ideas around publics and publicity in *Publicity's Secret*.

38   Passavant, "The Strong Neoliberal State."

39   For elaboration, see Žižek, *The Ticklish Subject*; Dean, *Publicity's Secret*.

40   Lacan introduces the four discourses following the events of 1968 and elaborates them in Seminar XX, in *On Feminine Sexuality, The Limits of Love and Knowledge, 1972–1973*, 16–17. See Fink, *The Lacanian Subject*, 130; and Dean, *Žižek's Politics*. See also Žižek's discussion of the shift in Lacan, a discussion heavily influenced by Jacques-Alain Miller's reading of Lacan, in Žižek, *Organs without Bodies*, 101; and Žižek, "Class Struggle or Postmodernism?," 116–17.

41   Monbiot, "This is a Dazzling Debunking of Climate Change Science. It Is Also Wildly Wrong."

42   Suskind "Faith, Certainty, and the Presidency of George W. Bush."

43   Hardt and Negri, *Empire*.

44   Information available under "Charts & Trends: Household & Family Structure" at http://www.censusscope.org.

45   In 1983, 20 percent of workers belonged to a union. Information available at http://www.bls.gov.

46   For a discussion of civil society and new social movements, see Arato and Cohen, *Civil Society and Political Theory*.

47   Alexander R. Galloway views computer protocols as additional such mechanisms of contemporary control; as conditions for access and communication, protocols encode appropriate behavior in advance, as it were. See *Protocol*. Galloway's work makes particularly clear why it is the case that "control" should not be thought of in simple binary terms such that something is either under control or not, but should rather be understood as codes, techniques, and arrangements that distribute and manage.

48   Žižek, *The Ticklish Subject*, 368.

49   Žižek refers to this as the "direct super-egoization of the imaginary ideal," *The Ticklish Subject*, 368. For an account of the superego as commanding enjoyment, see Žižek, *The Plague of Fantasies*, 114, and Dean, *Žižek's Politics*, 32–41.

50   The classic account of ideological interpellation comes from Althusser, "Ideology and Ideological State Apparatuses."

51   Žižek, *The Parallax View*, 310.

52   One might want to argue that the illegal immigrant provides yet another imaginary identity. The very use of the term *illegal*, however, draws our attention to the way that neoliberalism relies on the image of the criminal as a strange attractor for combining those disadvantaged through and by neoliberal globalization.

53   See Žižek, "Class Struggle or Postmodernism?," 116.

54   Schor, *The Overspent American.*

55   Brown "Quality of Life," and Taylor, "The Personal Level"; Frank, *Luxury Fever.*

56   Munck, "Neoliberalism and Politics," 65.

57   Miller, *A Theory of Shopping.*

58   Kane, "The Bankruptcy Bill and Debt Obesity."

59   Louie, " 'Black Friday' Shopping Frenzy."

60   Garland, *The Culture of Control,* 10.

61   Passavant, "The Strong Neoliberal State."

62   Garland, *The Culture of Control,* 15. (Subsequent page references are given parenthetically in the text.)

63   Simon, " 'Entitlement to Cruelty,' " 127.

64   The most influential theorization of the centrality of political identity is in the work (together and separately) of Ernesto Laclau and Chantal Mouffe. In his recent writing, for example, Laclau writes, "The construction of a 'people' is the *sine qua non* of democratic functioning," *On Populist Reason,* 169.

65   Žižek writes, "What prevents the radical questioning of capitalism itself is precisely *belief in the democratic form of the struggle against capitalism,*" *The Parallax View,* 320; original emphasis.

THREE Democracy

1   For a thorough discussion of Žižek's critique of democracy, see Dean, *Žižek's Politics.*

2   I am drawing here from Ernesto Laclau's discussion of universalization under conditions of uneven power relations; see Laclau, "Stucture, History, and the Political." Laclau argues that when power relations are uneven, universality depends on particularity, on the possibility of a particular element coming to stand for something other than itself. The supposition of democracy disavows the incommensurability necessary for universality as it presumes itself to be the solution to its problems—the answer to any problem with democracy is more democracy. For elaboration of this point, see Dean, "Secrecy since September 11th."

3   Buchstein and Jörke, "Redescribing Democracy."

4   Habermas, "Discourse Ethics," 66.

5   See, for example, Chambers, *Reasonable Democracy.*

6   This point applies to theories of radical democracy such as Laclau's and Mouffe's as well.

7   See Schmitt, *The Crisis of Parliamentary Democracy,* especially chapter 2.

8   There are of course good historical reasons for the primacy of "one" discourse. While an adequate account of these reasons is beyond the scope of this essay, such an account would necessarily draw out the connections between scientific discourse, Enlightenment accounts of reason, and critiques of absolutism anchored in a reason with claims to universal validity because of their kinship with science. Thomas Hobbes, then, would figure in such an account.

9   Lacan, *On Feminine Sexuality*, 16–17; Žižek, *Iraq*, 131–57.

10   Žižek, *Iraq*, 144.

11   Ibid.

12   See, for example, "Remarks by the President at the 20th Anniversary of the National Endowment for Democracy," November 2003, available at http://www.whitehouse.gov (accessed July 28, 2008).

13   Gutmann and Thompson, *Why Deliberative Democracy?*, 7. (Subsequent page references are given parenthetically in the text.)

14   Post from February 28, 2005, http://jdeanicite.typepad.com.

15   For the sake of clarity, I've omitted the specific Lacanian formulae for each of these discourses. A thorough elaboration appears in my *Žižek's Politics*.

16   Žižek, *Iraq*, 133–45.

17   Diane Rubenstein also reads Bush's relation to law as perverse. See *This Is Not a President*, 193–96.

18   Claude Lefort, *Democracy and Political Theory*.

19   Text of address available at http://www.whitehouse.gov.

20   "Bush: 'I'm the decider' on Rumsfeld," April 18, 2006. Available at http://www.cnn.com.

21   In Joan Copjec's words, "The pervert is a pure, pathos-less instrument of the Other's will," *Imagine There's No Woman*, 229.

22   See Žižek, *Tarrying with the Negative*, 122–24.

23   Ibid., 122.

24   Ibid.

25   For a more thorough argument on this point, see Dean, "Enemies Imagined and Symbolic."

26   Žižek, *Iraq*, 134.

27   Ibid., 139.

28   See Schmitt, *The Concept of the Political*, 35.

29   Gutmann and Thompson are thus incapable of responding to one of Schmitt's central claims: "The political entity is by its very nature the decisive entity, regardless of the source from which it derives its last psychic motives. It exists or does not exist. If it exists, it is the supreme, that is, the decisive case, the authoritative entity," *The Concept of the Political*, 43–44.

FOUR Resolve

1   David Frum recounts the process through which Bush's speech was written,
    highlighting the thinking that went into his adoption of the phrase "axis of
    hatred" and Bush's chief speechwriter, Michael Gerson's, substitution of "evil"
    for "hatred." See *The Right Man*, 231–39.

2   My theorization here is informed by Slavoj Žižek's reading of Hegel. See, for
    example, Žižek, *For They Know Not What They Do*, 33–46, and Žižek, *The
    Ticklish Subject*, 88–89.

3   Susan Friend Harding writes, "Fundamentalists, and born-again Christians gen-
    erally, do not simply *believe*, they *know*, that the Bible is true and is still coming
    true, that God speaks to them, and that Jesus dies so that they may live," *The
    Book of Jerry Falwell*, 272. In using the terms *believe* and *know*, I am follow-
    ing Žižek's account of Lacan's *subject-supposed-to-know* and *subject-supposed-to-
    believe*. See Žižek, *The Plague of Fantasies*, 106–9.

4   I am not saying that those who heard Bush's speech necessarily agreed with him.
    That resolve championed by conservatives was heavily criticized by more mod-
    erate, less unilateral voices. Rather, my aim is to account for (provide the
    conditions of possibility for) the use of a specific phrase. I am attempting to
    make explicit or bring to the fore the differing and likely contradictory supposi-
    tions that could underlie the sense of White House speechwriters, administra-
    tion officials, and political pundits that such a phrase would capture the mo-
    ment, accomplish their goals, or resonate in powerful ways.

5   Perhaps a third possible explanation might be found in what Michael Rogin
    refers to as "political demonology" and the "countersubversive tradition" in
    American politics. He uses these terms to designate "the creation of monsters as
    a continuing feature of American politics by the inflation, stigmatization, and
    dehumanization of political foes"; see *Ronald Reagan, the Movie and Other
    Episodes in Political Demonology*, xiii. While Bush's use of the term *evil* can be
    viewed in light of this feature of American politics, my concern is with the actual
    word *evil* rather than demonization more generally. For a critique of Rogin's
    reading of Reagan as a sign (and consequent failure to grapple with what is
    epistemically significant about Reagan as a hyperreal object), see Rubenstein,
    This Is Not a President, chapter 2.

6   See, for example, Nordlinger, "Ashcroft with Horns."

7   For an account that emphasizes the loss of a sense and language of evil, see
    Delbanco, *The Death of Satan*.

8   See, for example, Kurtz, "Postmodernism Kills." Kurtz, a research fellow at the
    Hoover Institution at Stanford University, insists not only that "postmodernism
    can kill you" but also that postmodern professors believe "that America is an *evil*
    imperialist power which it would be immoral to aid in any way" (emphasis in
    original).

9   From the standpoint of the hawks in the Bush administration, the link between

these regimes is clear: they are rogue regimes bent on developing weapons of mass destruction. These are the three regimes Condoleezza Rice identifies as rogues and threats to U.S. interests in "Promoting the National Interest." There she urges the United States to mobilize whatever resources it can to remove Saddam Hussein. And she refers to North Korea as the "evil twin of a successful regime just across its border" (60). Analyzing the first Gulf War, Michael J. Shapiro points out the use of the term *weapons of mass destruction* as enabling "a geopolitical category that is aimed at saving our identity-affirming cartography." See *Violent Cartographies*, 104. Clearly, WMDs function in Rice's essay as the content enabling the category "rogue regime" and securing as well the imaginary moral geography of the "axis of evil."

10 Survey results from "The 2004 Political Landscape," Pew Research Center for the People and the Press, released November 5, 2003 and available at http://people-press.org (accessed July 28, 2008).

11 One who would and does deny the political impact of the religious right is Ann Coulter, in *Slander*. Coulter argues that the religious right is a "mythical enemy" created by liberals "to justify their own viciousness and advance their agenda," 211. "Loathing of the religious right has become an end in itself," she writes, "a consuming passion. Liberals denounce Christian conservatives for being moralistic, for imposing their morality on others, for not separating morality from politics, and for bringing religious zeal to public life—and then work themselves into a frothing frenzy of righteous, moralistic zeal over their own moral excellence for being so rational, calm, and detached," 247.

12 Some of the best studies in this large and fascinating field include Apostolidis, *Stations of the Cross*, and Harding, *The Book of Jerry Falwell*.

13 Baugh, *The Battle for Baptist Integrity* (Austin, Texas: Battle for Baptist Integrity, Inc., no date). Copies may be requested by fax: (512) 327–0944.

14 Frum, *The Right Man*, 238.

15 Fineman, "Bush and God," 22 ff.

16 See Jane Bennett's and Michael Shapiro's introduction to *The Politics of Moralizing*. They write: "The diagnosis of moral depletion—defined as a loss of shared values—makes the most sense in relation to an ideal of cultural life as an organic whole whose parts tend toward a state of equilibrium," 2.

17 Thus, Susan Neiman, powerfully rereads the history of continental philosophy as a struggle with the reality of evil in the world. See her *Evil in Modern Thought*.

18 See Žižek's discussion in *The Ticklish Subject*, 290–97.

19 See, for example, Morrow, *Evil*. This collection of short pieces on evil is less an investigation than a set of lists, reflections, and narratives of pain and horror to establish the permanence of evil and the importance of recognizing "evil for what it is," 13. A typical claim: "Evil is the most powerful word in the language, and the most elusive," 7.

20 Morrow, "The Real Meaning of Evil," 74.

21 For an account of performative contradictions, see Habermas, *Moral Conscious-*

ness and Communicative Action, especially 79–92. For a discussion of the symptom as "a particular element which subverts its own universal foundation," see Žižek, *The Sublime Object of Ideology,* 21.

22   Frum, *The Right Man,* 231.

23   Delivered on January 28, 2003 and available at http://www.whitehouse.gov. For a compelling discussion of torture in terms of perversion, one that helps clarify the Bush administration's own infatuation with torture, see Copjec, *Imagine There's No Woman,* 228–29.

24   Bennett and Shapiro, *The Politics of Moralizing,* 4.

25   Bercovitch, *The American Jeremiad.*

26   All presidential inaugural addresses can be found at http://www.bartleby.com.

27   This speech is available in Merrill and Patterson, eds., *Major Problems in American Foreign Relations,* vol. 2, 220–22.

28   Ibid., 221.

29   Harry S. Truman, "Annual Message to the Congress on the State of the Union, January 8, 1951." Available at http://www.trumanlibrary.org.

30   This pattern applies even to his famous "military-industrial-complex" speech in which evil does not appear.

31   Available at http://www.bartleby.com.

32   Frum reports that Bush hung a portrait of Eisenhower in the Cabinet Room and placed a bust of him in the Oval Office. "Why Ike? It might have been Bush's way of reminding his critics that he was not the first president to be ridiculed for his mangled syntax. But I think there was something more to Bush's choice: Eisenhower represented the kind of president that Bush wanted to be—a leader above party, a leader who drew his power from personal authority," *The Right Man,* 53–54.

33   See, respectively, "Commencement Address at American University," June 10, 1963, and "Remarks in the Rudolph Wilde Platz," West Berlin, June 26, 1963. Both are available at http://www.kennedylibrary.org.

34   "Radio and Television Address to the American People on the Nuclear Test Ban Treaty," July 26, 1963. Available at http://www.kennedylibrary.org.

35   "Address Before a Joint Session of Congress," November 27, 1963. Available at http://www.lbjlib.utexas.edu.

36   See his "Commencement Address at Howard University: To Fulfill These Rights," June 4, 1965. Available at http://www.lbjlib.utexas.edu.

37   Nixon's first inaugural address was delivered on January 20, 1969, and is available at http://www.nixonlibraryfoundation.org. Predictably cynical comments at this point might treat Nixon's appeal to listening in less lofty terms by emphasizing that this was how Nixon could hear the "silent majority" or why he embraced wire-tapping.

38   Ford's address is available at http://www.ford.utexas.edu.

39   President Jimmy Carter's "Crisis of Confidence" speech was delivered on July 15,

1979. A transcript is available at http://www.pbs.org/wgbh/americanexperi ence, accessed November 18, 2008.

40 See the speeches collected at http://www.reagan.utexas.edu.

41 Rogin, *Ronald Reagan*, xv. I should note here that Rogin is discussing a specific speech Reagan gave about Nicaragua. Insofar as Rogin treats this speech as indicative of Reagan's general position as a representative of the American countersubversive tradition, however, my critical point applies.

42 Ibid., xvii.

43 See, for example, Reagan's "Remarks on Rewarding the Presidential Medal of Freedom to the Late Senator Henry M. Jackson of Washington," June 26, 1984. Reagan observes, "Henry Jackson understood that there is great good in the world and great evil, too, that there are saints and sinners among us. He had no illusions about totalitarians, but his understanding of the existence of evil didn't sour or dishearten him. He had a great hope and great faith in America." Available at http://www.reagan.utexas.edu.

44 Asking whether freedom must "wither in a quiet deadening accommodation with totalitarian evil," Reagan, in a speech before the British House of a Commons in June 1982, invokes a moral struggle between the forces of good and the forces of evil. The speech was widely criticized for its apocalypticism, primitivism, and its outrageous admixing of religion and politics. Text of the speech is available at http://odur.let.rug.nl/usa/P/rr40/speeches/empire.htm; the speech can be heard at http://www.americanrhetoric.com.

45 In a radio address given during Easter, three years after the "evil empire" speech, Reagan notes that few commentators properly contextualized his point about opposing totalitarian and communist dictators. Reagan explains that he had been talking about America's own spiritual problems and its legacy of evil with respect to racism, anti-Semitism, and other forms of intolerance. See "Radio Address to the Nation on International Violence and Democratic Values," March 29, 1986. Available at http://www.reagan.utexas.edu.

46 "Interview with Henry Brandon of the London Sunday Times and News Service on Domestic and Foreign Policy Issues," March 18, 1983. Available at http://www.reagan.utexas.edu.

47 "Democracy's Next Battle," Oxford Union Society Address by Ronald Reagan, December 4, 1992. I was unable to find a copy of this speech online. The Reagan Library, however, kindly faxed me a copy. Their phone number is (800) 410-8354. I'm indebted to Desiree Harvey for her diligence in securing this text. See also "Reagan: 'Evil Still Stalks the Planet,'" *Washington Post*, December 5, 1992, a19.

48 Rogin describes a number of Reagan's movies and roles, reading them, however, as a confusion between life and film rather than as an alliance between the imaginary and the Real in the wake of the decline of symbolic efficiency.

49 Fineman, "Bush and God," 24.

50   See also Rubenstein's discussion of Bush in terms of perversion, *This Is Not a President*, 192–96.

51   Žižek, *The Ticklish Subject*, 248. See also my discussion in *Publicity's Secret*, chapter 4.

52   Bruni, *Ambling into History*, 32.

53   Ibid., 88.

54   Ibid., 87.

55   Rubenstein highlights Bush's frequent verbal slip-ups—"I know how hard it is to put food on your families"—as evidence of his failed introjection of the father function and hence perverse psychic structure, *This Is Not a President*, 181–82.

56   Frum, *The Right Man*, 273–74. See also Bruni, *Ambling into History*, 239–43.

57   For a compelling analysis of the biblical sources of Bush's rhetoric (an analysis that usefully compares Bush's language to Osama bin Laden's), see Lincoln, *Holy Terrors*.

58   Frum, *The Right Man*, 148.

59   Bruni, *Ambling into History*, 255.

60   George W. Bush's speech to a joint session of Congress, September 20, 2001, can be heard at http://www.americanrhetoric.com.

61   "Terror Coverage Boosts News Media's Images," Pew Research Center for People and the Press, survey report released November 28, 2001. Available at http://people-press.org (accessed July 28, 2008).

62   Žižek, *The Plague of Fantasies*, 63.

63   "Powell, Rice Defend Bush's 'Axis of Evil' Speech," CNN.com, February 18, 2002. Available at http://www.cnn.com (accessed July 28, 2008).

FIVE Ethics

1   Butler, *Giving an Account of Oneself*, 108. Hereafter cited in the text as *Giving*.

2   See Žižek, "Neighbors and Other Monsters," 137.

3   Foucault, "Governmentality," 102.

4   Butler, *Excitable Speech*, 78. Hereafter cited in the text as *ES*.

5   See Passavant, *No Escape*.

6   I should note here that Žižek does not view this closure as final; rather, throughout his work he emphasizes possibilities for rupture, as in, for example, the radical act that changes the coordinates of a situation, in Lacan's feminine formulae for sexuation that present a logic of the non-all, and in the gaps and ruptures inherent in the material structures in which we find ourselves. In what follows, I draw from Eric Santner's specific figuring of these gaps as stresses that call to and excite the subject.

7   Žižek, *The Ticklish Subject*, 369.

8   Butler, *Precarious Life*, 20. Hereafter cited in the text as *PL*. I am not sure how new these bases are. Judith Shklar, for example, theorizes liberalism by prioritizing a fundamental hatred of cruelty. See her *Ordinary Vices*.

9   Passavant, "The Strong Neoliberal State."

10   Ibid.

11   Sassen, *Losing Control?*

12   Žižek, *The Fragile Absolute*, 40.

13   See Žižek, *The Parallax View*, 297.

14   See Dean, *Žižek's Politics*, chapter 4.

15   *The Parallax View*, 10.

16   Ibid., 370.

17   "Neighbors and Other Monsters," 159–60.

18   Ibid., 160.

19   Santner, "Miracles Happen," 86–87.

20   Ibid., 89.

six   Certainty

1   "Half of New Yorkers Believe U.S. Leaders Had Foreknowledge of Impending 9/11 Attacks and Consciously Failed to Act; 66% Call for New Probe of Unanswered Questions by Congress of New York's Attorney General, New Zogby International Poll Reveals," Zogby International, August 30, 2004. Available at http://www.zogby.com, accessed February 20, 2009.

2   "Americans Question Bush on 9/11 Intelligence," *Angus Reid Global Monitor*, October 14, 2006. Available at http://www.angus-reid.com, accessed November 24, 2008.

3   Hargrove and Stemple, "Anti-Government Anger Spurs 9/11 Conspiracy Beliefs."

4   In *Aliens in America* I take up belief in extraterrestrial life and alien abduction as a way of exploring the construction of a consensual space via the exclusion of competing conceptions of the real.

5   Fetzer, "Scholars on its First Anniversary."

6   Žižek, *The Parallax View*, 61.

7   Ibid., 61–62.

8   I am indebted to Mladen Dolar for this formulation.

9   Dunbar and Reagan, eds., *Debunking 9/11 Myths*, xv.

10   Ibid.

11   Brooks, "The Paranoid Style," A31.

12   Krugman, "Who's Crazy Now?" Krugman also points out that critics of the Bush administration have often been disparaged as conspiracy theorists.

13   Available at http://www.whitehouse.gov.

14   "The Top September 11th Conspiracy Theories," America.gov, October 25, 2006. Available at http://www.america.gov, accessed February 20, 2009.

15   DeMott, "Whitewash as Public Service," 36.

16   Describing the emergence of a network of independent researchers after 9/11 in "Intersecting Facts and Theories on 9/11," Joseph P. Firmage writes, "While the research involved in this truly *independent* investigation are of varying discipline

and credentials, there is little question that the best of them have done a highly
competent job of: (1) employing only credible sources to assemble as complete
a picture of 9/11-related facts as is possible without access to classified material."

17   See Dean, *Aliens in America.*

18   Nancy Jo Sales, "Click Here for Conspiracy."

19   Grossman, "Why the 9/11 Conspiracies Won't Go Away."

20   "Scholars Repudiate Official Version of 9/11," Scholars for 9/11 Truth press
     release, January 27, 2006. Available at http://twilightpines.com, accessed No-
     vember 24, 2008.

21   A version of this paper appears as Jones, "Why Indeed Did the World Trade
     Center Buildings Completely Collapse?"

22   Gravois, "Professors of Paranoia?"

23   Pope, "9/11 Conspiracy Theorists Thriving."

24   Victoria Ashley, "Steven E. Jones: A Physics Professor Speaks Out on 9/11;
     Reason, Publicity, and Reaction," 9–11 Research.com, January 14, 2006. Avail-
     able at http://911research.wtc7.net, accessed February 20, 2009.

25   Twohey, "UW Lecturer's 9–11 Media Blitz Is Rapped."

26   Comment posted at http://www.alaskafreepress.com/msgboard/board/10,
     accessed January 27, 2007. Website no longer available.

27   Fetzer, "An Open Letter about Steve Jones."

28   Wood and Reynolds, "The Scientific Method Applied to the Thermite Hypoth-
     esis"; and "Why Indeed Did the WTC Buildings Disintegrate?"

29   "The Scientific Method Applied to the Thermite Hypothesis."

30   Wood and Reynolds, "Why Indeed Did the WTC Buildings Disintegrate? A
     Peer-Review of Steven E. Jones' 9/11 Research," No More Games.Net, August
     23, 2006. Available at http://nomoregames.net (accessed February 20, 2009).

31   See Wood's website, http://drjudywood.com (accessed November 24, 2008).

32   Transcript, "The Dynamic Duo with Jim Fetzer," January 2, 2007. Available at
     http://www.911scholars.org, accessed January 27, 2007.

33   Holmgren, "Scholars for 9/11 Plagiarism and Disinformation."

34   Available at http://members.iinet.net.au/%7Eholmgren/intro.html, accessed
     January 27, 2007.

35   Cited in Žižek, *The Fragile Absolute,* 114.

36   Santner, *My Own Private Germany.* (Subsequent page references are given pa-
     renthetically in the text.)

37   Lacan, *The Psychoses, 1955–1956,* 74. This source is hereafter cited in the text.

38   Santner, *My Own Private Germany,* 11.

39   See Žižek, *The Parallax View,* 174.

40   Ibid., 344.

41   Ibid., 167.

Althusser, Louis. "Ideology and Ideological State Apparatuses." In *Mapping Ideology*, edited by Slavoj Žižek, 100–140. London: Verso, 1994.

Apostolidis, Paul. *Stations of the Cross: Adorno and Christian Right Radio.* Durham: Duke University Press, 2000.

Arato, Andrew, and Jean L. Cohen. *Civil Society and Political Theory.* Cambridge: MIT Press, 1992.

Arestis, Philip, and Malcolm Sawyer. "The Neoliberal Experience of the United Kingdom." In Saad-Fiho and Johnston, eds., *Neoliberalism: A Critical Reader*, 199–207.

Armitage, John, and Joanne Roberts. "Chronotopia." In *Living with Cyberspace: Technology and Society in the Twenty-First Century*, edited by Armitage and Roberts, 43–54. London: Continuum, 2002.

Barabási, Albert-László. *Linked.* New York: Plume, 2003.

Bauman, Zygmunt. *The Individualized Society.* Cambridge: Polity, 2001.

Bennett, Jane and Michael Shapiro, eds. *The Politics of Moralizing.* New York: Routledge, 2002.

Bercovitch, Sacvan. *The American Jeremiad.* Madison: University of Wisconsin Press, 1978.

Bigelow, Gordon. "Let There Be Markets: The Evangelical Roots of Economics." *Harper's Magazine*, May 2005, 33–38.

Boyd, Andrew. "The Web Rewires the Movement." *Nation*, August 4, 2003.

Brand, Stewart, and Fred Turner. *From Counterculture to Cyberculture.* Chicago: University of Chicago Press, 2006.

Brooks, David. "The Paranoid Style." *New York Times*, May 4, 2006.

Brown, Clair. "Quality of Life." In Juliet Schor, *Do Americans Shop Too Much?*, edited by Joshua Cohen and Joel Rogers, 53–56. Boston: Beacon, 2000.

Brown, Wendy. "American Nightmare: Neoliberalism, Neoconservatism, and De-Democraticization." *Political Theory* 34, no. 6 (December 2006): 690–714.

———. "Neoliberalism and the End of Liberal Democracy." *Theory and Event* 7, no. 1 (2003): n.p.

———. *States of Injury.* Princeton: Princeton University Press, 1996.

Bruni, Frank. *Ambling into History: The Unlikely Odyssey of George W. Bush.* New York: HarperCollins, 2002.

Buchstein, Hubertus, and Dirk Jörke. "Redescribing Democracy." *Redescriptions* 11 (2007): 178–201.

Butler, Judith. *Excitable Speech: A Politics of the Performative.* New York: Routledge, 1997.

———. *Giving an Account of Oneself.* New York: Fordham University Press, 2005.

———. *Precarious Life: The Powers of Mourning and Violence.* London: Verso, 2003.

Butler, Judith, Ernesto Laclau, and Slavoj Žižek. *Contingency, Hegemony, Universality.* London: Verso, 2000.

Campbell, Al. "The Birth of Neoliberalism in the United States: A Reorganization of Capitalism." In Saad-Fiho and Johnston, eds., *Neoliberalism: A Critical Reader,* 87–98.

Chambers, Simone. *Reasonable Democracy: Jürgen Habermas and the Politics of Discourse.* Ithaca: Cornell University Press, 1996.

Clarke, Simon. "The Neoliberal Theory of Society." In Saad-Fiho and Johnston, eds., *Neoliberalism: A Critical Reader,* 50–59.

Cohen, Jean L. *Class and Civil Society: The Limits of Marxian Critical Theory.* Amherst: University of Massachusetts Press, 1987.

Cohen, Lizbeth. *A Consumers' Republic: The Politics of Mass Consumption in Post-War America.* New York: Alfred A. Knopf, 2003.

Colás, Alejandro. "Neoliberalism, Globalisation and International Relations." In Saad-Fiho and Johnston, eds., *Neoliberalism: A Critical Reader,* 70–79.

Coles, Romand. *Rethinking Generosity.* Ithaca: Cornell University Press, 1997.

Connolly, William E. *The Ethos of Pluralization.* Minneapolis: University of Minnesota Press, 1995.

Copjec, Joan. *Imagine There's No Woman.* Cambridge: MIT Press, 2002.

———. "May '68, the Emotional Month," In *Lacan, the Silent Partner,* edited by Slavoj Žižek, 90–114. London: Verso, 2006.

Coulter, Ann. *Slander: Liberal Lies about the American Right.* New York: Three Rivers Press, 2002.

Critchley, Simon. *Infinitely Demanding: Ethics of Commitment, Politics of Resistance.* London: Verso, 2007.

Crouch, Colin. *Post-Democracy.* London: Polity, 2004.

Dean, Jodi. *Aliens in America: Conspiracy Cultures from Outerspace to Cyberspace.* Ithaca: Cornell University Press, 1998.

———. "Enemies Imagined and Symbolic." *Philosophy and Social Criticism* 31, no. 4 (June 2005): 499–509.

——. "The Networked Empire: Communicative Capitalism and the Hope for Politics." In Passavant and Dean, eds., *Empire's New Clothes*, 265–88.

——. *Publicity's Secret: How Technoculture Capitalizes on Democracy.* Ithaca: Cornell University Press, 2002.

——. "Secrecy since September 11th." *Interventions* 6, no. 3 (2004): 362–80.

——. *Solidarity of Strangers: Feminism after Identity Politics.* Berkeley: University of California Press, 1996.

——. *Žižek's Politics.* New York: Routledge, 2006.

Debord, Guy. *Comments on the Society of the Spectacle.* Translated by Malcolm Imrie. London: Verso, 1998.

Delbanco, Andrew. *The Death of Satan.* New York: Farrar, Straus and Giroux, 1995.

DeMott, Benjamin. "Whitewash as Public Service." *Harper's Magazine*, October 2004, 35–45.

Derber, Charles. *People before Profit.* New York: St. Martin's Press, 2002.

Duménil, Gérard, and Dominique Lévy. *Capital Resurgent: Roots of the Neoliberal Revolution.* Translated by Derek Jeffords. Cambridge: Harvard University Press, 2004.

——. "The Neoliberal (Counter-)Revolution." In Saad-Fiho and Johnston, eds., *Neoliberalism: A Critical Reader*, 9–19.

Dunbar, David, and Brad Reagan, eds. *Debunking 9/11 Myths: Why Conspiracy Theories Can't Stand Up to the Facts.* New York: Hearst, 2006.

Dyer-Witheford, Nick. *Cyber-Marx.* Champaign: University of Illinois Press, 1999.

——. "E-Capital and the Many-Headed Hydra." In *Critical Perspectives on the Internet*, edited by Greg Elmer, 129–64. Lanham, Md.: Rowman and Littlefield, 2002.

Fetzer, James H. "An Open Letter about Steve Jones," November 19, 2006. http://www.scholarsfor911truth.org/OpenLetterToJones.html (accessed November 24, 2007).

——. "Scholars on its First Anniversary," November 25, 2006. http://www.911schol ars.org (accessed July 28, 2008).

Fineman, Howard. "Bush and God." *Newsweek*, March 10, 2003, 22ff.

Fink, Bruce. *The Lacanian Subject.* Princeton: Princeton University Press, 1995.

Firmage, Joseph P. "Intersecting Facts and Theories on 9/11." *Journal of 9/11 Studies* 2 (2006). http://www.journalof911studies.com (accessed July 28, 2008).

Foucault, Michel, "Governmentality." In *The Foucault Effect: Studies in Governmentality*, edited by Graham Burchell, Colin Gordon, and Peter Miller, 87–104. Chicago: University of Chicago Press, 1991.

Frank, Robert H. *Luxury Fever.* Princeton: Princeton University Press, 1999.

Frank, Thomas. *One Market under God.* New York: Doubleday, 2000.

——. *What's the Matter with Kansas?* New York: Metropolitan Books, 2004.

Freud, Sigmund, "Fetishism." In *The Standard Edition of the Complete Psychological Works of Sigmund Freud.* Volume 22 (1927–1931), edited by James Strachey, 152–58. London: Hogarth, and the Institute for Psychoanalysis, 1961.

Frum, David. *The Right Man: The Surprise Presidency of George W. Bush*. New York: Random House, 2003.

Galloway, Alexander R. *Protocol: How Control Exists after Decentralization*. Cambridge: MIT Press, 2004.

Gamson, Joshua. "Gay Media, Inc.: Media Structures, the New Gay Conglomerates, and Collective Sexual Identities." In *Cyberactivism: Online Activism in Theory and Practice*, edited by Martha McCaughey and Michael D. Ayers, 255–78. New York: Routledge, 2003.

Garland, David. *The Culture of Control*. Chicago: University of Chicago Press, 2001.

George, Susan. "A Short History of Neoliberalism." Paper presented at the Conference on Economic Sovereignty in a Globalizing World, Bangkok, March 24–26, 1999. http://www.globalpolicy.org/globaliz/econ/histneol.htm (accessed July 16, 2007).

Global Report on Human Settlements. *The Challenge of Slums*. United Nations Human Settlements Programme. London: Earthscan Publications, 2003.

Goldberg, Michelle. *Kingdom Coming: The Rise of Christian Nationalism*. New York: W. W. Norton, 2006.

Goodin, Robert E. *Reasons for Welfare: The Political Theory of the Welfare State*. Princeton: Princeton University Press, 1988.

Graham, Mary. *Democracy by Disclosure: The Rise of Technopopulism*. Washington, D.C.: Brookings Institution, 2002.

Gravois, John. "Professors of Paranoia?" *Chronicle of Higher Education*, June 23, 2006. http://chronicle.com (accessed July 28, 2008).

Grossman, Lev. "Why the 9/11 Conspiracies Won't Go Away." *Time*, September 11, 2006. http://www.time.com (accessed July 28, 2008).

Gutmann, Amy, and Dennis Thompson. *Why Deliberative Democracy?* Princeton: Princeton University Press, 2004.

Habermas, Jürgen. "Discourse Ethics: Notes on a Program of Philosophical Justification." In *Moral Consciousness and Communicative Action*. Translated by Christian Lenhardt and Shierry Weber Nicholsen, 43–115. Cambridge: MIT Press, 1990.

———. *The Theory of Communicative Action*. Volume 1: *Reason and the Rationalization of Society*. Translated by Thomas McCarthy. Boston: Beacon Press, 1984.

Harding, Susan Friend. *The Book of Jerry Falwell: Fundamentalist Language and Politics*. Princeton: Princeton University Press, 2000.

Hardt, Michael, and Antonio Negri. *Empire*. Cambridge: Harvard University Press, 2000.

Hargrove, Thomas, and Guido H. Stemple III. "Anti-Government Anger Spurs 9/11 Conspiracy Beliefs." Scripps Howard New Service, August 2, 2006. http://news polls.org (accessed July 28, 2008).

Harvey, David. *A Brief History of Neoliberalism*. New York: Oxford University Press, 2005.

Holmgren, Gerard. "Scholars for 9/11 Plagiarism and Disinformation," February 6, 2006. http://members.iinet.net.au/holmgren/scholars.html (accessed January 27, 2007).

Jones, Steven E. "Why Indeed Did the World Trade Center Buildings Completely Collapse?" *Journal of 9/11 Studies* 3 (September 2006). http://www.journal of911studies.com (accessed November 24, 2008).

Illouz, Eva. *Cold Intimacies: The Making of Emotional Capitalism.* London: Polity, 2007.

Kahn, Richard, and Douglas Kellner. "Oppositional Politics and the Internet: A Critical/Reconstructive Approach." *Cultural Politics* 1, no. 1 (2005): 75–100.

Kane, Tim. "The Bankruptcy Bill and Debt Obesity." Heritage Foundation Policy Archive, April 7, 2005. http://www.heritage.org (accessed July 28, 2008).

King, Samantha. *Pink Ribbons, Inc.: Breast Cancer and the Politics of Philanthropy.* Minneapolis: University of Minnesota Press, 2006.

Krugman, Paul. "Who's Crazy Now?" *New York Times,* May 8, 2006.

Kurtz, Stanley. "Postmodernism Kills." *National Review,* August, 12, 2002. http://www.nationalreview.com (accessed November 24, 2008).

Lacan, Jacques. *On Feminine Sexuality, The Limits of Love and Knowledge, 1972–1973: Encore; The Seminar of Jacques Lacan, Book XX.* Edited by Jacques-Alain Miller. Translated by Bruce Fink. New York: W. W. Norton, 1998.

———. *The Psychoses, 1955–1956: The Seminar of Jacques Lacan, Book III.* Edited by Jacques-Alain Miller. Translated by Russell Gregg. New York: W. W. Norton, 1997.

Laclau, Ernesto. *Emancipations.* London: Verso, 1996.

———. *On Populist Reason.* London: Verso, 2005.

———. "Stucture, History, and the Political." In Butler, Laclau, and Žižek, eds., *Contingency, Hegemony, Universality,* 182–212.

Laclau, Ernesto, and Chantal Mouffe. *Hegemony and Socialist Strategy.* London: Verso, 1984.

Lapavitsas, Costas. "Mainstream Economics in the Neoliberal Era." In Saad-Fiho and Johnston, eds., *Neoliberalism: A Critical Reader,* 30–40.

Lebowitz, Michael. "Ideology and Economic Development." *Monthly Review,* May 2004. http://www.monthlyreview.org (accessed November 24, 2008).

Lefort, Claude. *Democracy and Political Theory.* Translated by David Macey. Minneapolis: University of Minnesota Press, 1988.

Lemke, Thomas. " 'The Birth of Biopolitics'—Michel Foucault's Lecture at the Collège de France on Neoliberal Governmentality." *Economy and Society,* May 2001, 190–207.

Lenhart, Amanda, Mary Madden, Alexandra Rankin Macgill, and Aaron Smith. "Teens and Social Media." Pew Internet and American Life Project, December 19, 2007. http://www.pew internet.org/pdfs/PIP—Teens—Social—Media—Final.pdf (accessed November 24, 2008).

Lincoln, Bruce. *Holy Terrors: Thinking about Religion after September 11.* Chicago: University of Chicago Press, 2003.

Louie, David. " 'Black Friday' Shopping Frenzy: Holiday Shopping Season Begins," November 25, 2005. http://abclocal.go.com (accessed July 28, 2008).

Marcuse, Herbert. *One Dimensional Man.* Boston: Beacon Press, 1964.

Matic, Veran, and Drazen Pantic. "War of Words." *Nation*, November 29, 1999. http://www.thenation.com (accessed April 29, 2007).

Merrill, Dennis, and Thomas G. Patterson, eds. *Major Problems in American Foreign Relations*. Volume 2: *Since 1914*. 5th ed. Boston: Houghton Mifflin Company, 2000.

Miller, Daniel. *A Theory of Shopping*. Ithaca: Cornell University Press, 1998.

Mink, Gwendolyn. *Welfare's End*. Ithaca: Cornell University Press, 1998.

Monbiot, George. "This Is a Dazzling Debunking of Climate Change Science. It Is also Wildly Wrong." *Guardian*, November 14, 2006. http://www.guardian.co.uk (accessed July 28, 2008).

Morrow, Lance. *Evil: An Investigation*. New York: Basic Books, 2003.

——. "The Real Meaning of Evil." *Time*, February 24, 2003, 74.

Mouffe, Chantal. *The Democratic Paradox*. London: Verso, 2000.

——. *On the Political*. London: Verso, 2005.

Munck, Ronaldo. "Neoliberalism and Politics, and the Politics of Neoliberalism." In Saad-Fiho and Johnston, eds., *Neoliberalism: A Critical Reader*, 60–69.

Neiman, Susan. *Evil in Modern Thought: An Alternative History of Philosophy*. Princeton: Princeton University Press, 2002.

Nordlinger, Jay. "Ashcroft with Horns." *National Review Online*, July 24, 2002. http://www.nationalreview.com (accessed November 24, 2008).

Palley, Thomas. "From Keynesianism to Neoliberalism: Shifting Paradigms in Economics." In Saad-Fiho and Johnston, eds., *Neoliberalism: A Critical Reader*, 20–29.

Passavant, Paul A. *No Escape: Freedom of Speech and the Paradox of Rights*. New York: New York University Press, 2002.

——. "The Strong Neoliberal State: Crime, Consumption, Governance." *Theory and Event* 8, no. 3 (2005): n.p.

Passavant, Paul A., and Jodi Dean, eds. *Empire's New Clothes: Reading Hardt and Negri*. New York: Routledge, 2004.

Patelis, Korinna. "E-Mediation by America Online." In *Preferred Placement: Knowledge Politics on the Web*, edited by Richard Rogers, 49–64. Maastricht: Jan van Eyck Academie, 2004.

Perelman, Michael. *The Confiscation of American Prosperity*. New York: Palgrave Macmillan, 2007.

Pollin, Robert. *Contours of Descent*. London: Verso, 2005.

Pope, Justin. "9/11 Conspiracy Theorists Thriving." ABC News, August 6, 2006. http://abcnews.go.com (accessed July 28, 2008).

Poster, Mark. *What's the Matter with the Internet?* Minneapolis: University of Minnesota Press, 2001.

Radice, Hugo. "Neoliberal Globalization: Imperialism without Empires?" In Saad-Fiho and Johnston, eds., *Neoliberalism: A Critical Reader*, 91–98.

Ranciere, Jacques. *Disagreement*. Translated by Julie Rose. Minneapolis: University of Minnesota Press, 1999.

Rice, Condoleezza. "Promoting the National Interest." *Foreign Affairs,* January/ February 2000. http://www.foreignaffairs.org (accessed November 24, 2008).

Rich, Frank. *The Greatest Story Ever Sold: The Decline and Fall of Truth from 9/11 to Katrina.* New York: Penguin Press, 2006.

Rogers, Richard. "The Issue Has Left the Building." Paper presented at the Annual Meeting of the International Association of Internet Researchers, Maastricht, the Netherlands, October 13–16, 2002.

Rogin, Michael. *Ronald Reagan, the Movie and Other Episodes in Political Demonology.* Berkeley: University of California Press, 1987.

Rubenstein, Diane. *This Is Not a President.* New York: New York University Press, 2008.

Sales, Nancy Jo. "Click Here for Conspiracy." *Vanity Fair,* August 2006, 112–16.

Saad-Fiho, Alfredo, and Deborah Johnston, eds. *Neoliberalism: A Critical Reader.* London: Pluto, 2005.

Santner, Eric L. "Miracles Happen: Benjamin, Rosenzweig, Freud, and the Matter of the Neighbor." In *The Neighbor: Three Inquiries in Political Theology,* by Slavoj Žižek, Santner, and Kenneth Reinhard, 73–133. Chicago: University of Chicago Press, 2005.

——. *My Own Private Germany.* Princeton: Princeton University Press, 1996.

Sassen, Saskia. *Losing Control?* New York: Columbia University Press, 1996.

Schmitt, Carl. *The Concept of the Political.* Translated by George Schwab. Chicago: University of Chicago Press, 1996.

——. *The Crisis of Parliamentary Democracy.* Translated by Ellen Kennedy. Cambridge: MIT Press, 2000.

Schor, Juliet B. *The Overspent American.* New York: Harper Perennial, 1998.

Shaikh, Anwar. "The Economic Mythology of Neoliberalism." In Saad-Fiho and Johnston, eds., *Neoliberalism: A Critical Reader,* 41–49.

Shapiro, Michael J. *Violent Cartographies: Mapping Cultures of War.* Minneapolis: University of Minnesota Press, 1997.

Shirky, Clay. "Is Social Software Bad for the Dean Campaign?" Many-2-Many Blog, January 26, 2004. http://www.corante.com (accessed April 28, 2007).

Shklar, Judith. *Ordinary Vices.* Cambridge: Harvard University Press, 1984.

Simon, Jonathan. " 'Entitlement to Cruelty': The End of Welfare and the Punitive Mentality in the United States." In *Crime, Risk, and Justice: The Politics of Crime Control in Liberal Democracies,* edited by Kevin Stenson and Robert R. Sullivan, 125–43. Cullompton, UK: Willan, 2000.

Sunstein, Cass R. *Infotopia: How Many Minds Produce Knowledge.* New York: Oxford University Press, 2006.

——. *Republic.com 2.0.* Princeton: Princeton University Press, 2007.

Suskind, Ron. "Faith, Certainty, and the Presidency of George W. Bush." *New York Times Magazine,* October 17, 2004. http://www.nytimes.com (accessed July 28, 2008).

Taylor, Betsy. "The Personal Level." In Juliet Schor, *Do Americans Shop Too Much?*, edited by Joshua Cohen and Joel Rogers, 57–62. Boston: Beacon, 2000.

Treanor, Paul. "Neoliberalism: Origins, Theory, Definition," Paul Treanor's blog, December 2, 2005. http://web.inter.nl.net/users/Paul.Treanor/neoliberal ism.html. (accessed November 24, 2008).

Twohey, Megan. "UW Lecturer's 9–11 Media Blitz Is Rapped." *Milwaukee Journal Sentinel*, August 4, 2006.

Wark, McKenzie. *A Hacker Manifesto*. Cambridge: Harvard University Press, 2004.

White, Stephen K. *Sustaining Affirmation: The Strengths of Weak Ontology in Political Theory.* Princeton: Princeton University Press, 2000.

Wood, Judy, and Morgan Reynolds. "The Scientific Method Applied to the Thermite Hypothesis." *The Journal of 9/11 Research and 9/11 Issues*, December 14, 2006. http://drjudywood.com (accessed November 24, 2008)

——. "Why Did Indeed the WTC Buildings Disintegrate?" No More Games.Net, October 2006. http://nomoregames.net (accessed February 20, 2009).

Žižek, Slavoj. "Afterword: Lenin's Choice." *Revolution at the Gates*. London: Verso, 2002.

——. "Class Struggle or Postmodernism? Yes, Please!" In Judith Butler, Ernesto Laclau, and Žižek, *Contingency, Hegemony, Universality*, 90–135. London: Verso, 2000.

——. *Enjoy Your Symptom!* 2nd ed. New York: Routledge, 2001.

——. *For They Know Not What They Do: Enjoyment as a Political Factor.* London: Verso, 1991.

——. *The Fragile Absolute.* London: Verso, 2000.

——. *Iraq: The Borrowed Kettle.* London, Verso, 2004.

——. "Neighbors and Other Monsters." In Žižek, Eric L. Santner, and Kenneth Reinhard, *The Neighbor: Three Inquiries in Political Theology*, 134–90. Chicago: University of Chicago Press, 2005.

——. *Organs without Bodies: On Deleuze and Consequences.* New York: Routledge, 2004.

——. *The Parallax View.* Cambridge: MIT Press, 2006.

——. *The Plague of Fantasies.* London: Verso, 1997.

——. *Slavoj Žižek Presents Mao: On Practice and Contradiction.* London: Verso, 2007.

——. *The Sublime Object of Ideology.* London: Verso, 1989.

——. *Tarrying with the Negative.* Durham: Duke University Press, 1993.

——. *The Ticklish Subject.* London: Verso, 1999.

JODI DEAN is a professor of political science at Hobart and William Smith Colleges and the Erasmus Professor of the Humanities in the Faculty of Philosophy at Erasmus University, Rotterdam. Her previous books include *Žižek's Politics, Publicity's Secret: How Technoculture Capitalizes on Democracy*, and *Aliens in America: Conspiracy Cultures from Outerspace to Cyberspace*.

Library of Congress Cataloging-in-Publication Data
Dean, Jodi, 1962–
Democracy and other neoliberal fantasies : communicative capitalism and left politics / Jodi Dean.
p. cm.
Includes bibliographical references and index.
ISBN 978-0-8223-4492-6 (cloth : alk. paper)
ISBN 978-0-8223-4505-3 (pbk. : alk. paper)
1. Democratic Party (U.S.) 2. Politics, Practical—United States.
3. Political parties—United States. 4. United States—Politics and government—2001– 5. Democracy—United States. 6. Neoliberalism—United States. I. Title.
JK2316.D43 2009
324.2736—dc22   2009008983